THE EPIC OF THE FALL OF MAN

Genesis in anglico

The Glory-King of Hosts.

Frontispiece.

THE EPIC OF THE FALL OF MAN ✹ A COMPARATIVE STUDY OF CÆDMON, DANTE AND MILTON ✹

BY

S. HUMPHREYS GURTEEN, M.A., LL.D.

Graduate of the University of Cambridge ; Senior Canon of the Cathedral,
Davenport ; Author of "The Arthurian Epic," "Handbook
of Anglo-Saxon Grammar," etc., etc.

HASKELL HOUSE
Publishers of Scholarly Books
NEW YORK
1964

First published in 1896

HASKELL HOUSE

Library of Congress Catalog Card Number: 65-15879

Haskell House Catalogue Item # 561

PRINTED IN UNITED STATES OF AMERICA

PREFACE.

IN the following work, my object is to present, as I did in the *Arthurian Epic*, a comparative study of one most interesting niche in the poetic literature of England.

The former work was attacked by one critic, on the ground that I had failed to go outside of the lines which I had myself laid down as the limits of the inquiry; and I was accused of imperfect scholarship, because I did not drag into the study a discussion of myth-lore, or take notice of foreign developments of the narrative, when the avowed limits of the work excluded any such digressions. My object in the *Arthurian Epic* was simply to compare four distinct versions of the Arthur-story, viz., the Cambrian, the Breton, the Anglo-Norman, and the Tennysonian, as they exist at the present day; and with any speculations as to Sun-myths, or the consideration of any *foreign* versions or other extraneous, though highly interesting matters, I had no concern, in that work.

iii

Similarly, the present volume is simply a comparative study of one niche in the *sacred* poetic literature of England; and although I have included in this study the *Inferno* of Dante, I have done so only to bring out, in still bolder relief, the strong and weak points in Cædmon's and Milton's treatment of the subject. It is not, and does not pretend to be, a dissertation on the language of the Anglo-Saxons, or on their metrical system, or a *discursus* on the many interesting questions which have been raised and discussed, both in England and Germany, in reference to Cædmon's poem and Milton's epic.

It is a comparative study of two existing poems, and does not profess to touch upon any outlying questions, however fascinating or important they may be in themselves.

In this study I have taken, as the basis of my translation of Cædmon, the text of the Junian manuscript, edited by Mr. Benjamin Thorpe, F.S.A., for the Society of Antiquaries of London (1832), collated with the original manuscript, preserved in the Bodleian Library at Oxford.

The reduced fac-similes of the illuminations of the manuscript are taken from the fac-similes published in the *Archæologia* of the Society of Antiquaries of London (vol. xxiv., 1832), corrected and verified with the kind assistance of Mr. Horace Hart, Controller of the University Press at Oxford.

The modern English rendering of the passages from the *Beówulf* in the first Chapter of this work is taken, with slight changes, from the Rev. J. J. Conybeare's *Illustrations of Anglo-Saxon Poetry.*

The extracts from *Paradise Lost* are taken from Professor David Masson's scholarly edition of the works of Milton (Macmillan, 3 vols., 1874).

I am indebted to the Rev. Henry Francis Cary's admirable translation of Dante's *Inferno* for the extracts which appear in the following pages.

My translation of that part of Cædmon which relates to the "Fall of Man" does not pretend to be a *literal* translation. My object has been to give the *sense* of the original, and, in so far as possible, to keep to Anglo-Saxon modes of thought and of expression. In passages where the text itself is evidently corrupt, or where the wording or meaning is doubtful, I have endeavoured to express what, by long living among these relics of our ancestors, in study and thought, seems to me to be the most likely meaning of the words.

To Professor Masson I am indebted for far more than his valuable and able edition of the works of Milton. He was my earliest preceptor in literature when I was in the 'teens, and gave me my first impulse in literary studies, especially in the study of Milton; and I am glad of this opportunity to acknowledge a debt which it would be impossible ever to repay, and which in any case I should prefer to regard as a life-long obligation.

S. H. G.

New York, February 14, 1896.

CONTENTS.

vii

Contents

LIST OF PLATES.

LIST OF DIAGRAMS.

INTRODUCTION.

Historical Sketch of the Revival of Anglo-Saxon Learning in England.

THE deep interest which exists, at the present day, in all that has to do with the Anglo-Saxon period of English life, would be evident from the extent of the published literature on this subject, even if we had nothing further to guide us.

The language, the poetry, the history, the political institutions, the forensic system, the ecclesiastical polity, the social customs, and the antiquities in general of Anglo-Saxon England have, each and all, been explored, in recent years especially, by some of the ablest scholars in Europe, with the result of placing in the hands of the student of this period invaluable help in the prosecution of his subject.

But, perhaps, the best proof of the deep interest in Anglo-Saxon studies, which is evident to-day in both England and America, is to be found in the largely increased number of our prominent seats of learning in which Anglo-Saxon now forms part of the regular curriculum, and, as a consequence, in the greater number of educated men who can enjoy, as a recreation, the poetry of the Mead-hall and the cloister—the *Beówulf* and the so-called *Paraphrase* of Cædmon,—or who can read, in the original, for the purposes of their profession, such works as the *Saxon Chronicle*, Ælfric's homilies, or the Anglo-Saxon laws in Wilkins' digest, which, in a greater or less degree, are of a purely technical or professional character.

A brief survey of the gradual decay and final revival of Anglo-Saxon learning in England may serve to account for the widespread neglect which until very recent years, comparatively speaking, was the fate of Anglo-Saxon studies generally.

Previous to the Norman conquest, although the Anglo-Saxon ecclesiastics regarded Latin as the only language worthy of expressing their views on history, science and theology, yet the spoken language was the Anglo-Saxon. This was also the language of the laws and charters; and, judging from the numerous books of manuscript homilies described in monastic catalogues as *Sermones Anglici vetusti et inutiles*, it is reasonable to suppose that this class of writings was, for the most part, in the popular language of the country, as well as those poems which were intended for public recital by the *scops* or minstrels. The incursions of the Danes, during the ninth and two succeeding centuries, doubtless caused the destruction of much valuable Anglo-Saxon literature. These "slayers from the North," not able to discriminate between ecclesiastical and secular property, burned monastery and tower alike, and with the monasteries perished many a rich and noted library. These daring pirates could scarcely be expected to know or to care for the extent of the loss which they thus caused.* But this cannot be said in excuse of the Norman ecclesiastics, of whom we are about to speak. By the middle of the thirteenth century, when Anglo-Saxon had sunk into its modified form of Early English, pure Anglo-Saxon writings could no longer be understood. Anglo-Saxon was, to all intents and purposes, a dead language, even to those of Anglo-Saxon descent. The clerics were the only class, before the Revival of Learning, capable of mastering the literature of the past ; and they were too ignorant, too indolent, or too indifferent to attempt it. Hence, it came to pass that many an old manuscript was taken down from its dusty shelf only to be cleaned off with pumice in order to make room for some, then, more interesting Latin treatise. A case of this kind, came under our own observation not many

* *Vide* Note A.

years ago. In the library of Jesus College, Cambridge, there is an old manuscript which now contains Latin decretals; but beneath these, and
especially around the margins of some of the folios,
can be traced the remains of a fine copy of Ælfric's
Anglo-Saxon sermons. At other times, old Anglo-
Saxon manuscripts have been sewed together in
order to make covers for other works. Sir T.
Phillips, in some remarks prefixed to the table
of " errata," in his edition of *Fragments of Ælfric's
Grammar, Ælfric's Glossary, and a Poem on the
Soul and Body, discovered among the Archives of
Worcester Cathedral*, makes the following statement:
"The fragments having been found in the cover of
an old book (of which they, with some other fragments, constituted the sole stiffening), had been so
much smeared with a brown paste, to make them
adhere together, that it required much washing to
make them, in the least degree legible." From
these, and such like practices of illiterate clerics, we
can form some idea of the total neglect into which
Anglo-Saxon had fallen before the end of the fifteenth century.

At the period of the Reformation, and of the dis-
solution of the monasteries which followed, the
monastic libraries were scattered, and much that
was valuable was lost past recovery. At such a

crisis, when men's minds were intent upon the all-engrossing religious topics of the hour, what time could the ecclesiastics—the literary men of the time —find for such an apparently worthless study as that of Anglo-Saxon? If a man thought at all, it was upon the all-absorbing theological tenets of the day. It was not a time for the prosecution of trifling and useless studies. It was an exciting time, when every man who wrote, did so as if absolute truth were on his side, and absolute error on that of his opponent. Yet, strange as it may appear at first sight, this was the first time since the Anglo-Saxon had yielded to the Norman that the long-forgotten Anglo-Saxon writings were taken down from their dusty shelves and allowed to see the light. During this period of theological warfare the minds of men were absorbed in ransacking works on theology, philosophy, and science—everything, in fact—in support of their cherished opinions. In this way it came to pass that Anglo-Saxon writings attracted attention, their authority being called in to give weight to the innovations of the reformers.

Moreover, these writings were highly valuable, inasmuch as they could boast of antiquity, a very powerful weapon, when the contest turned, to such an extent as it actually did, on ancient traditions and customs. Yet, when the occasion ceased which had given rise to a study of the Anglo-Saxon, these works, which for a moment had been brought forth from the seclusion of the library, were once again consigned to oblivion. The occasion, moreover, was a religious one, and the theological writings of the Anglo-Saxon clerics were the only ones which were studied. Still, although Anglo-Saxon once again became forgotten, the old manuscripts suffered less at this, than at any previous period, owing to the eagerness shown by the reformers in collecting them for their own passing purpose.

This period, however, was succeeded by an age when a pedantic affectation of classical learning thoroughly permeated the upper ranks of society. The Queen, the courtiers, the courtly-makers (as the poets were called), even the clergy, felt the infection ; and the sermons of the day, like the small talk of the court, were full of quotations from profane writers. While the Queen was being flattered by men of high attainments ; while the courtiers and those of less favoured rank were pandering, in this particular, to the intense self-love of their sovereign ; while many of the clergy were bending to the fashionable whim of the day, in their desire to render themselves pleasing to those in power, it is no wonder that Anglo-Saxon literature was deemed of little moment, and was compelled to give way to the more highly polished literature of Greece and Rome.

But while classical studies received the patronage of the Queen, and formed the morning pastime of the court, Anglo-Saxon studies, under the leadership of Dr. Matthew Parker, Archbishop of Canterbury, began to show signs of revival. Archbishop Parker may justly be regarded as the restorer of Anglo-Saxon learning in England. He was one of the two great collectors of Anglo-Saxon manuscripts of that age, and to him is due the honour of having been the first to publish an Anglo-Saxon work in England. In 1567 Ælfric's Paschal homily was published under his personal direction, and shortly after, appeared the Anglo-Saxon version of the four Gospels. This work was brought out in 1571, with a dedication to Queen Elizabeth, by Foxe, the romancing martyrologist. It was the joint work of Foxe and L'Isle, who, at the instigation, and under the direction of Archbishop Parker, did all that men could be expected to do, who had to enter upon the task without dictionary and without grammar. The types for these works were cut by John Daye, by order of the Archbishop, and for neatness of style surpass any that were cast for many a long year afterwards.

We have said that Archbishop Parker was one of

the two great collectors of Anglo-Saxon manuscripts
of his day ; the other was Sir Robert Cotton.   Archbishop Parker, possessing the fine tastes of a true
antiquary, collected all the manuscripts he could find
from among the ruins of the dissolved monasteries,
and transferred them to his own collection ; nor, indeed, was this an especially difficult task when these
manuscripts were regarded as " old and useless."

Sir Robert Cotton, born five years before the
Archbishop's death, must ever be remembered with
affection by all lovers of our early literature.   At the
age of eighteen he began his noble work of rescuing
Anglo-Saxon manuscripts from the stalls of book-
sellers, or from the hands of private individuals ; and
at the time of his death, in 1631, he was zealously
engaged in the same work—a life spent in saving
from destruction these fine old relics of the past.

The Archbishop, upon his death, in 1575, be-
queathed his collection to his own University and
college, and they are now among the Parkerian
manuscripts in Corpus Christi College, Cambridge.
The collection of Sir Robert Cotton, more valuable
than that of the Archbishop, suffered a sad fate.
By the fire at Cotton House, in Little Dean's Yard,
Westminster, over a hundred manuscripts were lost,
burned, or totally defaced ; and the remaining ones,
among which may be mentioned the only existing

manuscript of the *Beówulf*, then known, were greatly damaged. The remains of this collection, having been deposited for a time in the old dormitory at Westminster, were afterwards removed, in 1753, to the British Museum, where they may now be seen.

But Sir Robert Cotton's indefatigable industry was not lost. It is true that this was the great dramatic era of England ; but amid all the gaieties and frivolities of the day, Anglo-Saxon was not altogether forgotten. In 1639, Sir Henry Spelman published his edition of the *Ecclesiastical Laws*, and, in the following year, his son edited the *Anglo-Saxon Psalter*. The former of these scholars was intending to establish an Anglo-Saxon professorship in the University of Cambridge, but his intention was thwarted. The country at that time became the wrestling ground for the champions of the King and the champions of the Commonwealth, and amid the tumult and confusion of the hour, men had but little time to devote to the past.

In 1644, Abraham Wheloc published at Cambridge the first edition of the Anglo-Saxon translation of Beda s *Historia Ecclesiastica* and parts of the *Anglo-Saxon Chronicle*, under the title *Chronologia Anglo-Saxonica*, together with a Latin translation. This work was printed from one of the Cottonian manuscripts, collated with one of the Parkerian in the library of Corpus Christi College.

About the middle of the seventeenth century, a handful of Anglo-Saxon scholars arose, who gave to the study a new impetus and a more distinctive character.

While Sir Robert Cotton was diligently engaged in his work of collecting manuscripts, Ussher, afterwards Archbishop of Armagh, was employed in a similar occupation, having been sent over to England to buy books for Trinity College, Dublin. At first, he worked in concert with Sir Thomas Bodley, who was collecting for his new library at Oxford; but shortly after, he returned to Ireland, and three years later again visited England, when he was able to number Sir Robert Cotton among his friends. During his book-hunting expeditions Ussher obtained the manuscript of a Scripture paraphrase in Anglo-Saxon, which he gave to Francis Dujon the younger, known in literature as Junius, the son of a Leyden divinity professor, and librarian to the Earl of Arundel. In 1650 this celebrated scholar left England on a visit to the Continent, and while there published, at Amsterdam, the copy of the Anglo-Saxon paraphrase which he had received from Ussher; nor did he hesitate to pronounce it the genuine, though long-lost work of Cædmon, mentioned by Beda, as the title indicates, *Cædomis Mona-chi Paraphrasis poetica Genesios ac præcipuarum Sacræ Paginæ Historiarum, abhinc annos MLXX. Anglo-Saxonice conscripta, et nunc primum edita a Francisco Junio, F. F. Amstelodami. 1655.**

It must not be forgotten, while speaking of Junius, that he laboured indefatigably to revive the study of Anglo-Saxon in England. At his own expense he procured, at Amsterdam, in 1654, a set of "Saxonic" types, which he brought with him upon his return, and presented, in 1677, to the University of Oxford.

Hitherto, as we have seen, although through the labours of Parker, Spelman, Wheloc, and Junius, some advance had been made in restoring attention to Anglo-Saxon writings, yet the student had been compelled to grope his arduous way in the dark, having no assistance at hand, and being without dictionary and without grammar. But now the darkness began to disappear, and a faint light arose to dispel the gloom in the Anglo-Saxon atmosphere. In 1659 the first Anglo-Saxon dictionary was published by Somner under the following title, *Dictiona-rium Saxonico-Latino-Anglicum voces, phrasesque præ-cipuas Anglo-Saxonicas, e libris, sive manuscriptis, sive typis excusis, aliisque monumentis tum publicis, tum privatis, magna diligentia collectas ; cum Latina et*

* *Vide* Note B.

Anglica vocum interpretatione complectens.   Adjectis interdum exemplis, vocum etymologiis, et cum cognatis linguis collationibus, plurimisque in gratiam linguæ Anglo-Saxonicæ studiosorum observationibus.   Opera et studio Guliel.   Somneri Cantuariensis. Fol. Oxonii. 1659. This work, though showing an indomitable perseverance on the part of the compiler, was very imperfect, and full of errors ; but this was only to be expected in a first attempt, and no student can feel otherwise than grateful to Somner for this result of patient toil.

In 1665 Dr. Marshall, a former pupil of Junius, (from whom, doubtless, he had acquired a taste for these studies), published at Dort the second edition of the Anglo-Saxon Gospels, together with the Gothic Gospels, as given by Junius.   It was a joint work of both, but printed with the types which Junius had brought from Amsterdam.

Twenty-four years later, and thirty-four years after the publication of the first Anglo-Saxon *dictionary*, appeared the first Anglo-Saxon *grammar*, that of Dr. Hickes, in the year 1689. We learn from the preface to this work that an Anglo-Saxon grammar by John Jocelin was in existence at the time ; but this has never been discovered. That such a work did exist, however, is evident from the fact that the index of it is mentioned in Wanley's *Catalogue of*

Saxon Manuscripts; and, moreover, the index itself is still preserved in the Bodleian Library. In the same collection, there are a few loose sheets of declensions by Marshall; but, as these are only fragmentary remains, we may consider the work of Dr. Hickes as the first Anglo-Saxon grammar published in England. It bears the following title, and is in Latin: *Institutiones Grammaticæ Anglo-Saxonicæ et Mæso-Gothicæ Auctore Georgio Hickesio Ecclesiæ Anglicanæ Presbytero. Grammatica Islandica Runolphi Jonæ. Catalogus Librorum Septentrionalium. Accedit Edvardi Bernardi Etymologicon Britannicum. Oxoniæ, e theatro Sheldoniano. 1689. Typis Junianis.*

It is worthy of remark, that Dr. Hickes owed his taste for these studies to the influence of Dr. Marshall, Rector of Lincoln College, of which Dr. Hickes was a Fellow, and so indirectly to the genius of Dujon.

About this time there arose at Oxford a clique of Anglo-Saxonists, who were among the brightest lights of Anglo-Saxon scholarship that had as yet appeared. In 1692 Edmund Gibson, afterwards Bishop of London, published a new edition of the *Saxon Chronicle*, much enlarged, and containing, in addition to a new Latin translation of the text, a preface, notes, and glossarial index.

Mr. Rawlinson, in 1698, brought out the first

edition of King Alfred's translation of the *De Consolatione Philosophiæ* of Boethius, the last man of genius produced by ancient Rome. It was copied from the transcript made by Junius, as the title informs us : *An. Manl. Sever. Boethi Consolationis philosophiæ Libri V. Anglo-Saxonice redditi ab Alfredo inclyto Anglo-Saxonum Rege. Ad apographum Junianum expressos, edidit Christophorus Rawlinson è Collegio Reginæ. Oxoniæ, è theatro Sheldoniano MDCXCVIII. Sumtibus editoris, typis Junianis.* Upon the death of Junius, in 1677, his transcript passed, together with his other manuscripts, into the possession of the University of Oxford, and Mr. Rawlinson simply performed the work that, if Junius had lived, would doubtless have been accomplished by the transcriber himself.

In 1701 Mr. Benson, another member of Queen's College, issued his *Vocabularium Anglo-Saxonicum*, a work founded upon Somner's dictionary, and showing the marked and steady advance in Anglo-Saxon scholarship that had been made during the preceding forty years.

In 1705 an enlarged edition of Dr. Hickes' work appeared under a new title : *Linguarum Vett. Septentrionalium Thesaurus Grammatico—Criticus et Archæologicus.* This *Thesaurus* was rendered still more valuable by the incorporation of Mr. Humphrey Wanley's *Catalogue of Saxon Manuscripts*, preserved in the libraries, public and private, of England. This *Catalogue*, or *Liber Alter*, is one of those works, the full effect of which it is difficult to overrate. It was invaluable at the period when it appeared, not merely as containing a description of manuscripts and their whereabouts, but as forming a valuable book of reference, pointing out to the scholar the quantity and nature of Anglo-Saxon literature which then remained in manuscript, and is of importance to the Anglo-Saxon scholar of to-day as indicative of manuscripts that may still be extant.

In 1699 Mr. Thwaites, the third Queen's man we have had occasion to mention in connection with this era, published the first and only edition of the *Saxon Heptateuch*, following it twelve years later by a small *Saxon Grammar*.

This, as we have already said, was the brightest period of Anglo-Saxon scholarship previous to the present century; but the crowning production of this age was the work of a lady. In 1715 appeared *The Rudiments of Grammar for the English-Saxon Tongue ; first given in English, with an Apology for the Study of Northern Antiquities, being very useful toward the understanding our Ancient Poets and other Writers. By Elizabeth Elstob.** This was the first

* *Vide* Note C.

Anglo-Saxon grammar written in *English*. Miss
Elstob, a niece of Dr. Hickes', is also to be remembered as the translator of the Anglo-Saxon homily
on the birthday of St. Gregory. This lady's Grammar of the " English-Saxon Tongue " is merely a
compilation from the previous works of Dr. Hickes
and Mr. Thwaites, and cannot lay claim to any great
amount of originality with respect to the substance
of the book; nor does it lay claim to any erudition
beyond that possessed by the originals. And yet,
in one respect, we deem it worthy of far higher
honour than its predecessors. At a time when the
majority of scholars slighted their mother tongue in
favour of a corrupt Latin, Elizabeth Elstob, though
herself a Latin scholar, put them to shame by her
practical proof that pure English is better than
scholastic Latin; and on this account, alone, we
think hers the crowning production of the age.

We have now arrived at the era of the Georges;
an era of comparative quiet. Already, we have
watched the gradual decay of pure Anglo-Saxon
after the Norman conquest; we have noted the
ignorant indifference on this subject of the Norman
clergy; we have traced the revival of Anglo-Saxon
studies under Archbishop Parker and his successors,
and have followed the advancement in Anglo-Saxon
learning down to its most brilliant period, namely,

the commencement of the eighteenth century. But now a relapse takes place. The eighteenth century is as barren, as the previous century was prolific, in Saxonists. During this long period we find but few zealous students writing works "useful toward the understanding our Ancient Poets and other Writers." The study of Anglo-Saxon seems gradually to have sunk into comparative oblivion, until at length it was very generally regarded as unworthy to occupy the serious attention of the literate. It is true that the history of the country explains this neglect, but we cannot stay to examine this point. There are, however, a few notable exceptions to the above statement. In 1721 Wilkins published his edition of the *Anglo-Saxon Laws*. King Alfred's translation of the *Historia Ecclesiastica*, together with the original, appeared in 1722, edited by John Smith, Canon of Durham. The Latin text of this edition is based upon that of the Jesuit Chifflet, but it is superior in every respect to any that had hitherto appeared. This by the way. The Anglo-Saxon translation of the Venerable Beda's work, as the reader will have remarked, had already been brought out by Wheloc in 1644. But the name of greatest note in connection with the eighteenth century is that of Edward Lye. The valuable grammar prefixed to his edition of the *Etymologicum Anglicanum* of Junius, and still

2

more, the great *Anglo-Saxon Dictionary* of Lye and Manning, published in 1752, evince the former's acquaintance with, and critical knowledge of, the Anglo-Saxon language.

In 1773 appeared, for the first time, King Alfred's translation of *Orosius*, edited by Daines Barrington, the least creditably executed work that had, up to this period, been given to the public.

One event connected with this subject, perhaps the most important of this age, was the foundation of the Anglo-Saxon professorship at Oxford in 1750. The statute creating this professorship did not come into effect till the year 1795, but when once in force the establishment of this chair may be regarded as one of the chief causes which led to the revival of Anglo-Saxon studies in the present century.

But there were other and more immediate causes which we have now to notice. In Wanley's *Catalogue of Saxon Manuscripts*, which formed part of the *Thesaurus* of Dr. Hickes, we find the earliest notice we possess of that grand old Anglo-Saxon epic, the *Beówulf*. Notwithstanding this notice, in which he calls it " *Tractatus nobilissimus poeticè scriptus*," its very existence seems to have been ignored by Anglo-Saxon scholars until Mr. Sharon Turner, at the beginning of the present century, gave some extracts from it in his *History of the Anglo-*

Saxons. Even after the publication of his work, this poem excited little or no interest, and it was not until the year 1815, more than a hundred years after the publication of Wanley's *Catalogue*, that an edition of the entire poem was given to the world by Dr. Thorkelin, a foreigner. At the latter end of the eighteenth century, this celebrated Danish antiquary visited England, and, while there, made a transcript of the *Beówulf* from the only known, existing manuscript in the British Museum. Upon his return to Denmark, he wrote a Latin translation and commentary, and the whole work was finished and ready for publication in 1807; but during the bombardment of Copenhagen the antiquary's house was destroyed, and with it the manuscript results of thirty years' incessant labour. Assisted and encouraged by the Count of Sanderumgaard, Thorkelin, then a septuagenarian, returned to England, and made a second transcript of the poem, which, together with a fresh Latin translation, was published in 1815 under the following title: *De Danorum Rebus gestis Secul. iii. et iv. Poema Danicum Dialecto Anglo-Saxonica. Ex Bibl. Cotton. Musæi. Britan. edidit, Versione Lat. et Indicibus auxit Grim. Johnson Thorkelin, Dr., etc.*

In the year 1817 Erasmus Rask published, at Stockholm, his *Angelsaksisk Sproglære,* or Anglo-Saxon Grammar, which, for advanced philological treatment of the subject, correctness of detail, and accuracy of the opinions expressed, cannot be too highly praised. In 1830 Mr. Thorpe translated this work into English, and thus conferred a boon upon the Anglo-Saxon student that can never be adequately acknowledged.

Thorkelin's edition of the *Beówulf*, together with Rask's *Saxon Grammar*, may be regarded as the immediate causes of the revival of the interest in Anglo-Saxon studies which characterises the present century. We acknowledge, though not without shame, that this second revival of Anglo-Saxon learning is due to the genius of foreigners ; still, we can turn proudly to the names of Parker and Cotton, Thorpe and Kemble, Conybeare and Ingram, Bosworth and Wright, to show that the descendants of the Anglo-Saxons have awakened to the fact that the language and literature of their ancestors is worthy of the attention of scholars, and that they will not allow other nations, although kindred, to carry off the palm in this particular.

Simply to enumerate the works upon every branch of the subject which have appeared during the past fifty years would tax the reader's patience to too great an extent, even if our space permitted. One fact is clear. A revival of Anglo-Saxon learning has taken place, and this in so thorough a manner that

we venture to predict it will not suffer another
relapse.   As the revival of classical learning in the
fifteenth century has resulted in a masterly investiga-
tion of the history, the laws, the politics, and the
social institutions of Greece and Rome, not to mention
tion the accurate scholarship of the day which has
produced these results, so, we believe, the time is
not very far distant when there will arise many a
fine Anglo-Saxonist to carry on the work begun by
Turner, Thorpe, and Kemble, until at length every
branch of the literature of Anglo-Saxon England
will be understood as thoroughly as are those of
ancient Greece and Rome.

CHAPTER I.

Advantages of the Study of Anglo-Saxon.

NOTWITHSTANDING all that has been accomplished during the past fifty years, especially in England and Germany, to facilitate and popularise the study of Anglo-Saxon, it is, nevertheless, a fact that, even at the present day, the subject has not the same fascination to the majority of students, (and we refer especially to University men,) as the study of the Classics, or even as the study of modern European languages; while by the masses of ordinarily well-educated people it is but too often regarded as a mere *virtuoso* affair, worthy only to amuse the idler hours of the antiquary.

We do not contend that a thorough knowledge of Anglo-Saxon literature is indispensable if one would attain to eminence in Letters, at the Bar, in the Senate, or in the Church; but we do hold that the advantages of the study to those who speak the English tongue can hardly be overrated.

The Anglo-Saxon literature, considering the state of civilisation to which Europe had attained at the time when it appeared, will bear comparison with any literature of the same age, and with a great deal that has appeared in later times. We must not compare it with the classic literature of Greece and Rome, which was produced after these nations had reached maturity and were in the very zenith of their intellectual greatness. This literature corresponds more exactly with the writings of that brilliant period in England, the dawn of which illumined the later years of the reign of Queen Elizabeth, and the full splendour of which is felt even at the present day. The Anglo-Saxon literature, though far from being so highly polished or showing so high a degree of intellectual culture as this, yet has charms of its own of a very marked character.

It is undeniable that it possesses intrinsic merit of a high order, and is therefore capable of affording pleasure to those who can look beneath the antique style, and seize upon the poetic and other treasures which lie embedded in the obsolete language and verse-systems of a by-gone age.

One fact concerning the writings of the Anglo-Saxon period does not seem to be generally appreciated, namely, that judging from the extant relics, which have already been discovered, they must originally have extended over a very wide field. They show the class of poetry that gave pleasure to the warrior in the Mead-hall, to the family in the *ton*, and to the *religious* in the monastery; they bring to light the quaint catechetical system of education generally adopted in the monastic schools, and disclose the extent of the scientific attainments of the *literati* of that day; and they comprise historic documents of high value, though but too frequently coloured by clerical bias or monastic prejudice. There are charters which explain many a point and unravel many a difficulty in constitutional history; there are codes of laws, civil and ecclesiastical, that, in many instances, show the basis of our modern canon and common law; there are Anglo-Saxon translations of the Gospels, the Psalter and other parts of the Holy Scriptures; there are renderings of the Decalogue, the Lord's Prayer, the Creed, the Ave Maria and of other parts of the Anglican service books; and finally, there are treatises on theology, and writings on philosophy, besides manuals of piety, and homilies of illustrious prelates. These works, considered simply as relics of an important past, might well excite curiosity, apart from their value to the *littérateur*, the historian, the divine, the lawyer and the general student, for the simple reason, before expressed, that they are works of intrinsic merit.

Among the poetry of the Mead-hall, the Saxons possessed, at least, one remarkable epic poem, a Christianised - pagan epic, or narrative of single-handed warfare, where "love is never introduced as a motive of action or intrigue as an instrument"; a graphic picture of early Anglian warrior life, commemorating noble deeds. We refer to the *Beówulf*. This grand relic of the heroic age in England, possesses especial claims upon the attention of the English-speaking nations, not only as being the first vernacular outburst of English song which has come down to us, but as opening up many a curious point, and shedding a new lustre on many modern peculiarities of language, character and customs, which otherwise might seem inexplicable. This monument, moreover, of the language and poetry of our ancestors is one of which any nation might well be proud. It is the oldest epic poem of which mediæval Europe can boast. It antedates the *Niebelungen-Lied*, the oldest epic of Germany, by several hundred years; and there is nothing in the early literature, whether of Scandinavia or of Germany, which can for a moment compare with this English poem, whether it be in power of imagination, in skill of construction, or in weirdness of detail.

A short analysis of this epic poem will show, in a
very distinct light, the leading features of Anglo-
Saxon *secular* poetry ; and, taken in connection with
the fuller analysis of Cædmon's *sacred* verse, which
we shall give later on, will show the justness of our
estimate that Anglo-Saxon literature possesses genuine, intrinsic merits.

We must ask the reader to imagine the interior
of an Anglo-Saxon Mead-hall * in the winter's evening, when the log fires are blazing on the hearths in
the centre aisle, and the dais is occupied by the
King and his cwén and the gleeman of noble
rank; when the long tables are lined with warriors
who drink their mead, and are eager to hear the
exciting tale that the *scop* is about to recite to the
notes of the harp. As the minstrel rises from his
stool, the din of laughter and talking is hushed, and
every eye is turned to the dais, as the gleeman,
striking a chord on his glee-beam, begins his recital :

> " Hark ! we have learnt a tale of other years,
> Of kings and warrior Danes, a wondrous tale,
> How æthelings bore them in the brunt of war."

The tale then begins with the reign of Hróthgár
who was King of the Danes in the North of England,
at the supposed era of the narrative ; and the poet

* *Vide* Note D.

sings of that monarch's kingly ancestors, of their heroic deeds, of his palace at Hart, and, finally, of a Mead-hall which Hróthgár had built, unsurpassed in size and beauty, by any that had ever been reared on English soil. The fame of this Hall is sounded far and wide. Men come from afar to see it and to witness the munificence of the King, who, with lavish hand, is known to deal out bracelet and ring and gold from the sacred " gift-stool." Here, as each night comes round, King and thanes are wont to meet, and

> . . . " oft uprose,
> Loud ringing through those bowers, the harp's glad
>   voice ;
> And oft the bard, whose memory's treasured store
> Was of the days and generations past,
> Waked the sweet song."

Year after year passes by, and naught occurs to disturb their happiness. The prowess of the Danish thanes guards their land from conquest, their palace and their Hall from plunder, and it seems as if their happiness is destined to be unending. But at length, their joy is turned to sadness. A terrible fiend appears, who wreaks on this happy band his dire and savage vengeance. This evil and mysterious enemy is the Grendel, one of a progeny of misshapen giants who had long warred against both

God and man.   This fiend, it seems, roamed the marshes in the lonely night, and held, as his domain, the fen-land, rocky fastness and dark morass.   His stature was enormous ; his strength far more than human ; his flesh invulnerable to all weapons of earthly mould ; and on his fingers were " hand-spurs," more like to steel than human nails.

This fiend hears, day after day, from his dark abode, the joyous revelry of the Danes.   He frowns in anger, and resolves that they shall be his prey. Erelong, under the earth-covering of Night, he stalks over the moors till he comes to Hróthgár's Mead-hall.   There being none to oppose his advance, he enters the building unheeded, and, as he treads its chequered floor, he sees, by the light of the smoul-dering fires, that company of æthelings asleep on their benches.   Grim and greedy, he soon is ready ; rugged and ruthless, he seizes in their sleep thirty of the noblest thanes, and, before ever a warning can be given, he is gone with their slaughtered bodies, back to his cavern home.

In the morning, a cry is raised that thirty thanes have been slaughtered, and the warriors sit in sad-ness when they behold, along the paths leading to the Grendel's den, the blood-traces of the accursed foe.   Scarcely is there one of that noble band but has lost some one of his kin.

After the space of one night the Grendel comes again. The band of æthelings who are on duty guarding that best of houses first feel the force of his murderous hand-grip. Then, a second time, he enters Hertha in stealth, and a second time accomplishes his mission of blood.

Night after night does this grim eoten visit the Mead-hall, and each time some fresh gap is made in the Danish band, and no force avails against his murderous assaults. So Grendel rules, and as often as the darkness comes, he wars against Hróthgár,—alone against all;—till at length the festive Hall stands empty, since none dares to battle with the unearthly foe and meet a certain death.

Twelve winters' tide was his rage endured, and it became known far and near, in sad songs, that Grendel waged unholy war against Hróthgár, and that no money-compromise could appease his savage rage. In perpetual night he held the misty moors, and Hertha, he occupied with its rich stalls; but the "gift-stool," alone, he might not so much as touch.

In spirit broken, Hróthgár sat many a time in his palace; many a time he sat on the sea-shore wrapped in saddest thought.

During these twelve long years, the "sad songs" relating to the Grendel's depredations had been sung

in every *ton* and hall and round-tower of England,
till at length, they had reached the ears of Higelác,
king of the Weder-Geáts, or Angles.   Here Beówulf lived, a thane of Higelác's court, and strongest
of the sons of men.   No sooner had the dire tidings
reached him, than he vows to be avenged upon the
Grendel.   He bids his men make ready a ring-prowed
ship, and determines to go " o'er the seabird's path " *
to seek the monarch, Hróthgár, in his hour of need.
He chooses thrice five bold warriors as his companions, men dauntless in fight, and who know every
landmark on the beaten coast.   Soon the ship is
ready ; her deep hold is filled with arms ; they leave
the shore ; and erelong, by the sea-girt cliffs, "e'en
as a bird," the boat cuts through the waves that
foam around her prow.   Before the second sun had
set, these warriors reach the coast of Hróthgár's
realm, and as they near the land they don their
glittering mail.   The warden of the coast had already espied their ship, and as soon as they had
landed, and he had learned the object of their coming, leads them an inland walk of two miles to
Hróthgár's palace, where they are forthwith ushered
into the presence of the King.   Then Beówulf
speaks in the self-confident, self-laudatory tones of a
true Homeric hero :

* *Vide* Note E.

        " ' King Hróthgár, hail !
I am the thane and kin of Higelác ;
One that have master'd in my day of youth
Full many a deed of gallant enterprise.
And now in mine own country have I heard
Bruited by loud report this Grendel's wrong :
For gleemen told, that, soon as evening's light
Beneath Heaven's vault sought its deep hiding-place,
Thy princely bower all emptied of its guests
Stood tenantless.   Then this valiant band and brave,
Counsell'd that I should seek thee at thy need ;
For they best knew my prowess, they had seen
What time I came deep dyed in hostile gore
From dread and perilous war ; then in one night
With hardy grasp I quell'd five savage Jutes,
And plunged them howling in the ocean wave.
And now with Grendel, with that guilty one,
Fiend though he be, alone will I assay
The mortal strife.

        " ' I have heard
That that foul miscreant's dark and stubborn flesh
Recks not the force of arms :—such I forswear,
Nor sword nor burnish'd shield of ample round
Ask for the war ; all weaponless, hand to hand

   .   .   .   .

Beówulf will grapple with this nightly foe.
There, as Heaven's righteous judgment shall award,
One of us falls.' "

While Beówulf is speaking, the aged monarch
gazes admiringly on the young warrior, and his eyes
seem to be rivetted on the bright coat of mail, " the

war-net sewed by the skill of the armourer," which
Beówulf wears. The King thanks him for his brave
offer, but cannot refrain from telling him of the
danger of the adventure which he has undertaken.

As evening approaches, Hróthgár and Beówulf
repair to the Mead-hall, and once more, after many a
long year, the fires on the hearths are kindled. The
monarch ascends the "gift-stool." His queen, the
beautiful Wealhtheów, sits at his side. His noble
"hearth-sharers" gather around him. The minstrel
strikes his "glee-beam." The war-men throng the
benches. The bright armour once again glistens in
the flicker of the log fires. The vats labour under
their burden of mead. Hertha as of old resounds
with merriment and song; there is laughter of men;
the din redoubles and words are winsome!

Wealhtheów, Hróthgár's queen, the gold adorned
one, greets the warriors in the Mead-hall, and the
buxom wife first gives the cup to her lord and bids
him be blithe at the feast. Then, on every side the
bracelet covered queen hands rich vessels, until she
bears the mead-cup to Beówulf. She greets the
Angles' lord, thanking God that the will had befallen
her to trust in any warrior for help. He, the fierce
war-man, drinks of the cup from Wealhtheów, and
then, eager for battle, Beówulf speaks:

"I resolved, cwén, when on the main I went, that

I alone would work your people's will or bow in death, fast in hostile grasps. I shall do deeds of noble valour or await my last day in this Mead-hall."

Wealhtheów liked the hero's proud speeches. Adorned with gold, went the joyful people's queen to sit by her lord until Hróthgár went to his evening rest. But he, the hoary monarch, well knew that in that high Hall there would be battle when murky night, the shadow-covering of creatures, came advancing dusky under the clouds.

When the evening's feast is over, the guests all arise. Hróthgár bids Beówulf hail, gives him command of the Mead-hall and adds, "Never before, since I could raise hand and shield, have I entrusted to any man the Danes' festive Hall, save now to thee, Beówulf. Have now and hold this best of houses; show thy mighty valour; watch against foes!"

Hróthgár then departs, but before he retires, he sets a band of æthelings to watch, and to give warning when the huge eoten is seen advancing. Beówulf, left alone with his companions, doffs his iron suit, gives his helm and rich sword to an attendant, and then retires to rest. Not a word is spoken by the warriors, as each one knows full well that many a thane, in that same hall, in days gone by, has met a horrid death. It is the silence which precedes the battle.

3

Before many hours have passed, there comes, stalking in the murky night, the shadow-walker. All of the Anglian warriors, appointed to defend that best of houses, are asleep; all of the Gothic band are deep in slumber;—all, save Beówulf. He, watching for the foe, in hate and angry mood, awaits the battle meeting. The fires smoulder on the hearths and the Hall is dark and cold. At length,

> ". . . beneath the hill of mists
> The Grendel came—a heaven-abandon'd wretch ;—
> The foul assassin thought in that high hall
> To gorge some human prey. Onwards he pass'd
> In darkness, till right near he might behold
> That princely bower, the nobles' golden seat
> Rich deck'd with many a mead-cup. . . . Soon he
>   reach'd,—
> A joyless guest, that hall ; soon, unopposed,
> With giant arm, fierce in his wrath, dash'd down
> Her iron-banded gates ; and now he trod
> Her chequer'd floor, angry of soul he moved,
> A fiendish foe ; and flamelike, as he strode,
> Shot from his eyes a sad and hideous light.
> There might he see the heroes at their rest—
> A band of brothers. Then his heart was glad,
> For sooth he thought, or ere the morrow dawn'd,
> From each man's corpse to drain the blood of life.
>
>   .   .   .   .
>
> ". . . Firm of soul meanwhile
> The thane of Higelác watch'd, full fain to prove
> How that foul fiend would fare beneath his grasp.

Nor long delay the murderer brook'd ; for still
In other days light effort had it cost
To slay the uncautious warrior in his sleep,
To crush the yielding bones, and from each vein
Draw the warm current.

    .   .   .   .

" Now strode he onward, and with slaughterous hand
Pounced on the wary chief.   He swift uprose
(Nor reckless of his aim nor weak of grasp)
And dash'd to that fair floor th' astounded foe.
Soon found that base one, that in the elder time
(Since first he roam'd the waste) he ne'er had coped
With sterner soul or hand of hardier grasp.
Care was upon his heart and sudden dread ;
Fain would he seek his own unhallow'd den,
And shroud himself in darkness, for he met
Such welcome as of old he wist not there.
Nor less bethought him of his evening pledge
The gallant thane of Higelác ; firm he stood,
And seized the monster.   Yet he might not triumph,
His hold was loosen'd, and the fiend was free.
Swift rush'd the hero forwards, all his care
Lest the dark murderer scape, and wing his flight
To fen and fastness.   Soon the Grendel felt
Beneath that grasp of power, that he had bent
In evil time his steps to Hróthgár's home.
Loud was the din, and fierce the champion's rage,
And keen the struggle."

The companions of Beówulf, fearing that their lord
is being overmatched, draw their swords and smite
on every side.   They know not that no war-blade

will cut into the fiend's flesh.   Vain are their effor..,
But Beówulf, stout of soul, has this foe of God in
his mighty hand-grasp, and,

> " Soon the dark wanderer's ample shoulder bore
> A gaping wound ; each starting sinew crack'd,
> And from its socket loosed the strong-knit joint.—
> The victory was with Beówulf ; and the foe,
> Howling and sick at heart fled as he might,
> To seek beneath the mountain shroud of mist
> His joyless home ; for well he knew the day
> Of death was on him, and his doom was seal'd."

In the morning, warriors come from far and near
to see the marvel.   The Grendel had left his track
as he fled, death-haunted and weary, to the Nicker's
mere.   There, near by, was to be seen the surge
boiling with blood ; for the miscreant had dyed it
after he had laid down his life in shelter of the fen.
The Mead-hall, too, bore many a mark of the great
night-battle.   The stalls, resplendent with gold, and
the couches, cunningly wrought, were uptorn from
their foundations where the wrestlers had borne them
in their angry mood.   The rich curtains that adorned
the walls were rent ; the chequered floor was broken ;
the tables were shattered ; and every part was in
wreck, save only the roof and heavy pillars.   Then
the King steps forth ; and the queen, as soon as it is
light, together with her lord, measures the meadow-

path encircled by her maidens. The warriors are merry, and run their fallow steeds in the race. The gleeman sings of the Goth's great deed, and Beówulf's praise is heard on every side.

Then is Hertha ordered to be adorned anew. The golden webs, (the embroidered hangings), shine once again on the walls, full of wondrous sights. The arm of the eoten with its hand, and "handspurs as of steel," is hung conspiciously forth as a trophy. The largest and noblest throng that had ever gathered in Hertha now fills the Hall. The mead-cup is borne around, and the King presents Beówulf with a helmet, decked with a wild boar's head in gold, a shield and coat of mail, and steeds such as the King himself used in the play of swords.

When the evening is come, the Hall again rings with the merriment of the warriors, and not till Hróthgár and Beówulf leave for the palace, does the revelry cease. Then, as of old, a guard is placed to watch the building; the war-men bow to sleep, and the bright shields hang glittering over their heads.

.   .   .   .

But in the dead of night, while all are asleep, there comes over that blood-stained mere, and stealing beneath the shade of mist and mountain fastness, the huge form of a second fell monster. This eoten does not bear the likeness of a man. It is *she*, the weird being who gave Grendel birth ; she, who inhabits the cold streams and hollow pools and watery caverns. Her eyes are wild, and, as she advances, a strange unearthly fire darts forth from them, shooting from place to place, as, with unsteady step and fitful bound, she takes her sorrowful journey, direfully to avenge her son.   The Hall is shrouded in darkness ; but only too well does she know the way thither. At length she reaches Hertha.   The Danes, without and within the Hall, unheedful of danger, are asleep ; yet it is a restless sleep.   It is as if a night Mara, with her horrid visions, were upon them.   The She-wulf rushes, unopposed, into the festive Hall ; but her unearthly step arouses the warriors, and in a moment, many a broad shield flashes in the light of the dying fires, and swords are drawn.   But she, the Grendel's mother, is in haste ; she is discovered ; she would save herself.   In an instant she seizes one of the nobles, Hróthgár's dearest thane, and before her hasty flight can be stopped she is off, and speeding her way over the cloud-enwreathed moor.   Then is a cry raised in Hertha ; the Danish men are aroused, and the hoary King is of angry mood when he learns that his dearest thane is dead.   Beówulf is quickly summoned to the presence-chamber.   Then speaks the King, the helm of the Danes : " Fresh sorrow is upon us, Beówulf ; he is dead whose arm has long upheld my realm. For that thou killedst Grendel yesternight, there is come another fell destroyer who has avenged her son. I have heard my people say that they have seen two such huge marsh-walkers, one in woman's likeness the other the Grendel." This

> "   .   .   .   foul spirit, howling as the wolves,
> Holds, by the perilous passage of the fen,
> Rude crag, and trackless steep, her dark abode.
> There from the headlong cliff rolls arrowy down
> The fiery stream, whose wild and wondrous waves
> The frequent and fast-rooted wood o'erhangs,
> Shrouding them e'en as with the warrior's helm.
> There nightly mayst thou see a sight of dread,
> A flood of living flame."

Her home is no holy place, continues Hróthgár. Its depth is such there liveth no man so wise who knows its lowest caves. Evermore there rise up from its depths dark storms, and the wind stirs hateful tempests, until the air grows gloomy and the heavens shed tears.

Beówulf, undaunted by the horrors of the place, undertakes to track the fiend to her home.

> " ' Here I swear,' he exclaims,
> ' She finds not refuge, nor in earth's deep caves,
> Nor in the forest's shades, nor in the abyss
> Of warring waters.   Fly she where she will,
> I vow revenge and pledge me to thy cause.' "

At these welcome words the aged monarch steps
from his throne, and with joy embraces Beówulf,
commands his steed to be immediately harnessed,
and, with a chosen band prepares to escort Beówulf
over the murky moor to the Grendel's home. The
warriors accordingly start, and, led by four trusty
guides, thread their way thither by cliff and cavern,
the dwelling of many a monster of the flood. At
length, they come to a halt, where, beneath the dark
shade of a far overhanging rock, the angry and
bloodstained stream rolls swiftly past. There, on
the naked brow of a crag across the stream, they
see the mangled head of Hróthgár's thane. Hróthgár turns away, sick at heart; but Beówulf burns
with a keener desire than ever for the approaching
battle, and forthwith prepares to plunge into the
flood in quest of the fiend, the She-wulf. His
companions, accordingly, help him as he dons his
armour: first, his bright helmet with its wondrous
charm "the head of the savage boar;" then his
coat of mail; and lastly his famous sword "Hrunt-
ing," the blade of which, steeped in herbs of strange
and magic virtue, has never failed him. As soon as
he is duly equipped, he turns to Hróthgár, and, in
case of a fatal termination of the adventure, com-
mends to his care the band of faithful warriors who
have accompanied him on the expedition. This

done, and without awaiting the King's reply, he plunges into the whelming surge.

For the space of a whole day he sinks through the waters, and at length strikes the rocky ground. In a moment, she, who had held the sovereignty of the flood for a hundred years, sees a man from above, exploring, springs upon him, and seizes the warrior in her horrid clutches; but although, at first, he is powerless to fight, yet she cannot break his ring-mail with her fingers, but fiercely drags him down towards her dwelling at the bottom of the flood. By this time Beówulf has sufficiently recovered his senses to notice his surroundings. He finds himself in a roofed hall where there is no water; a region, where " the fire-flood shed its deep and livid glare." Breaking loose from the iron grasp of his antagonist, Beówulf strikes blow after blow upon the misshapen fiend with his magic sword; but that blade, which had never failed him in battle, avails not against the unearthly flesh of the She-wulf. The angry fighter casts the weapon away, and resolves to rely solely upon his strength of hand. A terrible encounter ensues; she seizes him by the shoulder; he breaks away; she catches him with fierce grasps; throws him weary to the ground; presses him down, and draws her seax ready to avenge her son. But Beówulf's armour protects him. By a mighty effort he loosens her hold, and, seeing in that subaqueous realm, a sword of wondrous power, he springs away, seizes it, and deals such quick and terrible blows that at length the "bone-rings" of her neck break; the sword goes through her flesh, and she falls lifeless to the ground.

And now a marvellous sight presents itself. Instant, as though Heaven's glorious torch had suddenly shone, light is upon the gloom; a light that spreads itself throughout the inmost caverns of the eoten's stronghold and illumines its darkest recesses. Still grasping the mighty sword with which he had just killed the She-wulf, Beówulf wanders through this enchanted region, wondering at the sights and treasures which he sees, ready for any encounter that may await him, and eager to put an end to the Grendel should he still be alive. In one of the rocky chambers of this watery fastness, however, he finds the huge eoten lying dead. Wishing to present to Hróthgár some memorial of his victory, he proceeds to strike off the head of the Grendel. And now a second miracle ensues. At the first stroke of his sword the body springs far away from the head as the sword severs the two; and stranger yet, the steel of the sword melts away like ice as the giant's blood drips from it, leaving in Beówulf's hand naught but the rich sword-hilt. The warrior takes none of the treasures which surround him, but bearing in one hand the Grendel's head and the head of the She-wulf, and in the other the rich sword-hilt with its mystic runes, he prepares to return to his companions.

Hróthgár and his warriors, after Beówulf had plunged into the flood, stay at the water's edge to watch the issue of the adventure; but when, at length, they see the crimson blood rise to the surface, and the waters turned to a flood of fire, their courage fails them ; and fearing that Beówulf is slain, they depart, sick of mood, and bend their steps back to the Mead-hall.

The gallant band, however, who had followed their leader, Beówulf, still lingered on the strand. They had gazed long and eagerly, only to be disappointed, when all at once they see their Chief rise to the surface of the mere, and come swimming to land. No sooner is he safely landed than they help to loosen his helmet and coat of mail, and as they do so, the blood stained water, dripping from his person, dyes the very ground on which he stands.

Then a procession is formed. Four strong men can scarcely bear upon the deadly stake the heads of the conquered eotens. At length the heroes of the adventure reach the Mead-hall where the Danish warriors are drinking, but there is no sound of

revelry.   The harp is silent, and no merriment is to
be heard.   As they enter the Hall, however, a sudden shout of triumph and welcome resounds through
the building.   Beówulf advances to the "gift-stool;"
displays his hideous trophies; recounts his adventures; and ends by presenting to Hróthgár the
golden hilt, with its runic inscription, which he has
brought from the Grendel's den.   The King, in reply, indulges in a speech marked by true Nestorian
eloquence, acknowledging that Beówulf has re-
deemed his haughty pledge to free the country of its
superhuman pest.   Then the old monarch, with
royal munificence, deals from that "gift-stool" the
richest rewards in his power; the feast begins anew;
the gleeman improvises a lyric in honour of the hero;
the Mead-hall re-echoes the deep laugh and unbridled shouting of the warriors, and naught is heard
but the exultant cry, " Hertha is ransomed."

The helm of Night grows murky; the aged Hróthgár goes to his couch, and Beówulf is eager for rest.

When the black raven, blithe of heart, announces
the coming of the light on the following morning,
the heroes of this adventure resolve to return to
their own land.   Accompanied by the entire warrior band they leave Hertha, and bend their steps to
the shore.   The warden espies them coming,—a gallant band in sarks of netted mail,—and has their ship

in readiness, which it seems by the King's command has been

> " laden deep
> With warlike gear, steeds, arms, and treasured gold,
> The choicest meed of Hróthgár's ample store."

It is a brilliant sight that now presents itself on that Danish shore. There, stands the hoary monarch, resplendent in his kingly arms, first in age as well as in rank. Beside him, stands Beówulf, a mere youth compared with the Danish King, his face flushed with conscious pride ; and around them, stands that picked band of warrior-thanes, each one eager to do honour to the hero of the hour. The trusty warden draws near to inform the Anglian men that their ship is ready, when Beówulf advances and presents him with a jewelled sword in token of his esteem. The men embark ; the King kisses Beówulf, that best of warriors, and, as he bids him " God speed," he clasps him around the neck, his war-beaten face moistened with salt tears.

Soon the boat, harnessed for the sea, speeds through the waves, and, at length, the men see in the distance their native cliffs,—the well-known headlands of the Anglian coast. The torch of the world is shining when Beówulf reaches the Hall of his monarch Higelác. Immediately, a feast is prepared and

the Anglian men, bursting with curiosity, urge Beówulf to relate how it befell him on the way.

We may say, in passing, that the story of Beówulf
does not end at this point. The remainder of the
narrative, as it has come down to us in the Cottonian
manuscript, describes the further adventures of the
hero in his own land after the slaying of the Grendel; but this continuation of the legend, which is
virtually an independent tale, and but slightly connected with the adventure of the Grendel, is in all
probability the *residuum* of a much longer narrative,
and *may* have formed, at one time, part of an extensive cyclus. We have adduced enough, however, to
show the character of Anglo-Saxon secular poetry,
and to prove how valuable an insight such a poem
as this may give of certain phases of the social and
warrior life of our Anglo-Saxon ancestors.

But the advantages of a study of Anglo-Saxon
writings are not confined solely to the pleasure which
we derive from a perusal of the poetry which they
contain.

In the province of *language*, the pre-eminent advantage that an Anglo-Saxon scholar possesses over
the scholar of modern English only, in a thorough
understanding of the structure and resources of the
language, is unquestionable. The many apparent
anomalies of pronunciation, of spelling, and of struc-

ture, with which modern English abounds, can, in the majority of cases, be fully accounted for by referring back to the language in its pre-Norman stage.

The student of English who has mastered Anglo-Saxon has reached the fountain head of the English language, and can give both the "*an sit*" and "*cur sit*" of its grammar. It is true that in the English, as, indeed, in all the languages of the so-called Aryan family, the process of "phonetic decay" has been at work, so that terminations, originally significant words, have, after the lapse of time, either disappeared altogether, or have undergone so great a change from the falling out of letters, as to require a lengthened study to enable the student to recognise them. It is not pretended that a knowledge of Anglo-Saxon will disclose the full form of English inflections of which, perhaps, only a single letter remains at the present day. This is the province of comparative grammar. But it will, at any rate, disclose what a given form was, or must have been, at a much earlier stage of the language, and will throw light upon many a point which would sorely puzzle him who is unable to refer to the Anglo-Saxon.

Unfortunately, the works from which most people acquire their early grammatical ideas are, as a rule, based on Latin models, and show, throughout, how little such writers have understood the nature and structure of a Teutonic language. Those who place themselves under the direction of these Latinised guides, necessarily acquire views which are not only imperfect, but unsound into the bargain. A thorough acquaintance with Anglo-Saxon prevents or counteracts the effect of these erroneous teachings. But it accomplishes more than this. It has been well said, that to know the grammar of a language it is necessary to know the reasons of the grammar. It is not sufficient to know simply the forms of words; we ought to know why such forms exist, and why in their place we do not find some other forms; and this canon of the science of Language is one of universal application.

What can be easier to the Saxonist than to explain why the form " I sang " is more correct than " I sung "; or why the est in " livest " becomes t in " wilt "; or why such a sentence as " Neuyr after she coude be blythe," the form " coude " is more correct than the modern form " could "; or why, in the phrase " if any man say aught to you, ye shall say," the form " you " is used in one instance and " ye " in the other; or why we find " yes " in one place and " yea " in another; or " no " in one place and " nay " in another; or to explain the structure of such a phrase as " all the more "; or finally to explain why, in the universal use of the pronoun "it," educated Englishmen and Americans alike are as thoroughly "Cockney," from an etymological standpoint, as the veriest ignoramus born within hearing of Bow-church Bell?

It is the same in matters of *pronunciation*. Most of the peculiarities of modern English speech in this respect, which at first seem to court the criticism of those who are not of English birth, belong legitimately to the English nation as heirlooms of its Anglo-Saxon ancestry, and can be shown to be correct on strict philological lines.

At times too, a modern word, traced back to the Anglo-Saxon, will throw a perfectly electric light upon a point of language or of history or of national character. We call a sullen, dogged, obstinate boor a "churl." Whence this epithet? In Saxon times, the thanes, the ceorls, and the théows formed the three classes of society, corresponding to the nobility, the yeomanry, and the domestic slaves of a later age. The ceorl or yeoman was the ancestor of that sturdy race of freemen which has grown into the powerful "middle class" of our own day; the lineal ancestors of the men who, from the time of King John to the present hour, have fought the great battle for civil liberty, till to-day they form the bone and sinew of England and, in spite of the clamour of the demagogue, are more truly the "ruling classes"

than the mightiest peers of the realm.   Such was the
Saxon ceorl or churl.   How, then, has this word of
true nobility become degraded from its high meaning ?   The history of the Norman period in England
supplies the true answer.   The haughty barons,
holding their lands, however small, by military tenure, looked down upon and despised, as beneath
contempt, these sturdy Saxon tillers of the soil, and
treated them as low-born.   The ceorl, in turn, hated
with bitter hatred the insolent foreigner whose iron
arm was crushing him to the earth.   Helpless, yet
high-spirited, he repaid *hauteur* with blunt words
and sullen looks, till the Norman, in deep disdain,
exclaimed " Churl,"—and the word has lived.

Seclusiveness of character and love of privacy are
often laid to the charge of those of Anglo-Saxon
descent; and in England, where these characteristics
are very distinctly marked, they are invariably attributed by foreigners to national vanity or personal
affectation.   The most elementary knowledge of
Anglo-Saxon social life would show that the English
come rightfully by this characteristic, and that it is
no mark of mere pride or affectation, but was a characteristic of the whole of the Teutonic race, which
did not escape the keen notice of Tacitus.   Speaking of the Germans, before the Saxon invasion of
England, this writer says : " They dwell in villages,

not according to our custom, formed of houses one adjoining the other, but each man surrounds his own home with an open space." And this seclusiveness of character the Saxons carried with them to Britain. Anyone who has travelled in England must have noticed that it is pre-eminently the land of hedges and enclosures,—

" Little lines of sportive wood run wild "

whereas, on the Continent, almost the first thing that one notices is the absence of the hedge-rows of England. If, now, we examine English local names, (one of the surest tests by which to arrive at the national characteristics of a by-gone age,) we shall find that for more than a thousand years England has been distinctively the land of hedges or enclosures. The termination *ton*, which so frequently occurs on both sides of the Atlantic, proves how eager every Anglo-Saxon was to possess some spot which he could call his own, and guard from the intrusion of his neighbour. The primary meaning of this suffix *ton* * is an enclosure, or that which is bounded by a hedge ; and originally signified the single homestead or farm which the owner or occupant desired to mark out as his *hám* or home or sacred spot. This restricted meaning of the word *ton* or town was

* Anglo-Saxon *týnan* to enclose, hedge in, etc.

current even in the time of Wycliffe for he translates the passage in the Gospel according to St. Matthew c. xxii., v. 5 : " But thei dispisiden, and wenten oon to his *toun*, another to his marchaundise "; where the modern Anglican translation has, " They made light of it, and went one to his *farm*, and another to his merchandise." Even at the present day, there are single farm houses in England the names of which end in *ton*, still pointing to this Anglo-Saxon seclusiveness. In many cases, however, the isolated *ton* became the nucleus of a village, and the village grew into a town ; and last stage of all, the word *ton* or town has come to signify, not the one small farm, enclosed from the forest by the Saxon settler, but the dwelling-place of a vast population greater than that of which the whole of Saxon England could boast. Still, though Botolph's *ton* has grown into Bo'ston, yet the love of seclusion and impatience of intrusiveness characteristic of the first settlers have descended as an heirloom to each inhabitant of the modern Boston, and, carried across the Atlantic, by the first Puritan settlers in this country, are to this day the characteristics of its American namesake.

In the study of the origin of national *social customs*, a knowledge of Anglo-Saxon literature often discloses points of especial interest. It is well known that Anglo-Saxon notions of hospitality, though well intentioned, were inimical to sobriety. It was considered the duty of the host to offer mead or wine to every guest of distinction who might be journeying past his home. The kings and nobles, on their journeys of state or pleasure, stopped to drink at every house on their sparsely settled route; and as, at such times, they were exposed to the danger of assassination by secret foes, a system was introduced, the rememberance of which, has permeated the whole of our literature, and the vestiges of which remain in many of the pleasant amenities of the English social life of to-day.

Spenser, in the *Faerie Queene*, speaking of the mariner, says:

> Soone as the port from far he has espide,
> His chearfull whistle merily doth sound,
> And Nereus crownes with cups; his mates
> Him *pledg* around.

Similarly, Ben Jonson sings in his often quoted lines:

> Drink to me only with thine eyes
> And I will *pledge* with mine.

Here the word "pledge," to a modern reader, would convey but a very small amount of meaning; but to the Anglo-Saxon student this word is full of significance. When a Saxon warrior, travelling through the country, stopped to quench his thirst with a glass of mead at the nearest *ton* he might pass on his road, he was exposed to the danger of assassination by unsuspected enemies. The Saxon drinking-cups were large and horn-shaped, and required to be held in both hands. While the hands were thus in use, and the head raised in the act of drinking, a warrior offered a fine opportunity to the assassin. Hence a custom was introduced as a protection to life. A Saxon about to drink, asked his companion to be his *pledge*, or guardian, while so doing. The pledger, accordingly, drew his sword and protected the drinking man, who, in his turn, guarded his companion while he drank. When personal security became better ensured this practice died out, and the sword gave place to the various substitutes of modern times.

As an instance of the survival, in England, of this custom in the social usages of the present day, we may mention the passing of the " Loving Cup," which is observed at many of the more formal functions at the English Universities ; and more particularly at the Lord Mayor's banquets at the Mansion House, where both the customs and dress of an earlier age are scrupulously maintained. At such entertainments, when the Loving Cup is passed around, the ceremony brings vividly to mind the Anglo-Saxon custom of olden times. The guest whose turn it is to drink, rises from his seat, and receiving the Loving Cup in both hands from the guest on his left hand, turns to the guest on his right, who removes the massive lid; the guest on either side standing guard while he drinks the accustomed toast, in accordance with the traditions of an earlier age.

To the student of language, of literature, and of social observances, this study is all-important. But it has practical bearings as well. A strong and steady light may be reflected from this quarter on many points of municipal and common law; the theory of our political constitution; and the internal history of our Church polity. The Saxon charters and laws throw a strong light upon the Saxon political and religious institutions, and enable us to gain a tolerably clear insight into Saxon times. They show the rank, the rights, and the duties of the several orders of society; they disclose to us the mode in which our ancestors punished public wrongs or redressed civil injuries; they explain the constitution and jurisdiction of the several courts; they discover interesting facts respecting the tenure of land; and they show the amount of authority possessed by the Anglo-Saxon Church. The whole fabric of our laws, indeed, ecclesiastical as well as civil, is built upon an Anglo-Saxon foundation. To the lawyer who is not content with simply the practical knowledge of modern law requisite for the every-day business of life, but who aspires to a thorough mastery of any particular branch of his profession, a knowledge of Anglo-Saxon law is as indispensable as a knowledge of Roman law. "Where," asks an eminent authority on this subject, "is the lawyer who will not derive an accession of solid information from a perusal of the Anglo-Saxon laws published by Lambard, Wheloc, and Wilkins, not to mention the various charters and legal instruments that are still extant, together with the ancient records of our county courts, on the foundation of which is erected the whole superstructure of our forensic practice? What patriot is there whose heart does not burn within him while he is reading the language in which the immortal Alfred, and other Saxon kings, composed the elements of our envied code of laws, and portrayed the grand outlines of our free constitution?" And yet how few even of our most prominent members of the Bar have ever read one line of these, although the contents of the *Corpus Juris Civilis* may be as familiar to them as Blackstone or Kent! The lawyer who possesses this intimate acquaintance with his subject will not only have the personal satisfaction arising from a consciousness of superior knowledge, but will possess, in addition, a power of illustration and argument not attainable by the student whose attainments are confined to a knowledge of the principles of modern forensic practice only.

Moreover, our political institutions, which excite the admiration of all who have devoted attention to the subject, although they have been modified by Norman feudalism; although they have been rendered more secure by baronial or popular opposition to royal tyranny or absolutism; and although they have been improved and perfected by the wisdom of succeeding ages, still, even nowadays, are essentially Anglo-Saxon in all their main features. The originals of most of these institutions upon which the English race most prides itself at the present day, no less than the beginnings of many of the best principles of national constitutional government, and local self-government, to which both England and America owe so much of their greatness, are to be found in the charters and laws of the pre-Norman era. The statesman who has clearly before his mind the history of the grand constitutional principles of his country, and who can trace them back to a time when they existed only in germ, will have a broader view of the bearings of any attempt at innovation or reform, and be better entitled to an opinion upon any important question of statesmanship, than those who are prevented by ignorance from casting their observation beyond the narrow circumference of their own age.

At the present day, too, when questions of Church discipline, Church doctrine, and Church practice are commanding the attention of intelligent men—the laity as well as the clergy—they who can turn to the religious writings of the Anglo-Saxons may gain from them an insight into the doctrine and polity of the early Anglican Church which those cannot possess who take the Tudor period as their starting point. And where is the clergyman who will not derive advantage from a perusal of the ecclesiastical laws, the ecclesiastical history, the homilies, and the various works of piety and devotion of Anglo-Saxon England, of which so many specimens are extant?

But, perhaps, the crowning advantage of a knowledge of Anglo-Saxon consists in the pleasure it affords the lover of English literature, by enabling him to enjoy the earlier, no less than the more modern, writings of England's greatest writers. Let the student, who has mastered the Anglo-Saxon stage of our language as it passes sluggishly through Saxon times, follow it through the so-called Semi-Saxon, as it begins in Layamon's *Brut* to break loose from the trammels of grammatical forms; let him watch it, as it bounds through the Norman times, throwing off in its progress first one incumbrance and then another, till gaining power by the very oppression it has endured at the hands of its Norman tyrants, it bursts forth in the literature of the Early English period, giving promise of its future greatness; let him track it for a hundred years, as it changes its course, now tending to the Northern now to the Southern dialect, till, at length, in Middle English, it is powerful enough to express the highest flights of the genius of Chaucer; let him still follow it, as, impatient of restraint, it carries away in its progress the remaining imperfections which hide its true strength, until finally it shows its majestic power in the works of Spenser, Shakespeare, and Milton; then the student will have gained a correct notion not only of the gradually increasing power of the *language*, in its passage from a synthetic to an analytic structure, he will, further, have gained a view of the gradual unfolding of the *mind* of the English nation as reflected in the ever increasing brilliancy of the national literature, that can never be attained by one whose reading is restricted by a knowledge of modern English only.

CHAPTER II.

The Life and Times of Cædmon and Sketch of the Junian Manuscript.

THE earliest specimen which has come down to us of the English *metrical* Romance or Epic, carries us back, like the earliest specimen of the English *prose* Romance or Novel, to the very dawn of English life and history.

In tracing to its source the story of King Arthur and his knights of the Round Table, (and it is with this tale that English prose Romance begins), we have to retrace our steps and explore the dim past of bardic times when the Cambrian poets sang of the warlike deeds of kings and heroes in the death struggle then being waged between the Kelt and the Saxon.

And this, *cæteris paribus*, is equally true of the metrical Romance, whether secular or sacred; whether it be the Christianised-pagan romance of the *Beówulf* or the Scriptural romance of Cædmon's "Fall of Man." Both of these, take us back in thought to early Anglo-Saxon times, when England was dense with forests, when the woods were filled with the wolf, the elk, and the bear, and when only here and there a solitary dwelling in the field or feld, *i. e.* the clearing, marked the habitation of human beings.

The little that we know of the life of Cædmon, and the strange story of the sudden revelation of high poetic powers possessed by this hitherto unknown ceorl, would be unintelligible should we fail to understand the social and ecclesiastical conditions of the times in which he lived.

It is difficult, no doubt, to reproduce in imagination, even approximately, the everyday life of an age long gone by and enter into the spirit of its daily thought; and yet this must be attempted if we would study intelligently the literature of any past epoch. The history, the religion, the language, and the social customs of any given age are mutually explanatory, and one and all, must be made subsidiary if the literature of the past is to stand out before the mind as a living picture.

In the short account of the life of Cædmon which has been handed down to us by the Venerable Beda in his *Historia Ecclesiastica*, and which unfortunately is the only one that we possess, there are references to certain phases of Anglo-Saxon life that we must glance at before going farther, in order to render intelligible Beda's narrative of this remarkable man.

The Anglo-Saxon *scop* or gleeman,—a profession
corresponding to that of the bard of the Keltic era
and to that of the minstrel in the Norman era,—was
a kind of protean character. At times, he was the
companion of king and courtiers, holding the rank of
thane or nobleman ; an accomplished poet, entitled
to a high seat in the king's hall and the proprietor
of estates, whose presence was required at battles
when the prizes of valour were to be awarded, and
at court festivities to chant the heroic deeds of
his patron or of his patron's guests. The king's
scop or earl's gleeman, was the favourite of the
court ; the one indispensable guest at every banquet
and every courtly gathering ; whose skill with the
glee-beam or harp spread joy throughout the festive
hall, and whose memory was stored with soul-stirring
tales of great deeds, the recital of which could not
fail to fire the hearts and quicken the pulses of
young and old alike. It was the duty of the court
gleeman to know the genealogy of his patron, the
traditions of his house, the past history of his race,
and every fact or legend that could enhance his
dignity or flatter his pride. After dinner, when there
was " song and music together, and the glee-beam
was touched," he was the chief centre of attraction.
If the board was honoured by the presence of a distinguished guest it was his duty to be ready with

verses in his praise. This point is brought out very clearly in the story of Beówulf. On this hero's return to Hróthgár's court, after the conquest of the Grendel, the bard, "the King's thane, a man laden with lofty themes, thoughtful of song, he who a great multitude of old traditions remembered, who invented new ones fitly composed, this man now began Beówulf's adventure skilfully to relate." This function of the gleeman was styled "the right of bestowing praise," and earned for the *scop* a wide influence among a warlike and illiterate class of nobles.

But the gleeman was not always fortunate enough to be the retainer at a king's court, or the noble guest of the Mead-hall. At times, he appears as a wandering narrator of verse and tale, straying from *ton* to hamlet, from hall and monastery to cottage and ale-house ; he was passionately beloved by the laity, high and low, rich and poor, and even by the lower orders of the clergy. These gleemen, were the story-tellers, the news gatherers, the scandal-mongers, and gossip-bearers, in times when there were neither newspapers nor post offices ; the chief medium, from their vagrant mode of life, of hearing, bearing, and retailing the latest "domestic and foreign intelligence." Their profession procured them easy access to the camp, the ale house, and, occasionally, even to the monastery. It is not probable that any but very lax abbots or abbesses would have sanctioned their performances in monasteries; yet in the middle of the eighth century we know from authentic records, that the *religious* were not averse to being amused by " the sportive arts of poets, musicians, harpers, and buffoons." If the gleemen were popular with the laity and lower orders of the clergy, they were the reverse with the bishops and higher ecclesiastics, who regarded them as children of the devil, mockers and vagabonds, and, indeed, thought no name too bad for them. They are rarely spoken of, in ecclesiastical chronicles, as *scops* or gleeman, but as " ale-poets," " tumblers," " jesters," " players," and " mimics."

The ale-house, however, was the place that the wandering gleeman most liked, and in which he was most appreciated. Here, he had to suit his entertainment to the vulgar taste of boors, utterly incompetent to enjoy anything beyond the most palpable and coarsest of fun :—" Media inter carmina poscunt aut ursam aut pugiles,"—something rougher than song and music.

But the Anglo-Saxons, like all of their *confrères* of the Teutonic race, were fond of music and song, and at their convivial gatherings, even when the gleeman was not present, it was customary to pass the glee-beam, and for each guest in turn to do his share towards the entertainment of his fellows. This, which seems to have been a universal custom among the Anglo-Saxon ceorls at their feasts, is brought out very distinctly in Beda's account of the "Coming" of Cædmon as we shall subsequently see.

Another phase of Anglo-Saxon life, which it is most important to understand in this connection, is the monastic system then in vogue among the *religious*. It was the early days of Christianity in England, when the dogmas of the Church were held with the tenacity of a cloudless faith, and when the dazzling vista of the future life had lost none of its glamour under the disenchanting touch of rationalism. It was an age when the country was young and poetic; when kings and nobles thought to atone for the vices and blood-stains of a life-time by making large bequests to the Church; and when the faithful believed in the possibility of chastity and a pure heart. The religious and social conditions of the age rendered possible the existence of *double monasteries*, as they have been styled, *i. e.*, retreats for the *religious* of both sexes; and these establishments, not infrequently, were presided over by an abbess of royal or noble birth. The early English monastery was the centre of mission work, the centre of educational work, and the centre of all the medical and

5

relief work for miles around. Moreover, in these early days, when pilgrims on foot or on palfrey were constantly passing from one part of the country to another on their way to some famous shrine; or, when some regal or other party was making a " progression " through the country, it often happened that the monastery became the place of lodgment, (hotel, hospice, hospital), where travellers were always welcome, and entertained in good old Catholic style, with all the hospitality of the monastery. The double monastery was virtually a necessity of the age, and for many a long year was held in the highest estimation by our early Anglo-Saxon ancestors. The most distinguished of the Saxon female saints, and many of the most eminent prelates of that age, were educated in these establishments. The strictest precautions were enforced to keep the Sisters within the spacious precincts of their convent, and to prevent any man from entering within their enclosure, unless it were on some exceptional occasion; and then, only with the permission of the abbess, and in the presence of witnesses. Of this strict discipline, as it was observed at the double monastery at Wimborne, we have a minute account by a contemporary, Ralph of Fulda, in his life of St. Lioba, written in the beginning of the eighth century. He tell us : " There were two monasteries at Wimborne, formerly erected by the kings of the country, surrounded by strong and lofty walls, and endowed with competent revenues. Of these, one was designed for the clergy, the other for females; but neither, (for such was the law of their foundation), was ever entered by any person of the other sex. No woman could obtain permission to come into the monastery of the men; nor any of the men to come into the convent of the women, with the exception of the priests, who entered to celebrate Mass and withdrew the moment the service was over. If a female, desirous of quitting the world, asked to be admitted among the sisterhood, she could obtain her request, be she who she might, on this condition only, that she should never seek to go out, unless it were on some extraordinary occasion, which might seem to justify such indulgence. Even the abbess herself, if it were necessary that she should receive advice or give orders, spoke to men through a window; and so desirous was she to remove all opportunity of conversation between the Sisters and persons of the other sex, that she refused entrance into the convent, not only to laymen and clergymen, but even to the bishops themselves."

It is unquestionable that, at first, both clerics and nuns who had dedicated themselves solely to the service of God bore, as a rule, the highest reputation for chastity, self-denial, charity, and devotion; but in the course of time abuses crept in, and a system which, originally, was of the greatest service to the people at large, became later, the cause of gross scandal to the Church. The besetting sin of the Anglo-Saxon *men* was excessive drinking; although it is well to remember, in using this expression, that the common beverages of the Anglo-Saxon, the mead, the ale, and the wine were innocent compared with the strong alcoholic beverages of to-day. The besetting sin of the Anglo-Saxon *women* was, naturally, an excessive love of dress and admiration, and these national failings intruded themselves, at length, within the sacred enclosures of the monastery.

By the Council of Cloveshoe (747) all inmates of monasteries, both clerics and monks, were forbidden to drink to excess themselves, or to encourage such excess in others; they were to be content with sober cheer, and to exclude from their religious houses, delicate meats and coarse, unseemly amusements; to devote their cells to silence, study, and prayer, and never to allow them to become the resort of poets, gleemen, harpers, and buffoons, [*poetarum, citharistarum, musicorum, et scurrarum*]. With respect to convents of nuns, it was enacted that more attention should be paid to study and prayer, and less to the wearing and embroidering of works of vanity; and that the cells of the Sisters should be closed against lay society, superfluous visits, and private feasting. In short, they were forbidden to be *flammeæ puellæ* or women of fashion.

It is certain that the double monastery, even in its purest days, found but little favour with many of the Roman hierarchy. Pope Gregory, in one of his extant epistles, applauds Januarius for declining to establish a monastery for men adjoining a nunnery. Even some of the abbesses seem to have felt the grave responsibility which such an institution involved. The Abbess Ean.... the eighth century, writes to Wynfrith of the weighty care " universarum commissarum animarum promiscui sexus et ætatis." The Venerable Beda in an extant letter to his friend and patron the Abbot Albinus, St. Aldhelm, and others, notable in the Anglo-Saxon Church, denounced in no measured terms, the wrongdoings of these double conventual establishments; until finally, at the second Council of Nicæa, [A.D. 787], the system was authoritatively condemned by a canon forbidding the creation of double monasteries and enjoining the suppression of those already in existence.*

The story of Cædmon's life, however, carries us

* *Vide* Note F.

back to the " double monastery " in its purest and
best days, and presents a picture of the actual life
of the *religious* of that time, as chaste and earnest
and devout, as even pure fancy might have depicted it.

We do not propose to spoil the quaint, tender
narrative of Beda, by attempting a synopsis of his
account, but we shall give the story in full, as it has
come down to us, making such changes only as may
be necessary in translating the Latin original.

" In the year following, that is, in the year of the
Incarnation of our Lord 680, the most devoted servant of Christ, Hilda, abbess of the monastery that
is called Streoneshalh [Whitby], as we have before
related, after having performed many heavenly
works during her earthly life, passed thence, to
receive the rewards of the life eternal, on the 17th of
November, at the age of sixty-six years ; the first half
of which she spent most nobly, living in the secular
habit, and more nobly still, dedicated the remaining
half to our Lord in the monastic life ; for she was
nobly born, being the daughter of Herericus, nephew
to King Edwin, together with which King, she also
embraced the Faith and Sacraments of Christ at the
preaching of Paulinus, of blessed memory, the first
bishop of the Northumbrians, and kept the same

undefiled till she was worthy to attain to the Beatific Vision.

Resolving to quit the secular habit and to serve Him alone, she withdrew into the province of the East Angles, for she was allied to the King; being desirous to pass over from thence into France, to forsake her native country and all she had, and so live a stranger, for our Lord's sake, in the monastery of Cale, that she might with more ease attain to the eternal kingdom in heaven ; because her sister Heresuid, mother to Aldwulf, king of the East Angles, at that time living in the same monastery under regular discipline, was waiting for her eternal reward. Being led by her example, she continued a whole year in the aforesaid province, with the design of going abroad ; afterwards, Bishop Aidan, being recalled home, he gave her the land of one family on the north side of the river Wear ; where for a year she also led the monastic life together with a few companions.

After this, she was made abbess of the monastery called Herutea, which monastery had been founded, not long before, by the devoted servant of Christ, Heiv, who is said to have been the first woman that, in the province of the Northumbrians, took upon her the life and habit of a nun, being consecrated by Bishop Aidan ; but she, soon after she had founded

that monastery, went away to the city of Kalcacæs-
tir, and there fixed her dwelling.   Hilda, the servant
of Christ, being set over that monastery, began immediately to reduce all things to a regular system,
according as she had been instructed by learned
men; for Bishop Aidan, and other religious men
that knew her and loved her, frequently visited and
diligently instructed her, because of her innate wisdom and inclination to the service of God.

When she had for some years governed this monastery, wholly intent upon establishing a regular life,
it happened that she also undertook either to build
or to arrange a monastery in the place called Streoneshalh, which work she industriously performed;
for she put this monastery under the same regular discipline as she had done the former; and taught there
the strictest observance of justice, piety, chastity,
and other virtues, and particularly of peace and
charity; so that, after the example of the primitive
Church, no person was there rich, and none poor, all
being in common to all, and none having any property.   Her prudence was so great, that not only indifferent persons, but even kings and princes, as
occasion offered, asked and received her advice.
She obliged those who were under her direction to
attend so much to reading of the divine Scriptures,
and to exercise themselves so much in works of jus-

tice, that many might be thus found fit for ecclesiastical duties and to serve at the altar.

In short, we afterwards saw five bishops taken out of that monastery and all of them men of singular merit and sanctity.

.   .   .   .

Thus this servant of Christ, the Abbess Hilda, whom all that knew her called Mother, for her singular piety and grace, was not only an example of good life to those that lived in her monastery, but afforded occasion of amendment and salvation to many who lived at a distance, and to whom the fame was brought of her industry and virtue; for it was necessary that the dream which her mother Bregusuid had, during her infancy, should be fulfilled. At the time that her husband Hereric lived in banishment under Cerdic, King of the Britons, where he was also poisoned, she fancied in a dream, that she was seeking for him most carefully and could find no sign of him anywhere; but after having used all her industry to seek him, she found a most precious jewel under her garment, which, whilst she was looking on it very attentively, cast such a light as spread itself throughout all Britain; which dream was brought to pass in her daughter that we speak of, whose life was a bright example, not only to herself, but to all who desired to live well.

When she had governed this monastery many years, it pleased Him who has made such merciful provision for our salvation, to give her holy soul the trial of a long sickness, to the end that, according to the Apostle's example, her virtue might be perfected in infirmity.

Falling into a fever, she fell into a violent heat, and was afflicted with the same for six years continually; during all which time she never failed either to return thanks to her Maker, or publicly and privately to instruct the flock committed to her charge; for by her own example she admonished all persons to serve God dutifully in perfect health, and always to return thanks to Him in adversity or bodily infirmity. In the seventh year of her sickness, the distemper turning inwards, she approached her last day, and about cock-crowing, having received the *viaticum* of the most Holy Communion, and called together the handmaidens of Christ who were within the same monastery, she admonished them to persevere in evangelical peace among themselves, and with all others; and as she was uttering her words of advice she joyfully saw death approaching, or if I may speak in the words of our Lord, she passed from death to life.

That same night it pleased Almighty God, by a manifest vision, to make known her death in another monastery at a distance from hers, one which she had built that same year and is called Hakenes. There was in that monastery a certain nun called Begu, who having dedicated her virginity to God, had served Him upwards of thirty years in the monastic life. This nun, being then in the dormitory of the Sisters, on a sudden heard the well known sound of a bell in the air, which used to awake and call them to prayers when any one of them was taken out of this world, and opening her eyes, as she thought, she saw the top of the house open and a strong light pour in from above ; looking earnestly upon that light, she saw the soul of the aforesaid servant of God in that same light, attended and conducted to heaven by angels. Then awaking, and seeing the other Sisters lying round about her, she perceived that what she had seen was either in a dream or a vision ; and rising immediately in a great fright, she ran to the virgin who then presided in the monastery instead of the Abbess, and whose name was Frigyth, and with many tears and sighs, told her that the Abbess Hilda, Mother of them all, had departed this life, and had in her sight ascended to eternal bliss, and to the company of the inhabitants of heaven, with a great light, and with angels conducting her.   Frigyth, having heard it, awoke all the Sisters, and calling them to the church, admonished them to pray and sing psalms for her soul; which they did during the remainder of the night; and at break of day, the Brothers came with the news of her death from the place where she had died.   They answered that they knew it before, and then related how and when they had heard it; by which it appeared that her death had been revealed to them in a vision the very same hour that the others said she had died.   Thus it was by Heaven happily ordained, that when some saw her departure out of this world, the others should be acquainted with her admittance into the spiritual life which is eternal.   The monasteries are about thirteen miles distant from each other.

It is also reported that her death was, in a vision, made known the same night to one of the holy virgins who loved her most passionately, in the same monastery where the said servant of God died.   This nun saw her soul ascend to heaven in the company of angels; and this she declared the very same hour that it happened, to those servants of Christ that were with her; and awakened them to pray for her soul, even before the rest of the congregation had heard of her death.   The truth of which was known to the whole monastery in the morning.   This same nun was at that time with some other servants of Christ, in the remotest part of the monastery, where the women, newly converted, were wont to be upon trial till they were regularly instructed and taken into the society of the congregation.

There was in this Abbess's monastery a certain Brother, particularly remarkable for the grace of God, who was wont to make pious and religious verses, so that whatever was interpreted to him out of Scripture, he soon after put the same into poetical expressions of much sweetness and humility, in English, which was his native language. By his verses the minds of many were often excited to despise the world, and to aspire to heaven. Others after him attempted, in the English nation, to compose religious poems, but none could ever compare with him ; for he did not learn the art of poetry from men but from God , for which reason he never could compose any trivial or vain poem, but only those which relate to religion suited his religious tongue ; for having lived in a secular habit till he was well advanced in years, he had never learned anything of versifying ; for which reason, being sometimes at entertainments when it was agreed, for the sake of mirth, that all present should sing in their turns, when he saw the instrument come towards him, he rose up from table and returned home.

Having done so at a certain time, and gone out of
the house where the entertainment was, to the stable
where he had to take care of the horses that night,
he there composed himself to rest at the proper time,
when a person appeared to him in his sleep and salu-
ting him by his name, said, ' Cædmon, sing some
song to me.'   He answered, ' I cannot sing ; for that
was the reason why I left the entertainment and retired to this place, because I could not sing.'   The
other who talked to him replied, ' However, you shall
sing.' — ' What shall I sing ? ' he rejoined.   ' Sing
the beginning of created things,' said the other.
Hereupon, he presently began to sing verses to the
praise of God, which he had never heard, the pur-
port whereof was thus : ' Now are we bound to praise
the Maker of the heavenly kingdom, the power of
the Creator and His counsel, the deeds of the Father
of glory ; how He, being the eternal God, became the
author of all miracles, who first, as almighty preserver
of the human race, created Heaven for the sons of
men as the roof of the house, and next the Earth.'

This is the sense, but not the words, in order as he
sang them in his sleep ; for verses though never so
well composed cannot be literally translated out of
one language into another without losing much of
their beauty and loftiness.   Awaking from his sleep,
Cædmon remembered all that he had sung in his

dream, and soon added much more to the same effect in verse worthy of the Deity.

In the morning he came to the steward, his superior, and having acquainted him with the gift he had received, was conducted to the Abbess, by whom he was ordered, in the presence of many learned men, to tell his dream and repeat the verses, that they might all give their judgment what it was and whence his verse proceeded. They all concluded that heavenly grace had been conferred on him by our Lord. They expounded to him a passage in Holy Writ, either historical or doctrinal, ordering him, if he could, to put the same into verse. Having undertaken it, he went away, and returning the next morning, gave it to them composed in most excellent verse; whereupon the Abbess, embracing the grace of God in the man, instructed him to quit the secular habit and to take upon him the monastic life; which being accordingly done, she associated him to the rest of the brethren in her monastery and ordered that he should be taught the whole series of sacred history. Thus Cædmon, keeping in mind all he heard, and as it were chewing the cud, converted the same into most harmonious verse; and sweetly repeating the same, made his masters, in their turn, his hearers. He sang the Creation of the World, the origin of Man, and all the history of Genesis; and made many verses on the departure of the children of Israel out of Egypt, and their entering into the land of promise, with many other histories from Holy Writ; the Incarnation, Passion, Resurrection of our Lord and his Ascension into heaven; the coming of the Holy Ghost and the preaching of the Apostles; also, the terror of future Judgment, the horror of the pains of Hell, and the delights of Heaven; besides many more about the Divine benefits and judgments by which he endeavoured to turn away all men from the love of vice and to excite in them the love of, and application to, good actions; for he was a very religious man and humbly submissive to regular discipline, but full of zeal against those who behaved themselves otherwise; for which reason he ended his life happily.

For when the time for his departure drew near, he laboured for the space of fourteen days under a bodily infirmity which seemed to prepare the way; yet so moderate that he could talk and walk the whole time. In his neighbourhood was the house to which those that were sick and shortly likely to die were carried. He desired the person that attended him, in the evening as the night came on in which he was to depart this life, to make ready a place there for him to take his rest. This person, wondering why he should desire it, because there was as yet no sign of his dying soon, did what he had ordered. He accordingly went there, and conversing pleasantly in a joyful manner with the rest that were in the house before, when it was passed midnight, he asked them 'Whether they had the Holy Eucharist there?' They answered, 'What need of the Eucharist, for you are not likely to die since you talk so merrily with us, as if you were in perfect health?' 'However,' said he, 'bring me the Eucharist.' Having received the same into his hand, he asked, whether they were all in charity with him and without any enmity or rancour? They answered, that they were all in perfect charity and free from anger; and in their turn, asked him whether he was in the same mind towards them? He answered, 'I am in charity, my children, with all the servants of God.' Then strengthening himself with the heavenly *viaticum*, he prepared for the entrance into another life, and asked how near the time was when the brothers were to be awakened to sing the nocturnal praises of our Lord. They answered, 'It is not far off.' Then he said, 'Well, let us wait that hour'; and signing himself with the sign of the Cross, he laid his head on the pillow and, falling into a slumber, ended his life so in silence.

Thus it came to pass, that as he had served God with a simple and pure mind and undisturbed devo-

6

tion, so he now departed to His presence, leaving the world by a quiet death ; and that tongue which had composed so many holy words in praise of the Creator, uttered its last words whilst he was in the act of signing himself with the Cross, and recommending himself into His hands; and by what has been here said he seems to have had foreknowledge of his death."

Such is the remarkable account of the " Coming " of Cædmon preserved in the writings of the ablest and most trustworthy historian of the Anglo-Saxon era.

The historical truth of this account, however, and even the very existence of any such name as " Cædmon " have been called in question by at least one eminent English archæologist.* These and similar questions, although highly interesting to the antiquary, are in no sense of vital importance to the modern student of literature. Whether any such poet as Homer or as Shakespeare ever lived, or even if they did live, whether they wrote the works commonly attributed to them, are not matters of prime importance. The fact of the existence of these immortal works is amply sufficient, and although we should like to know somewhat of the life, the character, and the surroundings of the men who so largely

* *Vide* Note G.

contribute to our intellectual pleasure, yet, happily, our mental gratification is not limited by the possession of a knowledge of these facts.

It is so in the case of Cædmon. The poem *exists*, and from internal evidence can be proved to belong to the early days of Anglo-Saxon Christianity ; and whether Beda's account is strictly historical, or whether such a ceorl as Cædmon ever lived, are questions of little if of any moment.

At the same time, we are not left entirely in the dark as to these mooted questions. With regard to Beda's narrative we have *prima facie* evidence that the historian received it directly from some one of the members of the celebrated double monastery at Whitby, where Cædmon is stated to have lived and died. According to Beda's chronology, which cannot be gainsaid, Cædmon must have been living while the future historian was a child ; and the monastery in which Beda was reared and educated, being situated in the same section of the country as the lady Hilda's, viz., in Northumbria, must have had intimate relations with the latter. In this way, the traditions of one monastery would naturally be known, (and known in their original setting,) to the inmates of the neighbouring monastery.

The story of Cædmon's miraculously discovered gifts as a poet, which formed part of the legendary history of the monastery at Whitby, was doubtless the poetic rendering of an actual fact. The author of the Anglo-Saxon poem may, or may not, have had any such dream as the legend describes, but the existence of the poem is a fact ; and the tale of the bashful, super-sensitive hind leaving his companions because of his ignorance of music and falling into dreams of what he *might* have sung, is so true to nature that we may well regard it as the fanciful setting of a poetic age.

Nor is there anything strange in this development of legend-lore. The memory of the self-sacrificing life of the Lady Hilda has been preserved in story by the peasantry around her former home for more than a thousand years. An antiquary of Yorkshire tells us that when the sunbeams fall among the Abbey ruins, the spectators who stand on the west side of Whitby churchyard, so as just to see the most northerly part of the Abbey, imagine they perceive, in one of the highest windows there, the resemblance of a woman arrayed in a shroud ; and it is commonly believed among the peasantry, to be an appearance of the Lady Hilda in her glorified state. And so, she, who among an untaught people diffused the light of the Gospel and the warmth of its charity, still appears to the half-taught of to-day as a vision of sunshine in the old place of her toil.

As to the poem itself, it is certain from Beda's own statement, that he translated the opening lines of Cædmon's poem, as he gives them in his *Historia*, either from some manuscript which he had consulted, or from some version which he had heard recited and had committed to memory; and further, it is clear from his own statement that he did not attempt to give an exact translation of the original Anglo-Saxon but only a paraphrase. After quoting the lines in question, he says : " Verses never so well composed cannot be literally translated out of one language into another without losing much of their beauty and loftiness."

In the extant historical writings of the time between Beda and King Alfred, we do not recall any reference to Cædmon or his poem ; but in King Alfred's translation of Beda's *Historia* we have Beda's narrative repeated, and the opening lines of Cædmon's poem given in *Anglo-Saxon.*

Whether King Alfred's Anglo-Saxon version is a re-translation of Beda's Latin, or a transcript from the original Anglo-Saxon, has been questioned ; but on purely critical grounds we are convinced that King Alfred translated from the Latin, and did not copy from any Anglo-Saxon original.

This point will come out very clearly if we examine, side by side, the Latin wording of the *His-*

toria and the wording of the Anglo-Saxon translation of King Alfred.

" Nunc laudare debemus auctorem regni cælestis, potentiam creatoris et consilium illius, facta patris gloriæ; quomodo ille, cum sit æternus deus, omnium miraculorum auctor extitit, qui primo filiis hominum cælum pro culmine tecti, dehinc terram custos humani generis omnipotens creavit."

So writes Beda in his Latin version of Cædmon's opening lines.

In King Alfred's translation this passage is rendered as follows :

Nu we sceolan herian
Heofon-ríces weard
Metodes mihte
And his mód-gethonc
Wera wuldor-fæder
Swá he wundra gehwæs
Éce dryhten
Oord onstealde
He ǽrest gesceop
Eorthan bearnum
Heofon to hrófe
Hálig scyppend
Thá middangeard
Mancynnes weard
Éce dryhten
Æfter téode
Firum foldan
Fréa ælmihtig

Anyone who is familiar with the structure and rhythm of Anglo-Saxon poetry, would have little, if any, hesitation in deciding that these lines are not, and could not be, a copy of any original Anglo-Saxon verses; while a comparison of these two passages in Latin and Anglo-Saxon, apart from any other evidence, would show that they resemble each other so closely as to warrant the opinion that the Anglo-Saxon version is simply a translation of the Latin. Indeed, that this is the case, might almost be inferred from a comparison of the two passages in a modern English rendering:

" Now are we to praise the Maker of the heavenly Kingdom, the power of the Creator and His counsel, the deeds of the Father of Glory; how He, being the eternal God, became the author of all miracles, who first, as Almighty preserver of the human race, created Heaven for the sons of men, as the roof of the house, and next, the Earth."

Such is the English rendering of the opening lines of Cædmon's poem as given by Beda.

If, now, we compare this rendering with a literal translation of King Alfred's Anglo-Saxon version, the point which we are making will stand out in a very clear light:

> Now must we praise
> The Guardian of Heaven's kingdom,

The Creator's might,
And his mind's thought ;
Glorious Father of men !
As of every wonder He,
Lord Eternal,
Formed the beginning.
He first framed
For the children of Earth
The Heaven as a roof ;
Holy Creator !
Then mid-Earth,
The Guardian of mankind,
The Eternal Lord,
Afterwards produced ;
The Earth for men,
Lord Almighty !

We thus possess historic testimony, of the highest authority, that during Beda's boyhood a sacred poem on the subject of the " Fall of Man " had been produced by an inmate of the double monastery of the Lady Hilda at Whitby ; a poem so remarkable as to have commanded, in after years, the notice of a cleric and critic as learned as the Venerable Beda, and of such poetic excellence as to have elicited his highest commendation.

It would seem inexplicable, if we did not know the history of this early age, how a literary work of such importance should have been allowed to sink into total oblivion ; and even the manuscripts of the

poem have become wholly forgotten.   Still such was
the case.   The incursions of the Danes, and the
destruction of the monastic libraries which followed,
added to the ignorance and indifference of Anglo-
Norman ecclesiastics, and the ravages of time itself,
led, as we know, to the loss of many valuable writings.   It was not until the seventeenth century, as
we have before seen, that the manuscript of a sacred
poem, corresponding to the one described by Beda,
was discovered by Archbishop Ussher.   This manuscript was used by Somner in the preparation of his
Anglo-Saxon dictionary, and was subsequently presented by the Archbishop to Francis Dujon, known
to all the scholars of his day under the *nom de plume*
of Junius.

This famous manuscript, the only one now known
to exist in England, is in the Junian collection in
the Bodleian Library at Oxford, a small parchment
volume in folio, containing two hundred and twenty-
nine pages, the first two hundred and twelve of which
are apparently in the handwriting of the tenth century.

The illuminations, or rather drawings, which
accompany the manuscript, do not reach beyond
the ninety-sixth page, although in almost every succeeding page, to the very end of the volume, blank
spaces, intended to receive illuminations, occur, show-

ing that in the illustrations as well as in the text, the manuscript was left unfinished. In the whole series of fifty-three plates, the colouring of but one has been completed ; the others being drawn simply in black and white, with a view, apparently, of being coloured later by the illuminator. Where colours have been introduced they are simply outlines in brown, vermilion, and green.

Junius, in the preface to the edition of this manuscript, which he published at Amsterdam 1655, does not hesitate to pronounce it a copy of the long lost poem of Cædmon described by Beda in his *Historia ;* and he does so, and doubtless correctly, on the ground of the correspondence which exists between the Ussher manuscript and Beda's description, no less than from the structure and general characteristics of the language.

It is true that the opening lines of the Junian manuscript do not correspond *verbally* either with the Latin of Beda or with the Anglo-Saxon of King Alfred ; but as we have before stated, Beda did not pretend to give more than the *sense* of the passage, and Alfred avowedly copied from the original of Beda. Hence, it is not strange, but only what we might have expected *a priori*, that the manuscript of the poem, if ever discovered, although it might not agree *verbatim*, would agree substantially, with the passage as given by Beda and his translator, King Alfred. And this proves to be the case with regard to the Junian manuscript as the following comparison will conclusively show:

FROM KING ALFRED'S BEDA.	FROM THE JUNIAN MS.
Nu we sceolan herian	Us is riht micel
Heofon-ríces weard	Thæt we ródera weard
Metodes mihte	Wereda wuldor-cining
And his mód-gethonc	Wordum herigen
Wera wuldor-fæder	Módum lufien
Swá he wundra gehwæs	He is mægna spéd
Éce Dryhten	Heofod ealra
Oord onstealde	Heah-gesceafta
He ǽrest gesceop	Fréa ælmihtig
Eorthan bearnum	Næs him fruma ǽfre
Heofon to hrófe	Ór geworden
Hálig scyppend	Ne nu ende cymth
Thá middangeard	Écean Dryhtnes.
Mancynnes weard	
Éce Dryhten	
Æfter téode	
Firum foldan	
Fréa ælmihtig.	

In this fragment, consisting of but eighteen short lines, we have the following epithets of the Deity, all of frequent occurrence in the so-called *Paraphrase*:—Heofon ríces weard; Éce Dryhten; Hálig Scippend; Mancynnes weard; Fréa Ælmihtig; and there is scarcely a single phrase that is not common

to both compositions, while the same identity pre-
vails in their whole structure. The exordium of the
Poem conveys exactly the same thought as the
Hymn cited by Beda, and clothed very nearly in
the same mode of expression.

Few, if any, who have read the poem in the
original, and have given it the close study that its
intrinsic merits deserve, will refuse to accord to the
monk of Whitby the possession of high poetic gifts ;
while some few will not hesitate to accept, even in
this nineteenth century, the estimate of Beda, " *Et
quidem et alii post illum in gente Anglorum religiosa
poemata facere tentabant, sed nullus ei æquiparari
potuit. Namque ipse non ab hominibus, neque per hominem institutus, canendi artem didicit, sed divinitus
adjutus gratis canendi donum accepit.*"

" Others after him in the English nation were
wont to attempt to compose religious poems, but
none could compare with him, for he did not learn
the art of poetry by man, neither through man, but
was divinely aided, and through God's grace received
the gift of song."

CHAPTER III.

Analysis of Cædmon's " Fall of Man."

THE poem which we are about to analyse, is the earliest strain of sacred song that has come down to us from the distant past of England's poetic records.

It has been the fashion to style this famous relic of Anglo-Saxon literature a *Scripture Paraphrase*, but such a title is both inadequate and misleading. It is inadequate, since Cædmon's work though in the main based, as we shall subsequently see, on certain statements in the Hebrew Scriptures, on Biblical hints and Oriental imagery, is, nevertheless, in the form in which we have received it, virtually an original production, incorporating Rabbinical fancies, glosses, and comments, but still adorned with such innumerable touches of the poet's own imagination as to constitute it a distinct and independent version. Moreover, to designate it a *Paraphrase* is misleading, inasmuch as in the most highly finished portion of the work the author shows himself to be no mere paraphrast, but a man endowed with the soul and fire of the born poet.

But while this is true, not only of that part of the poem which treats of the " Fall of Man," but also of other portions where the expression, the versification and the rhythm evince careful elaboration, and the imagery is at its highest point of perfection, still, other portions of the work are comparatively so inferior to the major part of the poem, as to lend countenance to the commonly accepted title of " Paraphrase." Indeed, from a mere casual reading of the original, one is apt to form the opinion that the poem is the work of more than one writer ; and this, from the very unevenness of the style ; but a closer study shows conclusively that it is the work of a single mind, though written under differing conditions, some parts having been more carefully elaborated and more highly finished than others.

Whether that part of Cædmon's poem which relates to the " Fall of Man," can justly be entitled *an epic*, may be open to question. If an epic is a " metrical romance," no matter whether it be founded on history, on mythology, on theomachy, or on the purely imaginative creations of the poet, then it would be difficult to deny, to this part of Cædmon's poem, the lofty title of epic. It is a romance or narrative based on Hebrew mythology, interspersed with folk-lore on matters supermundane, mundane, and inframundane; on Bible hints and ecclesiastical imaginings; but still, a connected story of the traditionally received version of the Fall. It differs from the *Iliad*, the *Æneid*, and the Arthurian story, inasmuch as it is not a mere national epic, or an epic of purely national events. It is not a story of one planet alone, or even of the whole Starry Universe. In this, it differs from other prominent types of the Epic. Its field of action is infinite space, and its heroes are not human warriors, or even conventional demi-gods, but supernatural beings who can defy all the known laws of gravity, and can assume at will any form whatsoever, be it "toad" or "stripling cherub."

The central figure of the romance is an almighty Being, supposed to represent the Deity, who, in a burst of terrestrial anger, hurls from the Empyrean the angels who attempt to oppose His will, and subsequently suffers His newly created Man, who knows nothing of Sin, and less of Satan, to be exposed to the machinations of a criminal Archangel, whose colossal intelligence had made him the most conspicuous figure in the Empyrean, next to the epic Deity himself. This being is the true hero of the plot,—a Fiend who is bent on the most demon-like scheme of revenge that archangelic ingenuity could conceive.

Now, what does all this mean? It cannot be denied that, at the present day, Milton's poetic narrative of the Creation and Fall, are in possession of the imagination of the average amateur theologian; and of the intellectually immature masses of England, of America, and of the English-speaking races generally. It is not taken as a Talmud or commentary, or even as a supplementary Bible. It is the *only* narrative generally known; and if the tiny, authentic Scripture "original," which, in the course of centuries has grown into the modern fully developed *Epic of the Fall of Man*, were to be excerpted from the canonical Scriptures, as all that the Bible had to say on the subject, and this were to be presented, in its unconnected entirety, the result would not only cause a vacant stare of astonishment on the face of the average Protestant, but would be likely to arouse a suspicion that someone had tampered with the Bible, and had suppressed the larger part of a fine, old-fashioned Bible story.

What a distinguished writer has said of Milton's epic, we can apply with equal truth to Cædmon's poem: "In so far as *Paradise Lost* is an expression of Milton's habitual mode of thought, respecting Man and History, in relation to an eternal and unknown Infinity, it is so by way of what the Germans call *Verstellung*, viz., popular image or representation ; and not by way of *Begriff*, viz., pure or philosophic notion." Cædmon deals with his subject as a Verstellung. He represents, by popular image or representation, the traditional ideas of his day on this subject, and does not attempt to philosophise, or explain in the abstract his notion of the origin of Evil or of Death.

And it is so in Milton. Both, give in the popular imagery of their time, and in poetic form, the current theological traditions of the age. Cædmon reproduces sixth century, Catholic tradition in popular dressing. Milton, with all the theological developments and popular conceits of the Middle Ages behind him, with regard to Heaven, Purgatory, and Hell, presents, in more modern garb, the Protestant tradition of a thousand years later ;— a tradition which had been evolved, since the so-called Reformation, by the occult principle of Protestant selection.

Cædmon's poem is then an epic, a Verstellung, if we accord these titles to Milton's more ambitious work. It is an epic of the whole of creation ; of infinitude in space and in time ; and, in common with *Paradise Lost*, is charming, illogical, and at times incomprehensible.

Although Cædmon's work is not a mere paraphrase, but a grand sacred poem, yet it is to be borne in mind that the intention of the author was not, like Milton, to immortalise *himself*, but to instruct the people, by giving the clergy and gleemen, and through them the people at large, a poetic version of the traditionally received account of the "Fall of Man," and other sacred narratives.

Whence Cædmon obtained the information which he evidently possessed of Rabbinical learning, it is impossible to say; yet it is beyond doubt that he is indebted to some of the Oriental or Rabbinical commentators, for many an idea which he has made tributary. It is well known, that the Anglo-Saxon Church was in direct touch, ecclesiastically, with the East, and hence, it is perfectly supposable, that Cædmon obtained his rabbinical interpretations directly through Oriental sources. It is more probable, however, to suppose that the apostles of Roman Christianity in England, had carried with them the traditional Eastern exposition of the book of Genesis, and so had established a traditional *consensus* which formed the basis of the teaching on this subject in every monastery in the land.

In order to understand fully this poem of the monk of Whitby, it is absolutely necessary to picture to the mind the whole scene of the Creation and the

Fall, as conceived by the brilliant brain of the Anglo-Saxon *scop*.

The poet begins his sacred song with a description of Heaven or the Empyrean, where the Deity, the

Glory King of Hosts,

sits enthroned in Light, Majesty, and Bliss ineffable, and surrounded by the ten tribes of the celestial hierarchy.

This Heaven or Empyrean, as conceived by Cædmon, is not the "bright framework" of Earth and planets, or of Sun and starry systems, since none of these, as yet, had any existence ; but an imaginary sphere of infinite radius,—(the phrase is of course unthinkable),—divided into two concaves, Heaven or the Empyrean and Chaos or the Abyss.

The upper of these concaves of primeval space is to be imagined as a boundless region of Light, Joy and Glory, in the midst of which, the Deity, though omnipresent, has His visible dwelling. Here, He is the Chieftain of an infinitude of intelligences called the Angels, who, though dispersed throughout the ranges of Heaven's boundless domain, yet lead, severally, their mighty lives, performing the behests of Deity, or lost in the abandonment of adoration.

The other half or concave of primeval space, Chaos or the Abyss, is a limitless ocean of universal dark-

ness, uselessness, and lifelessness, wherein the primal
elements battle unceasingly in blustering confusion ;
no Angel having ever winged his way down into its
repulsive obscurities.   The opal floor of the Empyrean divides the two concaves ; while beneath,
unvisited of Light, Chaos howls and rages and stag-
nates eternally.

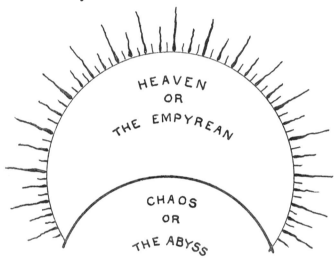

Before we proceed farther, however, in this analysis it may be well to emphasise one most important
point in the elucidation of the poem, viz. : that the
descriptions and illustrative diagrams which may be
introduced in this analysis are not mere fancies of
what Cædmon *may* have conceived in his scheme of
the poem, but are actually what he *must* have had,
and did have, in his mind when he began to write

his version of the " Fall of Man," and which he most tenaciously kept in view from first to last.

That such is the case may be conclusively proved from the words of the poem itself ; and often from the illuminations of the manuscript, which may be taken as a tenth-century commentary on the original text, by the artist of the Scriptorium, in which the manuscript was written.

In order to bring out this point in the clearest possible light, it will be necessary to adduce, in confirmation, such passages of the poem, and to introduce such of the illuminations of the manuscript, as may have a direct bearing on the views which will be advanced in the present examination of Cædmon's work.

In the opening lines of the narrative the poet tells us that the " Glory-King of Hosts "

> . . . ruled the *Heavenly concaves*, which at first,
> By power divine, were stretched out far and wide
> Throughout unbounded space, celestial Home
> Of those who guard the spirits of the just.

Here, the imagery in the term " Heavenly concaves " (A.-S. bósmas, Eng. bosoms), needs no comment, the two equal parts of the sphere being indicated with sufficient distinctness. But this is not all. In the following fac-similes of the illuminations of the manuscript, it will be seen that the artist of the Scriptorium leaves no doubt as to his understanding of the scheme of the poem. In the passage where Cædmon sings of the beginning of Creation that

> 　　　　　　.　.　.　o'er the Deep
> Was swiftly borne, on bright and radiant wing,
> The Spirit of the Lord,

the accompanying illumination shows the "Heavenly concaves" as the artist imagined Cædmon to have conceived them.

The same artistic interpretation of primeval space, occurs a few lines farther on in the poem, when Heaven's " All-glorious Chief "

> . . . severed Light from Darkness,

and bade

> Rise the bright framework of the glistening stars.

This illumination has a double representation of the " Heavenly concaves," in the upper one of which is depicted the Deity in the act of severing Light from Darkness, and in the lower one of which He is causing to rise the brilliant Firmament. In both, however, the same pictorial imagery is preserved. There is, in each representation, an upper concave, the Empyrean or dwelling of the Deity; and a lower one, which is swart and dark and dim, and is termed the Deep, or Chaos, or the Abyss.

We are not left, however, to the imagination of the illuminator for the portrayal of the physical aspect of the lower concave or Chaos. Cædmon, early in the poem, describes the swart Abyss in his own weird, graphic style:

As yet was naught beneath God's radiant Throne
But gloom as dark as in the cavern reigns,
And this wide-spread Abyss stood deep and dim
In idle uselessness, distasteful sight
To Him the source of all creative power.
The mighty King, in mind resolved, beheld
The joyless shade and saw the lowering cloud
Lie swart and waste, like an eternal sea
Of blackest Night, beneath the effulgent glow
Of Light ineffable.

It is all important to keep this primal imagery in mind, since, as we shall subsequently see, upon this point will depend the right understanding of the poet's idea as a whole.

The poem opens with a grand outburst of praise to the Deity ; a terrestrial *Gloria in Excelsis*, which forms a fitting exordium to the narrative which it introduces. The poet then describes, in brief, the treason of the proudest, most beloved Archangel in Heaven, and of the rebellious tribes, whose will he had subtly alienated from their rightful allegiance. The Archangel's proud boast,

> " In the North part of God's sublime domain *
> Will I a kingdom found, a palace rear,"

arouses the righteous wrath of the Deity, who forth-with forms a place of exile, and thither banishes the rebel host who have been faithless to their high estate,

> Down the dark, steep, unutterable path
> That leads to Hell.

It will therefore be necessary, now, to modify our diagram of primeval space. Hitherto, there have been but two concaves mentioned by Cædmon, the Empyrean and Chaos; but, with the formation of Hell, a small concave is carved, by the Almighty, out of the nethermost part of Chaos, as a torture-house for His traitor-Archangel and his band, and

* *Vide* Note H.

divided from the Empyrean by the broad belt of
Chaos. This "exile-house" is represented as a
vast region of fire, sulphurous lake, plain, and mountain, and of every form of fiery and icy torment.
The conditions of the poem require, therefore, now
three divisions of primeval space; the Empyrean,
Chaos, and Hell.

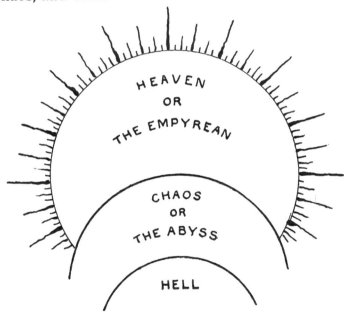

Among the illuminations of the manuscript, there
are two which show distinctly the artist's interpretation of the changed conditions of the picture.

In the following illumination the three divisions
of space are clearly delineated. The Deity, surrounded by adoring Cherubim and Seraphim, is

depicted as at rest within the concave of the Empyrean. Satan, chained to the floor of Hell, is paying
the penalty of his reckless ambition ; while between
the Empyrean and Hell the fallen Angels are being
hurled through Chaos to their place of doom.

In another of the illuminations, depicting the return
of Hell's Champion Fiend after the Fall of Man, the
blackness of Chaos is vividly represented as surrounding Hell proper, and the glare of the surging
fires within, darting upwards through the Gates of
Hell, like a fire-cloud seen through the mist, illu-

mines, for a small space, the lowest boundaries of Chaos.

In this, the first and introductory section of the poem, Cædmon gives a skilful and succinct statement of his theme, and adds such details of the setting of the narrative as would enable a monastic, or even a rustic, audience to picture to the mind, in correct perspective, the scenes which his imagination is about to portray. In other words, it is a masterly outlining of the whole argument of the poem, ending as a sub-climax with the " deep-racking pain " of the fiends in Hell.

The next section, which is the true beginning of the story, opens with the deep peace that reigned in Heaven after the expulsion of the rebel Angels; and depicts the Deity, as resolved in mind, to re-people with a better race the Northern quarter of His celestial domain, which had been left vacant by the fall of Satan and his followers. It is at this point, that the poet gives his fine description of the con-cave of Chaos, which we have already quoted; an eternal sea of blackest Night, forever surging and raging beneath the " vast celestial Firmament " or Empyrean.

Within this concave of seething elements and primal darkness, the Deity resolves to create a new World or Starry Universe and, at its centre, form an earthly Paradise as the abode of the favoured Being, whom He was about to make in His own image and similitude. The poet then sings successively of the creation of Light, the raising of the starry Firma-ment, and the separation of Land and Water, which, together, comprise the work of Creation of the first two and part of the third Days.

At this point, there is a break in the manuscript, and vestiges showing that three leaves of the poem have been cut out.

The narrative is then resumed with the account of the formation of Eve on the sixth and last Day of Creation, and the section ends with the greater Benediction, when the Deity blesses his masterpiece of creative skill, the new-formed Man, and utters His threefold mandate, to teem and multiply and fill the earth; to assume control over all creation; and strictly to abstain from the alluring fruit of the Tree of Death. This work accomplished, the Angels' Chieftain returns to the Empyrean, leaving to Man the earthly concave as his home.

The conditions of the setting of the narrative in this section of the poem, require one further change in the diagram of infinite space. The World or Universe, as conceived by Cædmon in his description of the Creation, is not the little planet that we call Earth, but the whole of the Starry Universe which surrounds us, as far as the eye can see, with its entire canopy of planets and suns and fixed stars, hung as it were at its highest point or zenith from the Empyrean. The Cædmonian diagram, as finally adapted to the necessities of the narrative, will henceforth consist of four concaves; the Empyrean or Heaven, the World or Starry Universe, Chaos or the Abyss, and Hell.

As, in the case of the other concaves which have already been described, so here, we are not left to mere conjecture, or to the play of our own imagination for our understanding of the poem; but have both Cædmon's verse, and the artist's drawings to guide us.

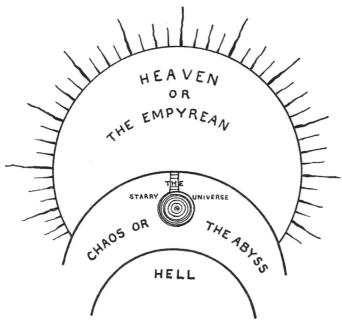

The poet tells us:

> Then Holy God resolved, *beneath the vast,*
> *Celestial firmament (tho' still within*
> *His boundless realms), to form a beauteous World*
> With overarching skies and waters wide
> And earthly creatures filled, in place of those
> Whom headlong He had hurled from His abode.

And the position of this Starry Universe in space, here so clearly defined, is rendered even clearer still, by the following illumination in the manuscript, descriptive of the formation of Eve from the side of Adam as he slept; and in order that the reader might make no mistake as to the interpretation of the drawing, the scribe has added, in the margins, a

brief statement of what was intended to be under-stood by each part of the picture. At the head of the illumination, in Anglo-Saxon, we are told " Here God's Angels proceed from Heaven into Paradise." On the right-hand side are the words, " Here the Lord cast sleep upon Adam and took a rib from his side and created his wife from that rib " ; and on the left hand we read, " Here the Lord created Adam's wife, Eve."

From this illumination, as well as from the wording of the poem, we must suppose that the poet intended this " Starry Sphere " as attached, at its north pole or zenith, to the Gates of the Empyrean by a celestial stairway, so that, along this channel of communication, a flood of light, darting downwards from the Empyrean into Chaos, through the opened Gates, and commingling with the shimmer of the Spheres below, would make the upper pole of this Starry Universe a blaze of golden mist.

The whole of this part of the poem, presupposes the Ptolemaic system of astronomy ;—the only system taught in Cædmon's day, or indeed for nearly a thousand years subsequently. Even so late as Milton's time, as we shall subsequently see, the Copernican system was far from being universally acknowledged by the scientific world, and both Dante and Milton built their poems, as Cædmon did, on the erroneous, though popular, astronomy of their own day.

According to the Ptolemaic system, what we have called the Starry Universe, hanging close by the Empyrean, was supposed to be an immense sphere cut or carved out of infinite space, and consisting of

8

eight concentric parallel Spheres, diminishing gradually in size, and wheeling one within the other, like a nest of Chinese balls, with our Earth, surrounded by its atmosphere, at the centre. The Ptolemaic system of astronomy, thus viewed the whole visible

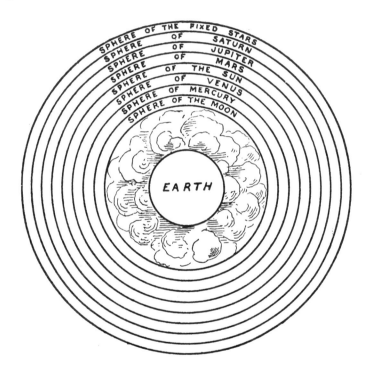

Universe from the Earth as the immovable centre of all things.

Such a sphere, as we have just described, if cut through at right angles to its polar axis, would show a plane or surface diagram similar to many which may be seen in the old text-books or manuals on Astronomy such as Milton used in teaching his pupils.*

At the centre, is the Earth, fixed and immovable while the eight concentric heavenly Spheres (represented on this plane surface as concentric circles) revolve around this fixed centre.

It is almost needless to say that the lines dividing the Spheres one from another, as marked out in the above diagram, are mathematical lines, i. e., popularly speaking, purely imaginary lines; each planet, sun or belt of fixed stars, keeping to its own well-defined Sphere or orbit, but with no visible lines of demarcation between such orbits.

To one descending the celestial steps from the Gates of the Empyrean, and gazing down into the heart of this great globe of concentric Spheres through the opening or entrance at its zenith, the scene presented would be one of surpassing grandeur. The first thing that would strike the eye would be the dazzling belt of the glittering dust of the Fixed Stars; then below, Saturn, Jupiter, and Mars bounding along in their enormous parallel Spheres or orbits; below this again, the blinding splendour of the circuit of the Sun; still lower, the calmer pathways of Venus and Mercury; then the Sphere of the

* *Vide* Note I.

pale Moon, the satellite, with her reflected silver
light ; and finally, at the centre, at the very heart of
these bewildering immensities of space, the impas-
sive Earth with her veil of atmosphere and fire and
water, the abode of God's creative masterpiece.

Of course, we know that, astronomically, this is all
wrong ; and yet it has served as the setting for three
of the grandest sacred poems of which literature can
boast.

In the third section of the poem, Cædmon returns
to the point at which he had broken off the narrative to describe the creation of Man ; and now resumes the thread of his story, recapitulating, with
fuller details, the origin of the rebellion in Heaven
and the expulsion of the rebel hosts.

He begins his fuller outburst of song by telling of
the creation of the ten Angel-tribes whom God had

Moulded in his own similitude,

and had endowed with every heavenly grace. One
of this angelic host, it seems, the Deity had raised
to the highest pinnacle of intelligence and power;
the most highly favoured subject of all the immortal denizens of the Empyrean. This Archangel, the
trusted Vicegerent of the Deity, in course of time,
begins to harbour dark and traitorous thoughts,
until, at length, he frowns and becomes a rebel.

The treason that is smouldering in his heart at length finds vent in a soliloquy of ambitious and self-proud thought, ending in a muttered resolve:

" No longer will I be His vassal-slave."

The Omnipresent One, knowing the innermost thought of the apostate Archangel, hurls the Fiend from his Empyrean throne, down the burning gulf to Hell. For three long days and three successive nights, are the Apostate and his guilty followers falling through Chaos, ere they reach the prison-house prepared by God as their place of exile. Here, amid the fiery torments of God's great torture-house, the traitor-angels lie stunned and prostrate in the deep, infernal gloom; till at length, aroused from their stupor, and seeing far off, through the gloom of Chaos, the distant glories of their former Seats, the supreme folly of the act their pride had allured them to perpetrate stands bare before them and, for a time, they resign themselves to the keen gnawings of relentless remorse.

In a sense, it is perfectly true, that the events related in this section are a recapitulation of the opening or introductory section of the poem; but a careful examination of the structure of the epic will show conclusively that Cædmon, far from evincing the crudeness of a tyro in his art, handles the materials at his disposition in a most masterly way, adopting the skilful device of announcing his theme in brief, at the outset, and subsequently filling in the colouring of the picture when the outline has been sufficiently perfected.

But to proceed. In the next section, having recovered from their stupor,—the result of their three days' fall through Chaos,—the Apostates hold a plenary Council in Hell. Satan, though manacled and foot-bound with twisted iron bands, is the first to break the horrid silence of the fiery concave, and in an impassioned speech,—one of the most dramatic and effective portions of the poem,—gives utterance to his already well-matured scheme of revenge. Fettered in his iron Throne in deepest Hell, prostrate and powerless to rise, the fallen Archangel first pours forth, in blasphemous apostrophe, his bitter wrath against the Almighty and against the unequal and unmerited punishment of his rebel Angels; and, as a climax to this part of his unholy tirade, he discloses his gigantic scheme of becoming a Devil; living, henceforth, the life of a fiendish iconoclast, frustrating when possible the grand designs of the Deity and shattering the highest ideals of divine love and workmanship. In vivid terms, he tells of a fair World beneath the Empyrean, decreed of old, though designed and created only in

later days, where the Almighty had already formed
the first of a new-born race of beings, akin in beauty
of form to the Angels, but of inferior intelligence,
with whom doubtless He intended to repeople the
Northern palaces of Heaven left vacant by the fall
of himself and his once princely retainers. To effect
the ruin of this earth-born Man, by whatever means
(so urges the Fiend), would foil the plans of the
Deity and ensure substantial revenge.

Having thus disclosed his scheme, and having out-
lined his own ideal demon-course for the future life
of his compeers, Satan suggests that they proceed
to discuss the best plan for the successful issue of
the proposed campaign.

As the inception of the idea of revenge, and the
determination of the most vulnerable point of attack,
are due to the arch-intelligence and brilliant brain
of Satan, and to him alone, it is not surprising that
in the peroration of his speech, when urging the importance of a well-defined plan of attack, he should
give, (as he does), a hint as to his own fully matured
views on the matter, and endeavour, in every possible way, to attain the object that he has in view.
He accordingly appeals to the false fidelity and false
loyalty of his followers in the past, and to his own
lavish munificence; and declares that in no way can
they repay his former regal generosity, now that he

is fetter-bound in Hell, than by efficient aid in carrying out his cherished scheme and effecting the eternal ruin of Man. Then, as though to inflame their drooping ambition, he holds forth the dazzling promise, sealed by his sovereign oath, that the daring one who should first proclaim the Fall of Man, seduced by devil-craft, should be rewarded with the gift of the second throne in Hell's dominion and be his (Satan's) sole Vicegerent.

At this point in the manuscript there are three leaves wanting, which doubtless contained the account of the deliberations of the Council in Hell. Still, although the original lines in this part of the poem are lost to us, yet we can easily and surely surmise, from the sequel, what the result of these deliberations, (according to Cædmon), must have been.

The continuation of the narrative shows that the scheme proposed by Satan met with the approval of the assembled fiends, and that one more crafty and more daring than his fellows was chosen to undertake the perilous adventure.

We next find the apostate Angel, warrior-armed for the desperate enterprise, with every clasp fast and secure. This done, he urges his way, by strength of wing and limb, upwards to Hell's Gates. Passing this barrier, he speeds, like a spiral column, onwards and upwards through the dark desolations of Chaos, till at length he descries far off the faint, soft light of the Starry Universe of which he is in search; and, entering at the zenith, or open point nearest the Empyrean, and passing downwards through the encircling Spheres, alights at length on the convex of Man's earthly Paradise.

With the opening of the fourth section of the poem, Satan's dark emissary, having reached the goal of his arduous journey, searches amid the luxuriant foliage of the Garden, for the newly God-created pair; and finally discovers them, reclining beneath the shade of two wide-spreading trees, the Tree of Life and the Tree of Death. With devil-craft he takes the body of a worm; entwines himself around the Tree of Death; and with the luring fruit of the tree in hand, addresses his first sin-fraught word to Adam.

It is, at this point, that the clever subtlety or "devil-craft," as the poet calls it, of Hell's delegate first appears. He does not approach the Man as his Maker's foe, but as an angelic *messenger* from Heaven, charged with a commission from the Highest to bid Adam eat of the fruit of the Tree of Death; and, this behest fulfilled, to return to the Empyrean bearing the prayers of God's favoured child for any boon, whatsoever, that he might desire.

In spite, however, of the apparent naturalness of the visit of an angel-ambassador, and the speciousness of his commission, Adam declines to recognise his pretentions ; and with scant courtesy tells him to be gone. Thus foiled in his first attempt, the Fiend turns, in angry mood, towards Eve; but concealing his wrath under a cloak of official indignation and sympathy with humanity, expresses his fear lest Adam's disloyalty to his sovereign King may entail God's righteous wrath, and bring upon them both untold ills. With words of flattery, and specious promises of increased mind-power, the Fiend inflames the woman's weaker intellect, until at last, led on by his crafty lies, she partakes of the deadly fruit. No sooner has she yielded to the Fiend's subtle influence and specious arguments, than the pledge which he had given her of celestial light is apparently fulfilled. A wondrous change comes over her. Her sight is able now to pierce even through the starry Spheres, surrounding the Earth, and to see and hear the worship of Cherubim and Seraphim within the concave of the Empyrean.

While under the spell of this illusion, the Fiend urges her to persuade her lord and spouse to retract the graceless and disloyal words that he had uttered and do his Sovereign's bidding. Thus urged, and thinking only of their mutual weal, she approaches

Adam, bearing in her hand the luscious fruit, and implores him to taste. To add to the force of her words, she assures him, that now she is convinced that the Messenger is, in very deed, God's Angel, for he had fulfilled his pledge to her of greater Light and wider range of Vision, and that no longer did she doubt that the fruit was sent by God with His command that they should eat.

At length, overborne by the Woman's pleading, Adam yields,

> . . . and all his heart
> Went forth to do her will.

His errand accomplished, the Fiend indulges in merriment at the success of his mission and, with a stroke of sarcasm, which none but a demon could have conceived, promises to take the thanks of them both to his liege lord.

This section is brought to a close with a soliloquy, addressed by the Fiend to his lord and Master, Satan, and his return to Hell, to report the successful termination of his fiendish adventure.

In the next section the poet describes the events immediately subsequent to the Fall. No sooner has the Fiend left the Man and the Wife to their ruined lives, than the subtle spell, which his devil-craft had cast over the mind of the Woman, is broken ; the glorious Light within disappears ; the wide-reaching vision of the Universe gives place to normal sight ; and the charm of the intensification of the power of hearing and of others of the senses, is seen to have been subjective only,—an illusion of the brain. Disenchanted, and plunged in deepest remorse for having listened to the artful lies of the tempter, at times, they bend the knee to God in heartfelt contrition, beseeching the All-Merciful that they, alone, may bear the consequences of their guilt ; at times, many a word of sadness passes between them,

> . . . for each shared deeply
> In the other's woe.

We may notice, in passing, that in this section of the poem, in which Cædmon describes the remorse and shame of the guilty pair, there are instances of the most exquisitely chaste pieces of dialogue to be found in any early English work. For example, after Adam has expressed his bitter sorrow for what has happened, and his fears for the future, Eve replies :

> Thú meaht hit me wítan
> Wine mín adam
> Wórdum thínum
> Hit the théah wyrs ne maeg
> On thínum hyge hréowan
> Thonne hit me æt heortan deth.

It is impossible to read the Anglo-Saxon of such a passage as this, even at this far off day, without feeling how perfectly the soft music and plaintive rhythm of the verse harmonise with the sentiment expressed. Even in a modern English rendering, these lines lose but little of their beauty, and may be taken as a good illustration of our meaning :

> " Well mayest thou upbraid me as thou dost,
> O Adam, my belovéd spouse, and yet
> Believe me, that thyself canst not bewail
> More bitterly the outcome of this deed
> Than I do in my heart."

But to return. At length, in shame and sorrow, the Man and the Woman seek the shelter of a neighbouring grove, and there, seated apart, await in silent dread, the coming of their King, and His sure sentence of full-merited doom.

After many days, the holy God descends to Earth, and walks at evening-time amid the glories of the Garden. No sooner do the Man and his sorrow-stricken spouse hear the voice of their Heavenly Chief, than they seek in conscious guilt the recesses of a deep-hidden cavern. Summoned by the Deity, Adam approaches his Maker, acknowledging his sense of woe and shame, and in answer to the questioning of his Sovereign Lord, acknowledges that, forgetful of divine Love, he had taken the deadly fruit from the hand of his virgin Wife, and had eaten in violation of his Lord's command. Eve, to the close questioning of her God, replies in deepest shame, that she was beguiled by

> . . . artful words of fairest import

and ate the fruit.

And so the fifth section ends.

The doom of the Fiend, in the similitude of the Worm, is then pronounced ; the Man and the Woman hear the sentence of their exile, and bending their steps from Paradise seek

> Another home, a realm more joyless far

than their native Paradise.

In the seventh and last section, the gates of Eden are closed behind the guilty pair. An Archangel, with flaming sword, guards the sacred enclosure to bar their return, and although Almighty God leaves them the radiant stars and the treasures of the Earth and Sea for their comfort and sustenance, they are sent forth to toil, to suffer, and to die.

If we consider this poem simply as the first strain of sacred song in Christianised England of which we have any record, written in an age of general illiteracy, and when few even of the clergy could be styled scholars in any real sense of the word, its high literary merit is remarkable. But we can go farther than this. Cædmon's work is not only meritorious by comparison with the rudeness of the age in which it was produced, but, intrinsically, it takes high rank in our literature. It is true that the poem contains but few similes; still the same may be said of the *Beówulf*, and of Anglo-Saxon poetry in general. In chasteness of diction, however, in smoothness of versification, in purity of thought, in the human sympathy which breathes forth in every line, no less than in the invention of incident, the arrangement of episodes, and the dignified tone of the ending, it is worthy of the high place which, in days gone by, it held in the estimation of the Venerable Beda, of King Alfred, and of the learned Dujon; and which it still holds in the heart of every lover of Anglo-Saxon poetry of the present day. Indeed, as we shall subsequently see, the poem, as a whole, will bear favourable comparison, in many respects, with the more elaborate epic of the erudite Secretary of the Commonwealth, and in more than one passage, evinces a chaste and delicate line of thought, while the corresponding passages in Milton, cannot fail to displease by their coarseness and repulsiveness.

CHAPTER IV.

Cædmon's Poem and Milton's Epic, a Comparative Study—Prologue and Creation.

IN the opening lines of *Paradise Lost*, when invoking the aid of the Heavenly Muse, Milton expresses the opinion that his " adventrous song " is a unique production in literature, involving,

> Things unattempted yet in prose or rhyme,

and it is beyond doubt that he fully believed in his own estimate of the sacred epic.

Nor do we propose to call this statement in question, as it must be acknowledged that, in a certain sense and under certain limitations, Milton's description of his own work is a true one.

That there existed a number of dramas and poems on the same subject as *Paradise Lost*, even at the time when the poet made the first rough outline of his future work [1639–42], and still more so when he began the actual writing of his epic [1658], has

128

been conclusively proved by quite a number of distinguished editors and critics of Milton's works; especially, by the Rev. Henry John Todd * in the Introduction to his *variorum* Edition, where he enumerates the claims of some thirty authors, German, Italian, Spanish, Portuguese, and Dutch, to the credit of having, probably or possibly, contributed something to the conception, the plan, or the execution of Milton's great poem. Voltaire, in his *Essay on Epic Poetry*, originally written in English [1727], during his stay in England, was the first to suggest that Milton had borrowed his " original " from a Scriptural drama that he had witnessed while in Italy [1638–9], entitled *Adamo*, written by a certain Giovanni Battista Andreini, the son of an Italian actress, and known, in both Italy and France, as a writer of comedies and religious poems. This hint of Voltaire's, led to the opening up of one of those, so-called, literary questions that, now and again, have diverted the attention of the scholar from the study of true literature into channels of worthless speculation and useless criticism. Indeed, for many a long year, the question of the particular author to whom Milton may have been indebted for hints and fancies in his *Paradise Lost*, continued to be a favourite topic of research ; and unfortunately, even

* *Vide* Vol. I., pp. 230–270, Edition 1852.

9

at this late day, the question, thus mooted, has not received its final *quietus.*

Leaving out of consideration this unedifying question of Milton's possible obligations to previous authors, and passing by even the perfectly legitimate literary question of Milton's "borrowings," and the sources of his poetic similes, illustrations, and images, all that we propose to do is to consider the only two works, written anterior to Milton's time, which can, by any stretch of the imagination, be compared, as literary works, with the celebrated epic of the Latin Secretary of the Commonwealth; we refer to the *Divina Commedia* of Dante and Cædmon's " Fall of Man."

That Milton was thoroughly familiar with the immortal work of the great Italian poet there can be no doubt, both from the fact of his well known familiarity with Italian literature, and from his evident "borrowings" from Dante. In the lines in which he describes Hell, as

> Regions of sorrow, doleful shades, where peace
> And rest can never dwell, *hope never comes*
> That comes to all,

we are, at once, reminded of the terrible inscription over the entrance to Inferno,

> " Lasciate ogni speranza voi che entrate."

So, again, the influence of Dante's healthier and less materialistic views on the punishments of Hell, as expressed in his *Inferno*, and his more philosophical, or psychological treatment of the subject, can be traced in many a passage of *Paradise Lost*, where the Italian's more metaphysical conception crops out quaintly from beneath the puritan theology of Milton's day. But granting all this, there is no "copying," no "original," but simply a suspicion of Dante's higher philosophy, flavouring, so to speak, the dry theology of the puritan poet.

With regard to Cædmon, however, the case is somewhat different. His "Fall of Man" is the only poem, so far discovered, that could be supposed for a single moment to have influenced Milton's brilliant and powerful imagination. As we have already seen, the discovery of this long lost manuscript, and its publication by Junius at Amsterdam in 1655, render it possible that Milton may have seen the work of the Anglo-Saxon poet, prior to the commencement of his *Paradise Lost*. Indeed, if we take into consideration Milton's insatiable appetite for reading, and his keen interest in all that was passing in the literary world of his day, it amounts to a moral certainty that the publication of such a literary curiosity as the long lost manuscript of Cædmon, must have found its way into Milton's quiet home in Petty

France, and have been read to him by one of his
acquaintances, if not by Junius himself.

However this may be, the two poems are sufficiently similar in plot and mode of treatment, to
indicate a common origin ; and sufficiently dissimilar,
to warrant the opinion that Milton, even if he had
seen the *Paraphrasis*, was but slightly, if at all, influenced by the perusal of the Anglo-Saxon poem.
At the same time, the points of coincidence between
the two poems, with regard both to the plot, the
incidents, the characters, and even some of the
speeches, are as remarkable as the points of divergence ; and hence the two poems offer a most
interesting field for critical comparison.

In order, however, to appreciate the true *status* of
Cædmon's verse and Milton's epic, we must bear in
mind the fact that Cædmon was not, so far as we
know, either a trained scholar or a trained theologian ; and we must suppose, if Beda's narrative is
to be taken literally, that his theological learning
and poetic skill, from what source soever derived,
were acquired with the easy assimilation of genius.
Milton, on the other hand, was a scholar in every
sense of the word. Educated at one of the two
most celebrated seats of learning in England, and
endowed by nature with talents of the highest order,
he became Latinist, Hellenist, Hebraist, a master of

Italian, and, like all great scholars, was endowed, in a very high degree, with the faculty of reproducing at will, the results of his wide reading. As a consequence, *Paradise Lost* is, perhaps, the most *learned* poem in the English language; while Cædmon's "Fall of Man," although it contains, like *Paradise Lost,* innumerable evidences of an intimate knowledge of the Bible, of Rabbinical writings, and of early Christian traditions, is charmingly free from every vestige of that ponderous learning which is a stumbling-block to the averagely intelligent reader of Milton.

Although, in this study, we propose to consider the works of Cædmon and Milton, not from a religious stand-point, but as literature, pure and simple, still, we may say in passing, that the theology of Cædmon is the healthy Christianity of the early Anglo-Saxon Church, and not, like Milton's, the peculiar and disenchanting theology of quasi-Arianism or of seventeenth century Puritanism.

But before entering upon our comparative study of the two works, it is essential to have a clear idea of the "setting," or environment, or background, of Milton's epic. We have already shown, in the last chapter, the "setting" of Cædmon's "Fall of Man," and we depicted, in a series of diagrams, the various changes in Cædmon's portrayal of infinite space that must have passed before the poet's imagination as the poem gradually unfolded itself before him.

And here we are met by the first, most striking, coincidence in the two poems. Milton's " setting " is identical with that of Cædmon's. Milton pictures infinite space as divided into two concaves, or *bósmas*, precisely as Cædmon had done a thousand years before ; and as in the case of Cædmon, so here, we are not left to our own unaided fancy to picture the poet's setting, but have Milton's own descriptions to guide us, and this, not only as regards the two concaves of original space or infinitude, but also as regards the further development of the diagram rendered necessary by the exigencies of the epic.

The diagram, on the page opposite, represents infinite space as conceived by both Cædmon and Milton alike.

The upper concave Milton describes as,

> . . . the empyreal Heaven, extended wide
> In circuit, undetermined square or round,
> With opal towers and battlements adorned
> Of living sapphire ;

and of the Angelic denizens of this Empyrean, the poet tells us, that

.   .   .   on such day
As Heaven's great year brings forth, the empyreal
    host
Of Angels, by imperial summons called,
Innumerable before the Almighty's throne
Forthwith from all the ends of Heaven appeared
Under their hierarchs in orders bright.
Ten thousand thousand ensigns high advanced,
Standards and gonfalons, 'twixt van and rear
Stream in the air, and for distinction serve
Of hierarchies, of orders, and degrees.

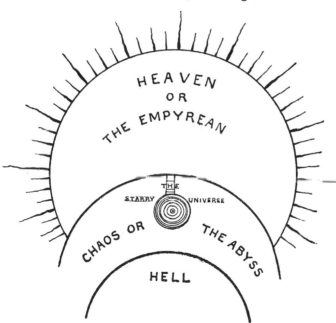

In the description of the wars in Heaven, when the
rebel hosts of Satan had been finally overcome,
Milton explains that the

. . . crystal wall of Heaven . . . opening wide,
Rolled inward, and a spacious gap disclosed
Into the wasteful Deep.

This " wasteful Deep," into which the rebel
Angels are hurled, lightning-struck, is Chaos,

. . . a dark
Illimitable ocean, without bound.

And in another passage, Milton describes it as a

. . . vast immeasurable Abyss,
Outrageous as a sea, dark, wasteful, wild,
Up from the bottom turned by furious winds
And surging waves, as mountains to assault
Heaven's highth, and with the centre mix the pole.

Into this Abyss, the rebels are forced to headlong
ruin, when,

. . . confounded Chaos roared
And felt tenfold confusion in their fall.
.   .   .   .   .   .

Nine days they fell ;
.   .   .   .   .   .

. . . Hell at last,
Yawning, received them whole, and on them closed,—
Hell, their fit habitation.

In these passages, we have a clear-cut outline of
Cædmon's three concaves, the Empyrean, Chaos,
and Hell.

Nor is the Miltonic conception of the Starry Universe any less distinct, or less picturable to the mind, than the Cædmonic.

Milton tells us,

> As yet this World was not, and Chaos wild
> Reigned where these heavens now roll, where Earth
> now rests.

But after the Creation of the World, and when Satan, bent on his mission of demon-revenge, had passed upwards through the Gates of Hell, and had arrived in the uppermost stratum of Chaos, Milton tells us that "the sacred influence of light" dawns on the Arch-fiend :

> . . . and from the walls of Heaven
> Shoots far into the *bosom* of dim Night
> A glimmering dawn.　Here Nature first begins
> Her farthest verge, and Chaos to retire.

At this point in his journey, Satan,

> Weighs his spread wings, at leisure to behold
> Far off the empyreal Heaven, extended wide
> In circuit,
>
> .　　　.　　　.　　　.　　　.　　　.
> And fast by, hanging in a golden chain,
> This pendent World, in bigness as a star
> Of smallest magnitude close by the moon.

That the "World" referred to in these lines is the Starry Universe, as in Cædmon, and not the tiny globe which we inhabit, is made perfectly clear by Milton's own verse, even if we had no other evidence to guide us.

We have already seen that the only system of Astronomy in repute in Cædmon's day was the Ptolemaic. According to this system, there were eight, and only eight, Spheres, the outermost one being the Firmament or Sphere of the Fixed Stars. But during the Middle Ages, in order to explain certain astronomical phenomena which the eight Spheres failed to account for, two additional Spheres were added, viz., the "Crystalline Sphere" and the "Primum Mobile," or "first moved." The Ptolemaic system, thus improved, was adopted in the thirteenth century by Alphonso X. of Castile, king and astronomer, and since that time, has commonly been styled the Alphonsine. It is this system that Milton adopts in *Paradise Lost ;* although a few passages can be pointed out in which he seems to hesitate between the old and the new—the Alphonsine and the Copernican. But, as a rule, it is the Alphonsine that he accepts, perhaps as being more poetical and hence better adapted to the requirements of his epic. In one passage, where he is describing the futile attempt of hypocrites to reach the Empyrean, he enumerates the Alphonsine Spheres in their usual order and by their accustomed names :

> They pass the planets seven, and pass the fixed,
> And that crystalline sphere whose balance weighs
> The trepidation talked, and that first moved.

A few instances of Milton's frequent reference to this, now antiquated, system of astronomy will suffice. When speaking of the Angelic hosts, he describes them as dwelling

> .   .   .   in Heaven, above the Starry Sphere,

where the " Starry Sphere," is the Firmament or Sphere of the Fixed Stars according to the Alphonsine system.

In the following extract, the Ptolemaic idea of concentric Spheres, enclosed the one within the other, is clearly depicted :

> Meanwhile, upon the firm opacous globe
> Of *this round World, whose first convex divides*
> *The luminous inferior Orbs enclosed*
> *From Chaos* and the inroad of Darkness old,
> Satan alighted walks.   A globe far off
> It seemed ; now seems a boundless continent.

After Satan has reached the opening at the zenith of the *Primum Mobile*, immediately beneath the Gates of Heaven, Milton tells us that the Fiend,

> .   .   .   without longer pause
> Down right into *the World's first region* throws

His flight precipitant, and winds with ease
Through the pure marble air his oblique way
Amongst innumerable stars, that shone
Stars distant, but nigh-hand seemed other worlds,—

a passage that would be unintelligible apart from a knowledge of Milton's astronomical tenets.

The imagery used by Cædmon in describing the pathway of communication between the Empyrean and the visible Universe, reappears in Milton, and the illumination in the Junian manuscript, depicting the celestial stairway, would be equally appropriate in a manuscript of *Paradise Lost.**

As the Arch-Fiend nears the confines of that Heaven from which he had fallen, lightning-like, into the Deep, he gains the first glimpse of the changed conditions of his former home :

                          . . . he descries,
Ascending by degrees magnificent
Up to the wall of Heaven, a structure high ;
At top whereof, but far more rich, appeared
The work as of a kingly palace-gate,
With frontispiece of diamond and gold
Embellished ; thick with sparkling orient gems
The portal shone, inimitable on Earth
By model, or by shading pencil drawn.

       .   .   .   .   .   .
Satan from hence, now on the lower stair,
That scaled by steps of gold to Heaven-gate,

* *Vide* page 112.

Looks down with wonder at the sudden view
Of all this World at once.

  .   .   .   .   .   .

The stairs were then let down, whether to dare
The Fiend by easy ascent, or aggravate
His sad exclusion from the doors of bliss ;
Direct against which opened from beneath,
Just o'er the blissful seat of Paradise,
A passage down to the Earth,—a passage wide,

that is, a passage opening at the zenith of the World
or Starry Universe and leading down through the
ten Spheres to Earth; or as Milton describes it
later on,

A broad and ample road, whose dust is gold,
And pavement stars, as stars to thee appear
Seen in the Galaxy, that milky way
Which nightly as a circling zone thou seest
Powdered with stars.

But one point remains to be noticed before we
leave this part of our subject, and enter upon our
comparative study of the general treatment of the
Epic of the Fall by our two poets, Cædmon and
Milton.

It will be remembered that in Cædmon's simple,
though artistic narrative, the Fiend, on the successful termination of his enterprise, returns to his
sovereign lord in Hell to relate the circumstances
and result of his demon adventure ; and apparently

retraces his steps along the same pathway and in the same supernatural manner by which he had journeyed thither. In Milton's more elaborate climax to this part of the narrative, Satan finds that his grim, bastard colleagues, Sin and Death, have built an adamantine bridge or causey, connecting Earth

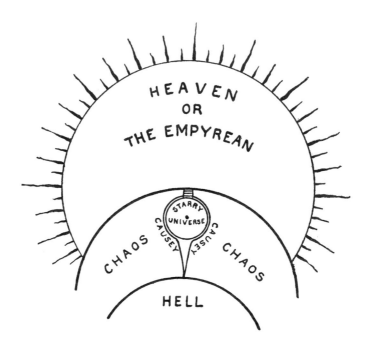

with Hell, just as the jewelled stairway, constructed by the Deity, connected Earth with the Empyrean.

Accordingly, this masterpiece of fiendish engineering requires a final change in our diagram of infinite space as conceived by Milton, and we shall henceforth have, not only the three concaves of Heaven, Chaos, and Hell, and the Starry Universe with its stairway to the Empyrean, but in addition, a weird structure conceived and fashioned by devil-skill to render more easy the descent to Hell of the human race, and to facilitate the intercourse of the demons between Hell and the Earth.

We are now in a position, with the aid of the diagram given here and those in the preceding chapter, to compare the creations of the two poets,—the chaste phantasies of Cædmon and the more brilliant imaginings of the blind bard ; and if we mistake not, each version will be found to aid in the understanding of the other, and to help to fix the other more firmly and distinctly, as a picture, in the mind of the reader.

In our analysis of Cædmon, we divided his poem into seven sections, (1) The Prologue, comprising a statement of the theme in brief; (2) The Creation; (3) The Account of the Rebellion and Expulsion in full; (4) The Council in Hell and departure of Hell's Delegate; (5) The Temptation and Fall ; (6) The events subsequent to the Fall, and anterior to the Sentence ; and (7) The Sentence and Banishment.

These, being essential parts of the poetic framework of the *Epic of the Fall of Man,* are, of necessity, common alike to Cædmon and Milton; but while the Anglo-Saxon poet adopts the natural or chronological order of events, as given above, Milton adopts a more artificial arrangement which, in many ways, was, doubtless, better adapted to his grander and more elaborate design. In Milton, there is a Prologue or Introduction similar to that in Cædmon, and presenting, in brief, a statement of the theme of the poem; but the next two sections Milton omits for the time being, and plunges at once " into the midst of things," as he himself expresses it in his " argument," laying the opening scene of his poem in Hell, and describing the plenary Council in Pandemonium—events which in Cædmon form the fourth section of the Epic. In the fifth, sixth, and seventh sections, Milton adopts the same chronological order as Cædmon, and hence the second and third sections are the only ones that demand our attention here.

What we have called the *second* section, viz., the history of Creation; and the *third* section, viz., the account, *in extenso*, of the Rebellion in Heaven and Expulsion of the rebel Angels, are placed by Milton after the narrative of the arrival of Satan within the precincts of the Garden of Eden, which ends the Fourth Book of *Paradise Lost*. It is not till we come to the Ninth Book that the direct narrative, broken off at the end of the Fourth Book, is resumed and the natural order maintained to the end of the poem.

This break in the narrative, at the point where Satan arrives in Eden, is peculiar to Milton, and deeply interesting, as it discloses some slight insight into Milton's method. Having determined in his own mind, to plunge "into the midst of things," and having, with fine, dramatic effect, introduced the hero of his epic as lying in a deadly stupor in deepest Hell, it was necessary for Milton to devise some way to account, to his readers, for the unceremonious expulsion and dread punishment of the angelic legions, and to explain the full *raison d'être* of the excursion of Satan to Earth. Milton, accordingly, represents the Deity as cognisant of Satan's journey and of its devilish object, and tells how He despatched Raphael to Eden to warn Man of his imminent peril. The arrival of this Heavenly messenger gives Milton the occasion to introduce the history of the Wars in Heaven; the expulsion of the Arch-Fiend and his followers; and to describe the creation of the Starry Universe. This ingenious arrangement of the narrative, enabled Milton to make a telling climax and anticlimax, thus giving additional interest to the events leading up to the second climax, viz., the final accomplishment of the

10

Fall of Man, and to the second anticlimax, the banishment from Eden.

The opening strain that falls from the lips of the
Anglo-Saxon monk is an ascription of praise to the
Highest :

> Most right it is to chant the ceaseless praise
> Of Him who guards the starry heights of bliss
> And ever, with enraptured hearts, adore
> The Glory-King of Heaven's Angelic host.
>
> High in His Majesty, with Justice clothed,
> Omnipotent to do His Sovereign will,
> He ruled the Heavenly concaves, which at first,
> By power divine, were stretched out far and wide
> Throughout unbounded space, celestial Home
> Of those who guard the spirits of the just.
>
> In Him alone, the Lord Eternal, dwells
> Might uncreated.   He is Head supreme
> Of all exalted creatures.   He alone
> Knew no beginning and shall have no end,
> Holding for evermore Almighty sway
> O'er Thrones and Principalities and Powers.

Milton, following classical methods and classical
models, which were the strict fashion in the literature
of the age, begins *Paradise Lost* with an invocation
of the Muse :

> Of Man's first disobedience, and the fruit
> Of that forbidden tree whose mortal taste

Brought death into the World and all our woe,
With loss of Eden, till one greater Man
Restore us, and regain the blissful seat,
Sing, Heavenly Muse, that on the secret top
Of Oreb, or of Sinai, didst inspire
That shepherd who first taught the chosen seed
In the beginning how the heavens and earth
Rose out of Chaos ;

.   .   .   .

. . . I thence
Invoke thy aid to my adventrous song,
That with no middle flight intends to soar
Above the Aonian mount, while it pursues
Things unattempted yet in prose or rhyme.

After his prologue, Cædmon gives in brief, a poetic forecast of his theme, and tells how accursèd pride moved the soul of the great Archangel to cause rebellion in Heaven :

No deadly sin or lurking, traitorous thought
Had dared assault their hearts ; in peace they lived
With their all-glorious Chief, and naught save Truth
And holy Rectitude upreared its head
Within the sacred battlements of Heaven
Till he, who lifted high above his peers,
The Guardian Angel of the Angelic tribes,
Fell through accursèd pride.   Full many then,
Holding in light esteem celestial Love,
Forgat their highest Good.   Presumptuous,
They thought to war against Almighty God
And erelong share, with High Omnipotence,

The unfading glory of that peaceful realm
Its sceptre, crown, and bright seraphic throng.

Vain was their hope, delusive was their dream ;
For in the stead of rebel victory and princely power,
Hatred and pride and racking pain befell
The rebel host, and such a rancorous mind
As he possessed who first moved discontent
And horrid discord.

And so in Milton, the poet himself tells us in his
" argument " that " the First Book proposes, first in
brief, the whole subject " ; and he carries out his
design in the form of a query addressed to the
Muse.

. . . what cause
Moved our grand Parents, in that happy state,
Favoured of Heaven so highly, to fall off
From their Creator, and transgress his will
For one restraint, lords of the World besides.
Who first seduced them to that foul revolt ?
The infernal Serpent ; he it was whose guile,
Stirred up with envy and revenge, deceived
The mother of mankind, what time his pride
Had cast him out from Heaven, with all his host
Of rebel Angels, by whose aid aspiring,
To set himself in glory above his peers,
He trusted to have equalled the Most High,
If he opposed, and, with *ambitious aim*
Against the throne and monarchy of God,
Raised impious war in Heaven and battle proud,
With vain attempt.   Him the Almighty Power

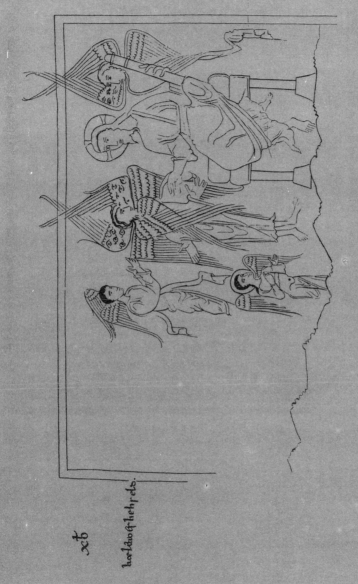

Then was God wroth with that rebellious host.

Hurled headlong flaming from the ethereal sky,
With hideous ruin and combustion, down
To bottomless perdition, there to dwell
In adamantine chains and penal fire,
Who durst defy the Omnipotent to arms.

In this opening section or Introduction to the poem, Cædmon enlarges somewhat on the subject of the treason which had long been smouldering in the heart of the Arch-Traitor, and its final outburst in open rebellion ; and the few words of bitter disloyalty which Cædmon ascribes to the " Angel of Presumption," as he styles Satan, are truly grand in their defiance :

          Then the Archangel spake,
His soul inflamed with dark, malicious thoughts :
" In the North part of God's sublime domain
Will I a kingdom found, a palace rear,
Such is my sovereign will."

The Anglo-Saxon poet brings this first section to a close by telling, in brief, the discomfiture and punishment of the rebel Angels:

             Then was God wroth
With that rebellious host, whom at the first,
With Heavenly glory and Angelic mien
He had endowed.   Forthwith, in ire, He formed
A place of banishment, an exile-house,
Filled with deep anguish and with hellish groans

And direful punishments ; a fell retreat
For those who faithless proved to their high trust.
Deep was the torture-house and void of joys ;
Home of perpetual Night, with sulphur charged,
With fire and cold intense, with lurid flame
And black Tartarean smoke.   The cold, He bade,
And direful flames increase a thousandfold
That by alternate tortures Hell itself
Might be henceforth doubly unbearable.
Then, through the rebel host could nought be heard
But horrid blasphemies and bitter cries
Against their righteous King, for taking thus
Grim retribution on His fallen foes ;
And in fierce raging mood each rebel sware
To wrest the Kingdom from Almighty God.
But when the Archangel's Sovereign high upreared
His mighty arm against that traitor band,
Their haughty boast deceived them, for the King
Sent terror in their hearts, and prone they fell
Powerless to fight.   For in His wrath He bent
Their vengeful pride, stripped them of might and state
And hoped-for triumph.   Then as abject thralls,
Joyless and shorn of Heaven's effulgent crown,
They stood examples of presumptuous pride.
In purpose stern and with relentless hand
The Almighty strongly grasped and might have crushed
And utterly destroyed His foe.   In lieu
He seized the realms and stately palaces
Their hands had reared, and from His Kingdom hurled
The faithless tribe and sent them wailing forth
Down the dark, steep, unutterable path
That leads to Hell.   No longer might be heard
The scornful vaunt ; for now their grandeur turned

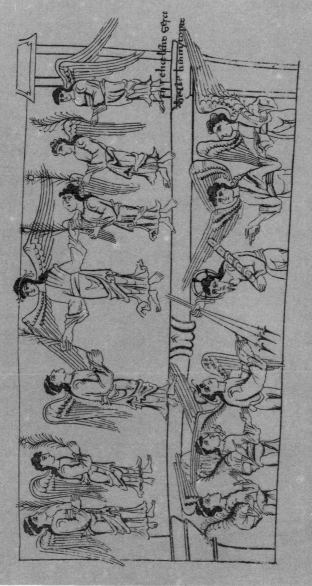

But when the Archangel's Sovereign high upreared
His mighty arm against that traitor band,
Their haughty boast deceived them.

To deepest infamy, their beauteous forms
By sin defaced, they urged their darksome way
To darker punishment.   In torments dire
Accursed they dwelt.   No longer did they raise
The loud derisive laugh ; for ceaseless woe,
Deep racking pain, grief unassuagable
And hydra-headed torture, all around,
Enthroned in blackest darkness, mocked their cries ;
Just retribution for the unholy war
They thought to wage against Almighty God.

In *Paradise Lost*, Milton passes by these preliminary events in his Prologue, and plunges *in medias res*, depicting his hero, together with his confederates, as "lying in the burning lake thunderstruck and astonished" after their fall from the Empyrean ; and he reserves all of this part of the narrative, viz., the incipiency of the rebellion in Heaven and the expulsion of the rebel hosts, to be related in full by Raphael, later on in the Epic,* when the Archangel gives at Adam's request, a circumstantial description of the wars in the Empyrean, ending in Satan's defeat and summary ruin.   To this part of Milton's narrative we shall refer in our comparison of corresponding passages when we come to Cædmon's fuller narrative in what we have styled the third section.

And now, that broad domain of Heaven's fair realm,
The fairest and most powerful to move

* *Vide* Book V, l. 561, etc.

Rebellious lust, in lonely grandeur stood ;
Its palaces so richly wrought and fair,
Conceived and fashioned by rebellious skill,
Stood tenantless.   Then thought the mighty God
How, once again, those bright Angelic seats
And beauteous realms, created by His will,
He might repeople with a better race
And nobler, than the vaunting myrmidons
Who lightly forfeited their heaven-born right.
Then Holy God resolved, beneath the vast,
Celestial firmament (tho' still within
His boundless realms), to form a beauteous World
With overarching skies and waters wide
And earthly creatures filled, in place of those
Whom headlong He had hurled from His abode.

So sings Cædmon, in the opening theme of his poem,
the creation of the Starry Universe and of Man.

In *Paradise Lost*, Adam beseeches Raphael, if it
be permissible, to relate,

How first began this Heaven which we behold
Distant so high, with moving fires adorned
Innumerable ; and this which yields or fills
All space, the ambient Air, wide interfused,
Embracing round this florid Earth ; what cause
Moved the Creator, in his holy rest
Through all eternity, so late to build
In Chaos ;

to which the " affable Archangel " replies :

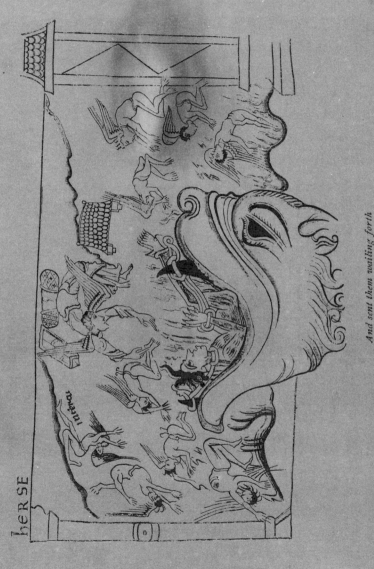

And sent them wailing forth
Down the dark, steep, unutterable path
That leads to Hell.

" Know then that, after Lucifer from Heaven "

.　　.　　.　　.　.　　.　　.

Fell with his flaming legions through the Deep
Into his place, and the great Son returned
Victorious with his Saints, the Omnipotent
Eternal Father from his throne beheld
Their multitude, and to his Son thus spake :

.　　.　　.　　.　　.　　.

.　.　.　‘ I can repair
That detriment, if such it be to lose
Self-lost, and in a moment will create
Another world ; out of one man a race
Of men innumerable, there to dwell,
Not here, *till, by degrees of merit raised,*
They open to themselves at length the way
Up hither, under long obedience tried,
And Earth be changed to Heaven, and Heaven
　　to Earth.’"

A very important point of divergence between the
two poems occurs in this part of the narrative. In
Cædmon it is the Deity, who with celestial majesty,
goes forth into Chaos to create the Universe ; and
in this, the poet is in perfect accord with both accounts of the Creation comprised in the first two
chapters of the book Genesis :

Here the eternal Lord, Head of creation,
In the beginning shaped the Universe,
The sky upreared, and this fair spacious Earth
By His strong might was stablished evermore.

Milton, on the other hand, with his peculiar an-
thropomorphic ideas of the divine Paternity, represents the Father as commissioning His Son, as a
celestial subject or prime minister, to accomplish His
behests:

> "And thou my Word, begotten Son, by thee
> This I perform, speak thou, and be it done!
> My overshadowing Spirit and might with thee
> I send along; ride forth and bid the Deep
> Within appointed bounds be heaven and earth."

We do not bring this forward from a theological
standpoint, but from a purely poetical point of view.
It seems to us to mar the dignity of the theme, for
the Omnipotent to send forth an inferior, although
delegated with sovereign power to perform the
marvels of such almightiness.

It is in this connection, that there occurs that fine
passage, to which we have before alluded, in which
Cædmon describes primeval Chaos:

> As yet, was nought beneath God's radiant Throne
> But gloom as dark as in the cavern reigns,
> And this wide-spread Abyss stood deep and dim
> In idle uselessness, distasteful sight
> To Him the source of all-creative power.
> The mighty King, in mind resolved, beheld
> The joyless shade and saw the lowering cloud
> Lie swart and waste, like an eternal sea

Of blackest Night, beneath the effulgent glow
Of Light ineffable ; till by the Word
And fiat of the King this World appeared.

The thought is the same in Milton. As the Son, accompanied by the angelic hosts, approaches the bounds of the Empyrean,

> . . . Heaven opened wide
> Her ever-during gates, harmonious sound
> On golden hinges moving, to let forth
> The King of Glory, in his powerful Word,
> And Spirit coming to create new worlds.
> On Heavenly ground they stood, and from the shore
> They viewed the vast immeasurable Abyss,
> Outrageous as a sea, dark, wasteful, wild.

Having passed in celestial state,

> Far into Chaos and the World unborn ;

the Vicegerent of the Almighty,

> Then stayed the fervid wheels, and in his hand
> He took the golden compasses, prepared
> In God's eternal store, to circumscribe
> This Universe, and all created things.
> One foot he centered, and the other turned
> Round through the vast profundity obscure.

In drawing their grand, poetic panorama of Creation, both Cædmon and Milton follow so closely the well-known artistic lines of the Hebrew cosmogony, that it will be unnecessary to do more, in this connection, than adduce a few passages which will bring out in bold relief the strong and weak points of the two versions.

The following passage in the Anglo-Saxon poem, descriptive of the creation of Light is as chaste and artistic, as the Anglo-Saxon poet's previous description of Chaos is weird and realistic :

Then o'er the Deep
Was swiftly borne, on bright and radiant wing,
The Spirit of the Lord.   The mighty King
Bade Light come forth far o'er the spacious Deep,
And instantly His high behest was done,
And holy Light shone brightly o'er the waste
Fulfilling His command.
In triumph then
He severed Light from Darkness and to both
The Lord of Life gave name ; and holy Light,
First born of all created things, beauteous
And bright, above all creatures fair
He called the Day.   Then was the Lord well-pleased
With this beginning of creative force,
For now He saw the black and swarthy shade
Subsiding o'er the deep and wide Abyss.
Then time passed o'er the quivering face of Earth,
And Even first, at God's command, dispelled
The radiant Day, till onward rolled the dark
And murky cloud which God Himself called Night,
Chasing away the Even's twilight gleam.
Thus, sundered by Almighty power, they stand

> .   .   .   Then o'er the Deep
> Was swiftly borne, on bright and radiant wing,
> The spirit of the Lord.

Subject to Heaven's decree, and evermore
Have done their Maker's will.

This passage, to our taste, is even finer than the corresponding passage in Milton:

> Darkness profound
> Covered the Abyss; but on the watery calm
> His brooding wings the Spirit of God outspread,
> And vital virtue infused and vital warmth,
> Throughout the fluid mass.
>
> .   .   .   .
>
> "Let there be Light!" said God; and forthwith Light
> Ethereal, first of things, quintessence pure,
> Sprung from the Deep, and from her native East
> To journey through the aery gloom began,
> Sphered in a radiant cloud—for yet the Sun
> Was not; she in a cloudy tabernacle
> Sojourned the while.   God saw the Light was good;
> And light from darkness by the hemisphere
> Divided: Light the Day, and Darkness Night,
> He named.   Thus was the first Day even and morn.

The description of the sublime work of the second Day of Creation, when the Firmament was upraised, is of especial interest as proving, by direct comparison of corresponding passages, the identity of the astronomical views of the two poets.   Cædmon tells us,

> Pale, heavenly Light,
> Succeeding Earth's first Darkness, ushered in
> The second Day.   Then bade the Almighty King,
> Forth from the bosom of the ocean flood,

Rise the bright framework of the glistening stars.
On every side the waters backward rolled,
And instantly, obeying God's command,
The mighty concave o'er the Earth rose high
A solid Firmament ; and the dark waves
Beneath the lofty vault of Heaven were reft
From those above, that all might dwell secure
Beneath God's wide, far-stretching canopy.

In this, and also in the following extract from Milton, the term " Heaven " is used to designate the Sphere of the Fixed Stars or Firmament, and not the Empyrean.

Again God said, " Let there be firmament
Amid the waters, and let it divide
The waters from the waters ! " and God made
The firmament, expanse of liquid, pure,
Transparent, elemental air, diffused
In circuit to the uttermost convex
Of this great round—partition firm and sure,
The waters underneath from those above
Dividing ; *for as Earth, so he the World*
Built on circumfluous waters calm, in wide
Crystalline ocean, and the loud misrule
Of Chaos far removed, lest fierce extremes
Contiguous might distemper the whole frame :
And *Heaven* he named the Firmament.   So Even
And Morning chorus sang the second Day.

This passage, which is one of eminent note in the study of *Paradise Lost*, leaves little room for doubt

Then bade the Almighty King,
Forth from the bosom of the ocean flood,
Rise the bright framework of the glistening stars.

as to Milton's conception of the relative positions of the " Earth," built " on circumfluous waters " ; and the " World," floating " in wide Crystalline ocean," *i. e.*, the Crystalline Sphere.

And what a contrast there is between the Anglo-Saxon poet's simple distant strain

> . . . Pale, heavenly Light,

and the grand apostrophe to Light, which like the low " thundering of organs," along a fretted roof, falls on the ear as the blind bard strikes the opening verse of the Third Book of his great epic.

> Hail, holy Light, offspring of Heaven first-born !
> Or of the Eternal coeternal beam
> May I express thee unblamed ? since God is light,
> And never but in unapproached light
> Dwelt from eternity,—dwelt then in thee,
> Bright effluence of bright essence increate !
> Or hear'st thou rather pure Ethereal stream,
> Whose fountain who shall tell ?   Before the Sun,
> Before the Heavens, thou wert, and at the voice
> Of God, as with a mantle, didst invest
> The rising World of waters dark and deep,
> Won from the void and formless Infinite !

It is impossible to read such a passage as this, without a thrill of intense sympathy for one who, when he framed these lines, could distinguish light from darkness—but nothing more.

Both Cædmon and Milton, when describing the
formation of Eve, adopt the second of the two distinct narratives of Creation * contained in the Hebrew cosmogony. It will be remembered, that in
the first of the two, (so-called), Mosaic accounts of
creation, the Hebrew chronicler does not enter into
any particulars of the formation of Man, but simply
states, " So God created man in his own image, in
the image of God created he him ; male and female
created he them."   But in the second narrative, we
have the fuller account of the moulding of Man out
of the dust of the Earth, and, as an apparent after-
thought, the unique creation of the Woman from
the side of Adam.

> Then to the Guardian of the skies it seemed
> Unfitting that the first-born of Mankind,
> The trusted Keeper of the new-formed World,
> Should longer dwell alone in Paradise.
> To primal Man, God's well-belovèd son,
> Was given a helpmate by his Sovereign Lord
> As aid and comfort in his mortal life ;
> For as he softly slept, the Almighty took
> A rib from Adam's side, *nor caused him pain*,
> *Since from the wound there flowed no drop of blood*,
> And therewith fashioned He a woman fair,

* The first account is given in the first chapter of Genesis and the
first three verses of the second chapter, which in the Anglican version, have been most absurdly divided from their context ; the second
account begins at the fourth verse of the second chapter and continues
to the end of the chapter.

As he softly slept, the Almighty took
A rib from Adam's side,
And therewith fashioned He a woman fair.

Inspired the form with life and placed within
A soul immortal, that at last, they seemed
Like to the Angels in their sinless youth
And peerless beauty clad.

So sings Cædmon.

The Eighth Book of *Paradise Lost* is chiefly occupied with the continuation of the conference
between the Archangel Raphael and Adam, during
which the latter relates, among other things, how
the Deity formed and fashioned the Woman, and
of his first meeting and nuptials with Eve.

"Mine eyes he closed, but open left the cell
Of fancy, my eternal sight ; by which,
Abstract as in a trance, methought I saw,
Though sleeping, where I lay, and saw the Shape
Still glorious before whom awake I stood ;
Who, stooping, opened my left side, and took
From thence a rib, with cordial spirits warm,
And life-blood streaming fresh ; wide was the wound,
But suddenly with flesh filled up and healed.
The rib he formed and fashioned with his hands ;
Under his forming hands a creature grew,
Man-like, but different sex, so lovely fair
That what seemed fair in all the world seemed now
Mean, or in her summed up, in her contained
And in her looks, which from that time infused
Sweetness into my heart unfelt before,
And into all things from her air inspired
The spirit of love and amorous delight."

It is impossible to refrain from admiring the dainty touch in the picture of the Anglo-Saxon poet where he tells us ;

> For as he softly slept, the Almighty took
> A rib from Adam's side, *nor caused him pain*
> *Since from the wound there flowed no drop of blood,*
> And therewith fashioned He a woman fair.

Indeed, as a matter purely of poetic taste, we prefer this passage greatly to the crude, though more realistic, delineation of the scene in Milton, where the Almighty takes,

> . . . a rib, *with cordial spirits warm,*
> *And life-blood streaming fresh.*

The closing incidents, in this section of the *Epic of the Fall*,—the greater benediction of the Deity, and the threefold mandate, so delightfully told in Cædmon, do not seem to have aroused the imagination of Milton, since here, he rises little, if at all, above the mediocrity of the Scriptural original of his story, and falls far short of it, in simplicity of thought and diction.

In Cædmon we read,

> Then the Creator blessed
> His latest triumph of creative might
> With blessings large, and words full fraught with peace.
> He blessed and said : " Teem now and multiply,

He blessed and said : " Teem now and multiply."

Fill with your heaven-born kin the verdant Earth ;
To you I give dominion o'er the Flood,
O'er all this vast creation sole control,
And in perpetual joy your days shall pass.
Hear, then, the mandate of Omnipotence ;
Whate'er the Ocean holds, whate'er the Earth
Brings forth of fowl or cattle or wild beast,
Whatever treads the Land or is endued
With mystic life, e'en whatsoever moves
Throughout the whale-path of the mighty Deep
All shall pay homage and obey your will."

Raphael, in the most prosaic verse, tells how the Deity,

> . . . then blessed mankind, and said,
> " Be fruitful, multiply, and fill the Earth ;
> Subdue it, and throughout dominion hold
> Over fish of the sea, and fowl of the air,
> And every living thing that moves on the Earth ! "

This absence of poetic inspiration, is equally apparent in Milton's rendition of the divine mandate to abstain from the forbidden fruit. In the Anglo-Saxon poem the writer represents the Deity as issuing the command:

> " All other trees enjoy, but from that one
> Strictly abstain and evermore beware
> Its luring fruit, lest it become erelong
> Unholy source of still unholier lust."
> They bowed their heads in deepest reverence
> Before their Heavenly King and praised His name

In sweetest melody, for all that Love
Divine had wrought or Wisdom had prescribed.
Forthwith departed Heaven's eternal King
Leaving to Man the Garden as his home.
And evermore, performing Heaven's behests
They dwelt in holy joy, nor sorrow knew ;—
Dear to the Lord their Maker while they kept
Inviolate His high decree.

The corresponding passage in *Paradise Lost* is not
among the happiest of Milton's verses :

. . . " but of the tree,
Which tasted works knowledge of good and evil
Thou may'st not ; in the day thou eat'st, thou diest.
Death is the penalty imposed ; beware,
And govern well thy appetite, lest Sin
Surprise thee, and her black attendant, Death."

In the *finale* of this part of the Epic Cædmon tells,
in a few words, how,

. . . the Creator gazed with blissful joy
Upon the grandeur of His new domain.
There stood, with beauty girt and filled with gifts,
Resplendent in the golden Light, Man's home
Of Paradise.

Milton's ending is fuller, richer in thought and
imagination, and more descriptive :

Here finished He, and all that He had made
Viewed, and, behold ! all was entirely good.
.   .   .   .   .   .

And evermore, performing Heaven's behests
They dwelt in holy joy.

Yet not till the Creator, from his work
Desisting, though unwearied, up returned,
Up to the Heaven of Heavens, his high abode,
Thence to behold this new-created World,
The addition of his empire, how it showed
In prospect from his throne, how good, how fair,
Answering his great idea.   Up he rode,
Followed with acclamation, and the sound
Symphonious of ten thousand harps, that tuned
Angelic harmonies.   The Earth, the Air
Resounded, ...
The heavens and all the constellations rung,
The planets in their stations listening stood,
While the bright pomp ascended jubilant.

From this passage, one might almost imagine that Milton had seen the illumination, or rather drawing, which accompanies this part of the Junian manuscript, where the Deity is represented as having returned to his high abode,

Thence to behold this new-created World.

Neither of these versions of Creation, however chaste or picturesque, can ever be said to rival the fine, old Hebrew legend, in the quaint simplicity of the story, in the strangely philosophical mode of expression in certain parts of the narrative, or to surpass it, in its utter untrustworthiness (if taken literally), as a historical document.

CHAPTER V.

The Fall of the Rebel Angels.

THE action of the epic of *Paradise Lost* opens abruptly, as we have already seen, with the awakening of the rebel Archangel amid

. . . whirlwinds of tempestuous fire,

whither he had been

Hurled headlong flaming from the ethereal sky,

. . . . . .
To bottomless perdition.

Here, as he raises his giant form, still half-stupefied by his fall through

. . . hideous ruin and combustion,

he casts his gaze around upon his " horrid crew " as they

Lay vanquished, rolling in the fiery gulf,
Confounded, though immortal.

At this point, the poet gives no detailed account of the treason of the rebel host, or of the wars in

Then the Creator gazed with blissful joy
Upon the grandeur of His new domain,

Heaven, reserving these cardinal points in the epic
to be related by the Archangel Raphael in the Fifth
and Sixth Books of the poem.

Cædmon, however, more naturally, and more in
accordance with classical models, (though not with
such strong dramatic effect), presents these incidents
more in their ideal, chronological order, and opens
this part of his narrative with an account of the origin of the ten Angel tribes :

> Of old,
> The King Eternal by His sovereign Might,
> Ordained ten Angel tribes, of equal rank,
> With beauty, power, and wisdom richly dower'd
> And in this host Angelic, whom in Love
> He moulded in His own similitude,
> He evermore reposed a holy trust
> To work His Will in loving loyalty,
> And added of His grace, celestial wit
> And bliss unspeakable.

We do not find, in Milton, any such numerical exactitude in his description of the angelic tribes as in
Cædmon, but he gives us to understand that there
were

> . . . mighty regencies
> Of Seraphim and Potentates and Thrones
> In their triple degrees.

Moreover, he depicts the Almighty Himself, when

calling together the heavenly hierarchy to hear His decree with regard to the Messiah, addressing them as,

" .   .   .   all ye Angels, Progeny of Light,
Thrones, Dominions, Princedoms, Virtues, Powers ; "

and similarly, Satan is represented as addressing his assembled host under the same titles,

" Thrones, Dominions, Princedoms, Virtues, Powers,"

so that in Milton's imagination these were, unquestionably, the main divisions of the angelic hierarchy. In both versions, however, the authors, following the lines of ancient tradition, have brought into unenviable prominence, either as hero of the Epic, or as chief instigator of the rebellion in Heaven, one of an exclusive caste of Archangels, pre-eminent for his gifts, both physical and intellectual. Cædmon depicts one of this favoured few as,

.   .   .   endowed with peerless might
And arch intelligence.   To him alone
The Lord of Hosts gave undisputed sway
O'er all the Angel tribes, exalted high
Above all Principalities and Powers
That next to God Omnipotent he stood,
O'er all created things, lone and supreme.
So heavenly fair and beauteous was his form,
Fashioned by God Himself, that by compare
Less glorious spirits grew dim ; e'en as the stars

Of God's fixed Sphere pale in the glowing light
Of more resplendent orbs.

Similarly, Milton describes his Archangel, Lucifer:

   . . . great indeed
His name, and high was his degree in Heaven ;
His countenance, as the morning star that guides
The starry flock,
   . . . brighter once amidst the host
Of Angels than that star the stars among.

He is also described by the poet as:

He, of the first,
If not the first Archangel, great in power,
In favour, and pre-eminence.

The analysis of the character of this august, spiritual deformity, as depicted respectively by Cædmon and Milton, we shall subsequently take up as a separate comparative study, and, in this connection, shall refer to his personal traits and motives of action, only in so far as may be necessary to render intelligible the main thread of the story.

And here, at the very beginning of the full action of the Epic, we are met by one of the most marked points of divergence between the two narratives.

Cædmon's Archangel of Presumption, seems to have been moved to secret treason, through a false, uncurbed ambition ; nor does the Anglo-Saxon poet

give us any insight into the remote or immediate
causes of the Archangel's open rebellion, except the
pride of conscious physical perfection, of conscious
strength of intellect, and of conscious powers of
leadership.

> Long had he reigned,
> August Vicegerent of the Heavenly King,
> But for presumptuous Pride which filled his heart
> With dire ingratitude and hostile thoughts
> Against the eternal Throne.   Then silent stood
> The great Archangel 'mid the Heavenly choir.
> No grateful anthem rose in meet return
> For gifts divine.   No joyful antiphon
> Burst forth responsive from his guilty lips.
> Nor was it hid from God's omniscient eye
> That His Archangel, though belovèd still,
> Began to harbour dark, presumptuous thoughts
> And in rebellion rise against his God.

This was the first stage in the apostasy of the
great Archangel; when the suggestion of treason
had gained entrance into the mind, and had found
harbour there, though as yet, the silent, inward
incipient thought was unexpressed in open word or
deed.

> .   .   .   thus he spake
> *Within his traitorous heart:*
> "No longer I,
> With radiant form endowed and heavenly mien

Will brook subjection to a tyrant God
Or be His willing slave.   Such power is **mine**,
Such goodly fellowship, I well believe
'T is greater e'en than God's own following."
With many a word of bold defiance, spake
The Angel of Presumption ; for he hoped
In Heaven to rear a more exalted throne
And stronger, than the seats he now possessed.
Then moved by traitorous guile *he built in thought*
Vast palaces within the Northern realm
And richer Western plains of Paradise,
And evermore he lived in doubtful mood
Whether 't were better in acknowledged war
To risk his high estate, or prostrate fall
Mock-loyal as his God's inferior.

But this smouldering treason, erelong, finds vent
in a bitter soliloquy, leading finally, to open rebellion :

At length the Archangel spake :
                              " Why should I toil
Who stand in need of no Superior ?
Marvels as great, ay, greater in renown,
Can I perform than our Omnific Chief ;
A Godlier throne than His and more sublime
Can I unaided rear.   Why, as a slave
Dependent on his lord for worthless gifts,
Should I His will obey and bow the head
In abject vassalage as to a King ?
I, too erelong may be a God as He !
Around me, even now, are strong allies
Who will not fail me in the crucial strife ;

Unflinching heroes, warriors of renown,
Who with accordant and full-tongued assent
Made me their chosen Chief. Such trusty friends,
With zeal inflamed and bound by common ties
To strict fidelity, will counsel well
And lure adherents from the opposing ranks.
Then, if I win this realm, I may become
The Angels' Chieftain, Sovereign of the skies.
Why should I then cringe to Almighty God
Who does me grievous wrong? I am resolved,
No longer will I be His vassal slave."

This idea of making Pride—the prince of the
deadly sins,—the motive of the treason and rebellion of the great, rebel Archangel, is not only in accordance with the Catholic teaching of the age in
which Cædmon lived, but is far more natural, far
grander, and far truer to human failings at their
noblest, than the motive of Jealousy—one of the
most unlovable of human failings—which Milton
attributes to his colossal hero. With his peculiar
anthropopathic conception of the Trinity, Milton
depicts the Deity as making a *pronunciamento* with
regard to his Son—

    " This day I have begot whom I declare
        My only Son, and on this holy hill
        Him hath anointed, whom ye now behold
        At my right hand. Your head I him appoint."

In consequence of this degree, Satan turns rebel,
and,

Around me, even now, are strong allies.

. . . fraught
With envy against the Son of God, that day
Honoured by his great Father, and proclaimed.
Messiah, King Anointed, could not bear,
Through pride, that sight, and thought himself impaired.
Deep malice thence conceiving and disdain,
Soon as midnight brought on the dusky hour
Friendliest to sleep and silence, he resolved
With all his legions to dislodge, and leave
Unworshipped, unobeyed, the Throne supreme,
Contemptuous.

As in Cædmon, so here, this heart-secreted treason at length finds vent in rebellious word and act.
In Milton, however, it is not in soliloquy that Satan
first gives expression to his disloyalty, but in a far
craftier way. Awakening his " next subordinate "
one celestial night, he approaches him with consummate skill and orders him to haste with all who fly
the banner of the great Lucifer,

Homeward with flying march where we possess
The quarters of the North,* there to prepare
Fit entertainment to receive our King,
The great Messiah, and his new commands,
Who speedily through all the Hierarchies
Intends to pass triumphant,

.   .   .   .

At length into the limits of the North
They came, and Satan to his royal seat

* *Vide* Note H.

High on a hill, far-blazing, as a mount
Raised on a mount, with pyramids and towers
From diamond quarries hewn and rocks of gold—
The place of great Lucifer.

In the speech which follows, Satan utters dark
hints of treason, when Abdiel, one of the Seraphim,
who was present at this gathering in the North and
remained loyal to the Deity, denounces, in no measured terms, the apostasy of his Chieftain. Stung
by this rebuff, the rebel Archangel throws off the
mask and openly advocates rebellion :

" Our puissance is our own, our own right hand
Shall teach us highest deeds, by proof to try
Who is our equal.   Then thou shalt behold
Whether by supplication we intend
Address, and to begirt the Almighty Throne
Beseeching or besieging.   This report,
These tidings, carry to the Anointed King ;
And fly, ere evil intercept thy flight."

In the description of the expulsion of the rebel
Angels from the Empyrean, we have a fine example
of the difference between the two poets in their
mode of treating a supernatural subject. Cædmon's
account, as we shall now see, is terse, graphic, and
mundane. He does not attempt the impossible.
He describes supramundane events as if he were
narrating human events, and apparently without

any consciousness of incongruity; and the result
is a seemingly natural narrative :

> When the All-powerful, in secret knew
> The great presumption of his Angel-chief
> And how, by folly moved, he sought to stir
> Unholy war within His joyous realm,
> The mighty God was wroth and straightway doomed
> The apostate Fiend to expiate his crime
> With sufferings greater than all mortal ills.
> (For Love divine was turned to sacred Hate)
> And heavenly Justice hurled him from his throne
> And cast him headlong down the burning gulf
> Which leads to deepest Hell.
>   *For three long days*
> *And three successive nights* the Apostate fell
> Together with his lone rebellious tribe,
> And all thenceforth to demons were transformed
> And doomed triumphless to the swart Abyss.
> There on the approach of each returning eve
> The fires, rekindled, fiercely rage anew,
> And Night appears immeasurably long.
> Then ere the dawn leads back the joyless light,
> Sharp biting cold and glacial blasts attack
> Their fervid forms, and evermore they writhe
> In lurid torture or deep, piercing cold.
> Such were the apostate fiends, who at the first
> Filled Hell's abyss, and such their punishment.

This simple narrative is expanded by Milton into
a detailed account of the Wars in Heaven, as related
by Raphael, and occupies the whole of the Sixth

Book. This part of *Paradise Lost* is an attempt to accomplish the impossible, and in our opinion is the least interesting portion of Milton's epic. The difficulties which Milton had to overcome were not only gigantic, they were insuperable. It is not only *difficult* to narrate in human language the happenings in a state of existence where time and space are unknown ; it is *impossible*, because it is unthinkable. It is not possible so much as to picture, even in imagination, either infinitude or boundless *space*, or eternity or boundless *time ;* nor is it possible to depict mentally any supernatural conditions whatsoever. We know, and can know, nothing about them, and have no language in which to express any such supernatural or problematical phenomena. That Milton, possessing, as he undoubtedly did, a philosophical training, must have been cognisant of these limitations of the human mind and of human speech, can be conclusively proved from his own words. When he describes the Empyrean as

. . . undetermined square or round,

it is simply the Miltonic way of expressing solemn nonsense. In the narrative of the expulsion of the Angels from the Empyrean, where the poet attempts to describe that which is not describable, he has either to use vague expressions, or to confine him-

And all thenceforth to demons were transformed
And doomed triumphless to the swart Abyss.

self to mundane language and imagery. When Lucifer is expelled from Heaven, how could Milton describe this fact? The diamond floor of the Empyrean "rolled inward"; but how could this be if there were no such artificial measurements as latitude or longitude?

Again, how could the rebel host *fall* when infinite space knows nothing of the laws of gravitation? It is true that Milton, now and again, avoids these inconsistencies by vagueness of expression and so gives *vraisemblance* to his narrative, as in the instance just adduced, where he describes Satan and his hosts as having been *hurled* from the Empyrean; but do what one may, it is impossible to think of *hurling*, apart from the idea of direction, viz., upwards or downwards or sideways; and accordingly, Milton himself speaks of their *fall*, where, if language is of any moment, the mundane idea of gravitation is retained.

Or, if we turn to the notion of *time*, we find Milton involved in difficulties no less insuperable. When Eve, addressing Adam, exclaims:

> "With thee conversing I forget all time,
> All seasons and their change,"

this is perfectly intelligible, because on this Earth of ours, we have the artificial arrangement by which we

12

measure what we call time. But when Milton speaking of the rebel angels tells us:

> Nine days they fell ; confounded Chaos roared,
> And felt tenfold confusion in their fall,

it is impossible to understand such a passage. That Milton himself felt the insuperable difficulty is clear by the manner in which he expresses himself in another passage where he says:

> Nine times the space *that measures day and night*
> *To mortal men*, he, with his horrid crew,
> Lay vanquished.

It would be perfectly possible to compile a chronological table showing the number of days, (as we count days), which are occupied with the events described in Milton's epic ; but with this we have no concern at present, our object being simply to show that the subject of Milton's epic, like that of Cædmon's poem, is a theme which could not possibly be treated consistently by the human mind or in human language. This thought comes out with especial prominence in Milton's attempted description of the Wars in Heaven, which Cædmon passes over so skilfully. Milton may give an idea of superhuman strength, when he describes the loyal angels as tearing up mountains by the roots (*sic*); or an idea of freedom from terrestrial restraints when armies might manœuvre, not only as squares or other plane figures, but as cubes or any figure of three dimensions ; and when their manual of tactics might involve vertical as well as horizontal movements ; but after all, we prefer the charm of mundane naturalness and human touch which Cædmon's poem preeminently possesses.

The conclusion of this part of Milton's narrative has little to commend it beyond that of Cædmon. The Messiah, (so the poem runs),

Drove them [the rebel angels] before him thunderstruck,

.   .   .   .

Nine days they fell.

.   .   .   .

Hell at last
Yawning, received them whole, and on them closed ;—
Hell, their fit habitation, fraught with fire
Unquenchable, the house of woe and pain.

We now come to one of the most interesting, as well as one of the most dramatic, portions of the Epic : the narrative of the Council in Hell and the choice of an emissary to accomplish the ruin of Man.

Cædmon begins this fourth section of his poem with a picture of the fiends lying prostrate and stupefied in the liquid fires of Hell :

But erelong deep remorse and envious thought
Made willing captive each rebellious heart ;
For while the false Archangel and his band
Lay prone in liquid fire, scarce visible
Amid the surging clouds of rolling smoke
And deep infernal gloom, the Angelic host
Who fell not from their love still held far off
The empyreal battlements of Heaven.
This, then perceived the traitorous fiends in Hell,
And in one moment stood their folly bare
In having thus exchanged celestial bliss
For the unending torments which their pride
And groundless arrogance had thus entailed.

In a similar strain, Milton tells how Satan,

. . . with his horrid crew,
Lay vanquished, rolling in the fiery gulf,
Confounded, though immortal.   But his doom
Reserved him to more wrath ; for now the thought
Both of lost happiness and lasting pain
Torments him : round he throws his baleful eyes,
That witnessed huge affliction and dismay,
Mixed with obdurate pride and steadfast hate.

.   .   .   .

His legions—Angel Forms, who lay entranced
Thick as autumnal leaves that strow the brooks
In Vallombrosa.

.   .   .   .

So thick bestrown,
Abject and lost, lay these, covering the flood,
Under amazement of their hideous change.

The Angelic host
Who fell not from their love still held far off
The Empyreal battlements of Heaven.

At this point in the narrative, the two versions, although sufficiently similar to show a common origin, differ considerably in mode of treatment. In the less artificial narrative of Cædmon, the Arch-Fiend is represented as being bound fast in iron bands in deepest Hell; and in this position, addressing the fallen Angels in a speech, which, for dramatic power, is unsurpassed even by Milton. It is true that in Cædmon there is no "high mount," no "glistening throne," no "dazzling palace of Pandemonium," "rising like an exhalation," and "built like a temple"; there are no spectacular effects; simply liquid fires, and chilling frosts, and horrid torments, and the vanquished Archangel—God's prisoner—held in adamantine chains, bemoaning his lost estate, in terms of deepest remorse mingled with threats of direst revenge.

Then Satan sorrowing spake:

> "This straitened place!
> Oh! how unlike those Heavenly seats where once
> In Heaven's high Kingdom we as princes reigned!
> But now expelled by Him, the Almighty One,
> That Heaven alas! which by divine decree
> Is destined for Mankind.   'T is this most grieves
> My anxious heart, that earthborn Man should hold
> My glorious seat and dwell in endless joy
> While we in Hell's avenging horrors pine.
> Oh! that my hands were free! that I might hence

But for a moment, for a winter's day ;
Then with this host would I—but now these chains
Press on me and these iron bands embrace !
Oh ! I am kingdomless !   Hell's fetters cling
Hard on each limb.   Above, beneath, the flame
Fierce rages.   Sight more horrible mine eyes
Ne'er yet have witnessed.   O'er these scorching deeps
The fire no respite knows.   The strong forged chain
With ever-biting links forbids my flight.
My feet are bound, my hands are manacled ;
Around my neck is forged this lattice-belt
Of iron strangely wrought by Angel-skill ;
And e'en the pathway to the Gates of Hell
Lies thick beset with foul and horrid Shapes
That bar all exit.   In this loathsome den
We, princes once, chained by a Tyrant's whim
Now suffer chastisement for fancied wrong.
'T is true we may not vent our dire revenge
On Him who thus denies us Heavenly light
And show our godlike strength in open war ;
Yet may we foil His will."

In the Anglo-Saxon version here quoted, it will
be seen that the rebel Archangel does not deign to
consult with any inferior as to his plan of revenge,
and not until he has fully matured his scheme, does
he broach his Arch-demon ideas to any follower.
Indeed, were it not for the fact that Cædmon's
Satan is represented as being bound by " Hell's
fetters " clinging " hard on each limb," his proud,
despotic nature would have spurned consultation

with even the highest of his fallen hosts, and he would simply have announced. his sovereign intention of undertaking the perilous adventure alone and single-handed.

In Milton's more elaborate version, however, Satan, recovering from his downfall through Chaos, into

> The fiery surge that from the precipice

of Heaven received them falling, sees by his side Beëlzebub,

> One next himself in power, and next in crime,

and discloses to him the first hint of his resolve,

> " To wage by force or guile eternal war,
> Irreconcilable to our grand Foe,
> Who now triumphs, and in the excess of joy
> Sole reigning holds the tyranny of Heaven."

During this talk with Beëlzebub, Satan formulates the crucial axiom of his demoniacal life:

> " To do aught good never will be our task,
> But ever to do ill our sole delight,"

and suggests that a Council be summoned of Hell's peers to discuss a plan of campaign,

> ". . . how we may henceforth most offend
> Our eneny, our own loss how repair."

The whole of this part of the narrative, which comprises the conference between Satan and Beëlzebub, and the enumeration and description of the

Powers that erst in Heaven sat on thrones,

but now are princes in Hell, is peculiar to Milton, and has no counterpart in Cædmon's poem.   But in the speech which Satan addresses to the fallen Angels, after having aroused them from their stupor, and still more, in his speech from the "throne of royal state" on the opening and at the close of the imperial parliament in Pandemonium, the two versions again run parallel and evince a remarkable similarity of thought.

But here a word of explanation may be necessary. In both poems the inception of the idea of the ruin of Man is *Satan's*—and his alone; but whereas, in the Anglo-Saxon poem, as it has come down to us, Satan is the sole speaker and advocate of the scheme of revenge; in Milton, the Council of war is conducted on less despotic lines, and each one of the chief princes of Hell takes part in the discussion. It is beyond doubt that Cædmon's poem originally contained the narrative of the debate; but in consequence of the break in the manuscript, at this point, and the excision of several leaves, we can only conjecture, from the sequel, the result of Satan's advice:

> " Begin we then, consult
> About this war."

One thing is certain. In both poems Satan is represented as the ruling mind in the Council, whose advice is finally adopted, whether as in Cædmon, the Arch-Fiend *himself* advocates his own scheme of war, or whether, as in Milton, Satan, with craftier statesmanship makes use of Beëlzebub and others to present and advocate his views, while he himself remains an apparently impartial listener.

The setting of the scene, when the ruined Archangel is about to speak to his fallen comrades for the first time, after their expulsion from the Empyrean, is pathetic and beautiful in the extreme :

> Then spake the haughty One, who erst in Heaven
> O'er all the Angelic hosts most brightly shone,
> Fairest of all God's creatures, most beloved
> By Him who made him.

This opening strain of Cædmon's describes the Arch-Traitor as he appeared while the august Vicegerent of Heaven.

Milton, on the other hand, depicts him as the " dread commander " of Hell:

> He, above the rest
> In shape and gesture proudly eminent,
> Stood like a tower.   His form had yet not lost
> All her original brightness, nor appeared

Less than Archangel ruined, and the excess
Of glory obscured ; as when the sun new-risen
Looks through the horizontal misty air
Shorn of his beams ;

 . . . . . .

       Darkened so, yet shone
Above them all the Archangel : but his face
Deep scars of thunder had intrenched, and care
Sat on his faded cheek, but under brows
Of dauntless courage, and considerate pride
Waiting revenge.   Cruel his eye, but cast
Signs of remorse and passion, to behold
The fellows of his crime, the followers rather
(Far other once beheld in bliss), condemned
Forever now to have their lot in pain.

In both versions, there is a touch in the description of Satan, as he first attempts to speak,—the expression of a thought,—so artistic, so natural, and so simple that one is apt to pass it by unnoticed.

Cædmon with the utter artlessness of true art tells us :

> Sátan mathelode, Sorgiende spræc.
>
> Satan then sorrowing spake.

Milton depicts the fallen Archangel as gazing for a moment upon the millions,

> . . . from eternal splendours flung
> For his revolt,

and tells us,

Thrice he assayed, and thrice, in spite of scorn,
Tears, such as Angels weep, burst forth : at last
Words interwove with sighs found out their way.

It is scarcely possible to conceive of anything more
grandly pathetic than this picture of the Archangelic
nature in ruins; the grandeur of the Archangelic
character shattered, yet retaining so much of its
former peerlessness in tears and muffled sobs.

It is during this first speech, delivered in the Stygian lake, and before the erection of the palace of
Pandemonium, that Satan gives the primal hint of
his plan of campaign, which is subsequently adopted,
and made the keynote of the speech of Beëlzebub :

.   .   .   " our better part remains
To work in close design, by fraud or guile,
What force effected not : that he no less
At length from us may find, Who overcomes
By force hath overcome but half his foe.
Space may produce new Worlds ; whereof so rife
There went a fame in Heaven that He erelong
Intended to create, and therein plant
A generation whom his choice regard
Should favour equal to the Sons of Heaven.
Thither, if but to pry, shall be perhaps
Our first eruption—thither, or elsewhere ;
For this infernal pit shall never hold
Celestial Spirits in bondage, nor the Abyss
Long under darkness cover.   But these thoughts
Full counsel must mature.   Peace is despaired ;

For who can think submission ?   War, then, war
Open or understood, must be resolved."

No sooner is " the high capital of Satan and his
peers " upraised, with roof of fretted gold," than the
heralds proclaim a solemn Council, and Satan, seated

High on a throne of royal state,

.   .   .   .

His proud imaginations thus displayed :
  " Powers and Dominions, Deities of Heaven !—
For, since no deep within her gulf can hold
Immortal vigour, though oppressed and fallen,
I give not Heaven for lost."

Then, having shown that their infernal kingdom
was safe from envious foes, he urges them to fresh
rebellion and proposes :

            " .   .   .   by what best way,
  Whether of open war or covert guile,
  We now debate.   Who can advise may speak."

In this speech, the dread Emperor of Hell makes
no allusion whatsoever to his own cherished scheme
of uncompromising revenge, but with consummate
craft, leaves the unfolding of his plan to his Minister
of State.

In the Anglo-Saxon version, however, Satan states
in bold, defiant, and unmistakable language, the most
vulnerable point of attack, if they would succeed in
accomplishing their revenge :

" . . . He hath devised,
'Twixt this swart Gulf and our ancestral Seats,
A beauteous World, if rumour be believed,
And hath already formed to dwell therein
A race with high intelligence endowed
And fashioned in His own similitude.
With this, His mignon tribe, He purposes
To fill the realms which our dread overthrow
And cruel fall left vacant. Here then lies
Our only hope of adequate revenge ;—
To ruin, if we may, this new-born Man
And on his race, eternal woe entail.
'T is futile now to cherish idle dreams
That God will e'er repent Him of His ire
Or soon restore the thrones and matchless realms
Which He has once usurped. Vain is the attempt
To move the Victor's mind. Whate'er we lost
Is lost beyond recall. Naught now remains
But to devise a scheme by which to thwart
The Victor's known intent and deftly strive
That Man possess not our escheated realm,
But urged by subtle craft to disobey
The stern command of his despotic God,
Forfeit celestial Grace. Then will He cast
These faithless creatures from His fickle heart,
And in one moment hurl them from their height
Of stainless bliss, down to this dark abode
To share our bitter torment and become
Our vassal slaves."

According to Milton, after Moloch and others of Satan's favoured peers, had counselled open war, mock submission, or golden ease, Beëlzebub,

. . . than whom,
Satan except, none higher sat—with grave
Aspéct he rose, and in his rising seemed
A pillar of state. Deep on his front engraven
Deliberation sat, and public care ;
And princely counsel in his face yet shone,
Majestic, though in ruin. Sage he stood,
With Atlantean shoulders, fit to bear
The weight of mightiest monarchies ; his look
Drew audience and attention still as night
Or summer's noontide air, while thus he spake :—
"Thrones and Imperial Powers, Offspring of Heaven,
Ethereal Virtues ! or these titles now
Must we renounce, and, changing style, be called
Princes of Hell ? for so the popular vote
Inclines—here to continue, and build up here
A growing empire."

Finally, obedient to the hint of his great Chief, Beëlzebub calmly deprecates each and all of the plans so far suggested, and, with a servile cunning worthy of a "pillar of state," unveils and advocates as his own counsel, the known views and wishes of his ruined Monarch. We can now compare the passage from the speech of Satan, given above, with the corresponding passage in Milton, where, although the speech is attributed to Beëlzebub, the "devilish counsel" was "first devised by Satan."

"There is a place
(If ancient and prophetic fame in Heaven

Err not)—another World, the happy seat
Of some new race, called Man, about this time
To be created like to us, though less
In power and excellence, but favoured more
Of Him who rules above ; so was His will
Pronounced among the gods, and by an oath
That shook Heaven's whole circumference confirmed.
Thither let us bend all our thoughts, to learn
What creatures there inhabit, of what mould
Or substance, how endued, and what their power
And where their weakness : how attempted best
By force or subtlety.   Though Heaven be shut,
And Heaven's high Arbitrator sit secure
In his own strength, this place may lie exposed,
The utmost border of his kingdom, left
To their defence who held it : here, perhaps,
Some advantageous act may be achieved
By sudden onset, either with Hell-fire
To waste his whole creation, or possess
All as our own, and drive, as we are driven,
The puny habitants ; or, if not drive,
Seduce them to our party, that their God
May prove their foe, and with repenting hand
Abolish his own works.   This would surpass
Common revenge, and interrupt His joy
In our confusion, and our joy upraise
In His disturbance ; when his darling sons,
Hurled headlong to partake with us, shall curse
Their frail original, and faded bliss,—
Faded so soon ! "

In these passages, we have a fine illustration of
the strong similarity in the mode of treating the

subject which characterises the two poets. This is
the more noticeable since in the narrative of the
choice of an emissary, which immediately follows,
the two versions diverge widely. In the Anglo-
Saxon poem, Satan is represented as manacled and
fettered, and hence, being unable to attempt the
enterprise in person, offers the highest reward,
within his gift, to any one of his heroes who should
achieve the adventure.

> " If I, of old, gave aught
> Of princely treasure or rich recompense
> To any warrior of my valiant host,
> While still we held our regal eminence,
> With naught more grateful could he now repay
> My former favour than by speedy help,
> And, passing hence through Hell's grim barriers,
> Soar upward through the clouds on mighty wing
> To Earth's dominion where, in bliss enthroned,
> This new-born Being reigns ; while we are doomed
> To bear the torture of this prison-house.
> As yet in God's esteem this Adam stands
> Pre-eminent, and may erelong possess,
> (For so it is decreed,) our rightful realm.
> If any one of this my sovereign host
> Can counsel and devise a crafty plan
> To lure his soul from loyal obedience,
> Then shall he be most hateful to his Lord ;
> His weal shall cease and some fell punishment
> Become his lot.
> " Deeply in mind revolve
> How he may be beguiled. If he but fall,

Then shall I rest me in these chains content
And he, the daring one, who first proclaims
The fall of Man, seduced by crafty words
I swear, by my eternal majesty,
Shall be exalted to the second throne
In Hell's dominion, and rewarded be
With whatsoe'er of state or wealth or power
In future ages may be proudly won
Within this fiery realm."

In the Miltonic version, no sooner is the plan out-
lined by Beëlzebub approved by the assembled
fiends, than he again rises, and, a second time, voi-
cing the known wishes of his Chief, asks:

    . . . " But, first, whom shall we send
In search of this new World ? whom shall we find
Sufficient ? who shall tempt with wandering feet
The dark, unbottomed, infinite Abyss,
And through the palpable obscure find out
His uncouth way, or spread his aery flight,
Upborne with indefatigable wings
Over the vast Abrupt, ere he arrive
The happy Isle ? what strength, what art, can then
Suffice, or what evasion bear him safe
Through the strict senteries and stations thick
Of Angels watching round ?   Here he had need
All circumspection ; and we now no less
Choice in our suffrage ; for on whom we send
The weight of all, and our last hope, relies."

 This said, he sat ; and expectation held
His look suspense, awaiting who appeared
13

To second, or oppose, or undertake
The perilous attempt.   But all sat mute,
Pondering the danger with deep thoughts ; and each
In other's countenance read his own dismay,
Astonished.   None among the choice and prime
Of those Heaven-warring champions could be found
So hardy as to proffer or accept
Alone, the dreadful voyage.

Unfortunately, there is a break in the Junian manuscript at the end of Satan's speech as given above, and we can only conjecture the drift of the subsequent debate as related by Cædmon. We know that it was an apostate Angel who dared the journey ; we know that it was not Satan ; but further than this we know nothing.   His very name is unrecorded, and how or why he was chosen for the desperate attempt, we must leave to surmise.

But Milton's narrative is complete, and presents a superb picture of self-conscious strength, and self-reliant intellect :

                              .   .   .   at last,
Satan, whom now transcendent glory raised
Above his fellows, with monarchal pride
Conscious of highest worth, unmoved thus spake :—
   " O Progeny of Heaven ! Empyreal Thrones !
With reason hath deep silence and demur
Seized us, though undismayed.   Long is the way
And hard, that out of Hell leads up to Light.

Our prison strong, this huge convex of fire,
Outrageous to devour, immures us round
Ninefold ; and gates of burning adamant,
Barred over us, prohibit all egress.
These passed, if any pass, the void profound
Of unessential Night receives him next,
Wide-gaping, and with utter loss of being
Threatens him, plunged in that abortive gulf.
If thence he scape into whatever world,
Or unknown region, what remains him less
Than unknown dangers, and as hard escape ?
But I should ill become this throne, O Peers,
And this imperial sovranty, adorned
With splendour, armed with power, if aught proposed
And judged of public moment, in the shape
Of difficulty or danger, could deter
Me from attempting. Wherefore do I assume
These royalties, and not refuse to reign,
Refusing to accept as great a share
Of hazard as of honour, due alike
To him who reigns, and so much to him due
Of hazard more as he above the rest
High honoured sits ? Go, therefore, mighty Powers,
Terror of Heaven, though fallen ; intend at home,
While here shall be our home, what best may ease
The present misery, and render Hell
More tolerable ; if there be cure or charm
To respite, or deceive, or slack the pain
Of this ill mansion : intermit no watch
Against a wakeful foe, while I abroad
Through all the coasts of dark destruction seek
Deliverance for us all. This enterprise
None shall partake with me."

After the break in the manuscript of Cædmon,
which we have just noticed, the poem continues
with the account of the starting of the chosen
Fiend on his adventurous journey:

Without delay, the apostate Angel donned
His glistening arms ; and tightly on his head
His helmet bound, secured with many a clasp.
Thus armed, and with a heart deep-versed in guile
He started on his fatal enterprise.
High toward the fiery concave first he shot,
A spiral column bright with lurid flame
Showed where he took his flight. The Gates of Hell
Were quickly left behind as lion-like
In strength and desperate in fiendish mood
He dashed the fire aside. The farthest bounds
Of that infernal kingdom passed, he urged
His venturous flight, tho' now with easier wing.
E'en as he upward sped, his crafty mind
Unceasingly revolved the subtlest words
Of specious flattery with which to lure,
To wicked deeds and deepest infamy,
The spotless subjects of the eternal King.
Onward he took his way and soon descried
Far off the trembling light of this fair World.

Although the narrative of this daring expedition,
as told by Milton, is far more elaborate, and more
highly finished in every respect than are the verses
of the Anglo-Saxon poet, yet who can read the two
versions, side by side, without according to the elder

Thus armed, with heart deep-versed in guile
He started on his fatal enterprise.

poet a high place in the realm of imagination.   Milton's Satan (so sings the poet),

> .   .   .   with thoughts inflamed of highest design,
> Puts on swift wings, and toward the gates of Hell
> Explores his solitary flight : sometimes
> He scours the right hand coast, sometimes the left ;
> Now shaves with level wing the deep, then soars
> Up to the fiery concave towering high.
>
> .   .   .   .
>
> At last appear
> Hell-bounds, high reaching to the horrid roof,
> And thrice threefold the gates ; three folds were brass,
> Three iron, three of adamantine rock,
> Inpenetrable, impaled with circling fire,
> Yet unconsumed.

Having appeased the Portress of Hell-gate,

> On a sudden open fly,
> With impetuous recoil and jarring sound,
> The infernal doors, and on their hinges grate
> Harsh thunder, that the lowest bottom shook
> Of Erebus.
>
> .   .   .   .
>
> .   .   .   the gates wide open stood,
>
> .   .   .   .
>
> .   .   .   and like a furnace-mouth
> Cast forth redounding smoke and ruddy flame.
> Before their eyes in sudden view appear
> The secrets of the hoary Deep—a dark
> Illimitable ocean, without bound,
> Without dimension.
>
> .   .   .   .

Into this wild Abyss the wary Fiend
Stood on the brink of Hell and looked a while,
Pondering his voyage.

. . . .

At last his sail-broad vans
He spreads for flight, and, in the surging smoke
Uplifted, spurns the ground.

. . . . . .

O'er bog or steep, through strait, rough, dense, or rare,
With head, hands, wings, or feet, pursues his way,
And swims, or sinks, or wades, or creeps, or flies.

Having been guided by Chaos and ancient Night
to where the Starry Universe is situated,

. . . Satan staid not to reply,
But, glad that now his sea should find a shore,
With fresh alacrity and force renewed
Springs upward, like a pyramid of fire,
Into the wild expanse, and through the shock
Of fighting elements, on all sides round
Environed, wins his way.

. . . . . .

But now at last the sacred influence
Of light appears, and from the walls of Heaven
Shoots far into the bosom of dim Night
A glimmering dawn. Here Nature first begins
Her farthest verge, and Chaos to retire.

. . . .

. . . Satan with less toil, and now with ease,
Wafts on the calmer wave by dubious light,

. . . .

Or in the emptier waste, resembling air,
Weighs his spread wings, at leisure to behold
Far off the empyreal Heaven, extended wide
In circuit, undetermined square or round,
With opal towers and battlements adorned
Of living sapphire, once his native seat,
And, fast by, hanging in a golden chain,
This pendant World, in bigness as a star
Of smallest magnitude close by the moon.
Thither, full fraught with mischievous revenge,
Accurst, and in a cursed hour, he hies.

The remaining portion of the journey of the Fiend, from the opening at the zenith of the Starry Universe down through the Spheres, is passed over by Cædmon with little more than mere mention :

Arrived, at length, he trod with fiendish joy
The verdant paths of Man's primeval home,
Impatient now to prove his mission crowned
With dark success.

Milton's description, on the other hand, of Satan prowling around the huge circumference of the Universe in search of a port of entrance, and the picture of Satan's flight down through Starry Space, are so brilliant and so grandly portrayed, that we do not hesitate to give them virtually *in extenso*. Moreover, the careful perusal of this passage, will tend to fix more firmly in the mind what we have already said regarding the peculiar astronomical views of *Paradise Lost :*

Meanwhile, upon the firm opacous globe
Of this round World, whose first convex divides
The luminous inferior Orbs, inclosed
From Chaos and the inroad of Darkness old,
Satan alighted walks.   A globe far off
It seemed ; now seems a boundless continent,
Dark, waste, and wild, under the frown of Night
Starless exposed, and ever-threatening storms
Of Chaos blustering round, inclement sky,
Save on that side which from the wall of Heaven,
Though distant far, some small reflection gains
Of glimmering air less vexed with tempest loud.
Here walked the Fiend at large in spacious field.—
          .   .   .   .

And long he wandered, till at last a gleam
Of dawning light turned thitherward in haste
His travelled steps.   Far distant he descries,
Ascending by degrees magnificent
Up to the wall of Heaven, a structure high ;
At top whereof, but far more rich, appeared
The work as of a kingly palace-gate,
With frontispiece of diamond and gold
Embellished ; thick with sparkling orient gems
The portal shone.
          .   .   .   .   .   .

Satan from hence, now on the lower stair,
That scaled by steps of gold to Heaven-gate,
Looks down with wonder at the sudden view
Of all this World at once.
          .   .   .   .   .   .

                    .   .   .   from pole to pole
He views in breadth,—and, without longer pause,
Down right into the World's first region throws

His flight precipitant, and winds with ease
Through the pure marble air his oblique way
Amongst innumerable stars.

. . . .

           But who dwelt happy there
He staid not to inquire : above them all
The golden Sun, in splendour likest Heaven,
Allured his eye.   Thither his course he bends,
Through the calm firmament.

Unable, however, to conjecture which of the dazzling planets that are bounding past him, each in his
appointed Sphere, is the Paradise of the newly-
created Man, he asks Uriel, Regent of the Sun,
one of the seven Archangels, whom he conveniently
happens to meet, to guide him, who replies :

" Look downward on that globe whose hither side
With light from hence, though but reflected, shines.

. . . .

That spot to which I point is Paradise,
Adam's abode ; those lofty shades his bower.
Thy way thou canst not miss ; "   .

. . . .

         . . .   and Satan, bowing low,

. . . .

Took leave, and toward the coast of Earth beneath,
Down from the ecliptic, sped with hoped success,
Throws his steep flight in many an aery wheel,
Nor staid, till on Niphates' top he lights.

CHAPTER VI.

The Temptation and Fall of Man.

AN especial interest gathers around the climax of
the story of the Fall of Man ; and the fascination of the narrative naturally deepens as the consummate devil-craft, which characterises severally
the Hell's Delegate of Cædmon and the Arch-Fiend
of Milton, is gradually unfolded by the poet, until
at length, the hellish design of foiling the Almighty
is accomplished, and the emissary departs, laughing
at the success of his infernal venture.

But more than this. The two versions of the
Temptation, the Fall, and the events immediately
subsequent to the Fall, present a wide field for
comparison and conjecture ; and, to the student of
comparative literature, furnish ample material for
far wider research than can be attempted in the
present work.

The hero of the Anglo-Saxon poem, having
alighted on the circumference of the tiny Earth,—
the fixed centre of the Spheres,—soon discovers the
primeval home of Man :

Erelong amid the shade
Of Eden's fair wide-spreading foliage,
He saw the parents of Mankind ; the Man
Whose comely form bespoke a wise design ;
And, by his side, radiant with guileless youth,
His God-created Spouse.   Above them spread
Two Trees rich-laden with immortal fruit,
The Trees of Life and Death implanted there
By Power divine, that Man might freely choose
Unending weal or never ceasing woe.
Far different were their fruits !   The one was fair
And glistening to the sight ; to touch most soft
And delicate.   Such was the Tree of Life.
And whosoever ate thereof would live
For evermore, neither by Age impaired,
Nor grievous sickness harmed, but live his life
And pass his days in joy ; and e'en on Earth
Would dwell beneath the smile of Heaven's high King,
And going hence in peace, would have decreed
Such honours as high Heaven alone can give.
Swarth was the other fruit and dim and dark
That on the Tree of Death hung temptingly,
Full fraught with bitterness.   (For mortal man
Must know the Evil and the Good.)   And he
Whoe'er should taste the baleful fruit that grew
On this accursèd Tree, his doom assured,
Must ever after live a life of pain
And sweating of the brow and sorrow dire.
Old age would from him take all youthful joys,
Bold deeds and lordly power, and at the last,
E'en Death would be one portion of his doom.
Awhile he might enjoy the carnal bliss
Of mortal life ; then seek that darkest land

With lurid flames illumed and be the slave
Of fiends—the direst danger of Mankind
And most enduring.
                This the foe well knew,
Satan's dark messenger who warred with God.
Then in the body of a worm he twined
With devil's craft around the *Tree of Death*,
Took of the fruit and turned his wily form
To where he knew the beauteous handiwork
Of Heaven's eternal King would surely be

So in *Paradise Lost*, Milton tells us that Satan,

            . . .   to the border comes
Of Eden,

    .   .   .   .

One gate there only was, and that looked East
On the other side. Which when the Arch-Felon saw,
Due entrance he disdained, and, in contempt,
At one slight bound high overleaped all bound
Of hill or highest wall, and sheer within
Lights on his feet.

    .   .   .   .

Thence up he flew, and *on the Tree of Life*,
The middle tree and highest there that grew,
Sat like a cormorant ; yet not true life
Thereby regained, but sat devising death
To them who lived.

Having been detected by Ithuriel, "squat like a toad," close at Eve's ear, as she lay asleep in the depth of night,

Assaying by his devilish art to reach
The organs of her fancy, and with them forge
Illusions as he list, phantasms and dreams ;
Or if, inspiring venom, he might taint
The animal spirits, that from pure blood arise
Like gentle breaths from rivers pure, thence raise
At least distempered, discontented thoughts,
Vain hopes, vain aims, inordinate desires,
Blown up with high conceits engendering pride,

and having been expelled from the Garden,

The space of seven continued nights he rode
With darkness,—thrice the equinoctial line
He circled, four times crossed the car of Night
From pole to pole, traversing each colúre ;—
On the eighth returned, and on the coast averse
From entrance or cherubic watch by stealth
Found unsuspected way.

.   .   .   .

.   .   .   and with inspection deep
Considered every creature, which of all
Most opportune might serve his wiles, and found
The Serpent subtlest beast of all the field.
Him, after long debate, irresolute
Of thoughts revolved, his final sentence chose
Fit vessel, fittest imp of fraud, in whom
To enter, and his dark suggestions hide
From sharpest sight :

.   .   .   .

Like a black mist low-creeping, he held on
His midnight search, where soonest he might find

The Serpent.   Him fast sleeping soon he found,
In labyrinth of many a round self-rolled,
His head the midst, well stored with subtle wiles :
Not yet in horrid shade or dismal den.

.   .   .   .

Fearless, unfeared, he slept.   In at his mouth
The Devil entered, and his brutal sense,
In heart or head, possessing soon inspired
With act intelligential ; but his sleep
Disturbed not, waiting close the approach of morn.

We have quoted these passages somewhat at
length, in consequence of their important bearing on
the after part of the Epic.   The Fiend in Cædmon's
poem, no sooner reaches the Garden of Eden than
he entwines himself in the guise of a worm [on
wyrmes líc], around the Tree of *Death*, [thone
deathes beám], *i. e.* the Tree of the Knowledge of
Good and Evil; while in Milton, the Arch-Fiend sits
like a " cormorant " on the Tree of *Life*.   In both
cases, the object of the Fiend seems to have been
the same, viz., to gain a point of observation and to
reconnoitre the situation ; for, as we shall shortly
see, neither does Cædmon's Fiend advance to the
attack as a " worm " ; nor does Milton's Satan approach Eve in his proper person, though eager, like
the cormorant, to devour his prey.   On the contrary, when the unequal struggle is begun, Cædmon's
Fiend assumes the garb of an *Angel* from the Em-

pyrean, while Milton's Arch-Fiend, not only assumes the *form* of a serpent, but enters the body of an *actual* serpent, and becomes the Devil incarnate *pro tempore*.   That Milton's Satan should have chosen the Tree of *Life* as his watch-point is intelligible, inasmuch, as it was,

> The middle tree and highest there that grew.

Similarly, we can understand why Cædmon's Fiend should have entwined himself around the Tree of *Death*, since that was the spot selected by himself as the trysting-place, where to test his vaunted prowess as the champion of Hell.

It is at this point in Milton's narrative, that Raphael is sent to warn Adam of the presence of the Arch-Fiend, and to prompt his continued obedience to his Maker; and that Adam, taking advantage of the visit of the Archangel, induces him to relate the history of the Wars in Heaven and the account of Creation.

In the opening verses of this life-drama of the Temptation, Milton depicts a pastoral scene of exquisite beauty, where the Man " goeth forth unto his work and to his labour until the evening," accompanied by the Woman, as soon as,

> . . . sacred light began to dawn
> In Eden on the humid flowers, that breathed

Their morning incense, when all things that breathe
From the Earth's great altar send up silent praise
To the Creator.

So luxuriant is the growth of plant and flower in
Eden, that Eve gains Adam's reluctant permission
to tend her favourite spot in Paradise, while he de-
votes his labour to a sturdier task; and so divide
between them the care of their Garden-home.

Cædmon has no passage corresponding to this,
and for the sufficient reason, that his version of the
Epic does not require it. In the Anglo-Saxon poem,
as we shall now see, the Fiend boldly approaches
Adam with his first overtures; and it is apparently
a matter of supreme indifference to him whether the
Woman is present or not. In other words, there
does not exist in this poem any reason to invent an
incident to account for the separation of the Man
and Wife when the Fiend begins his subtle onset.

But all this is changed in *Paradise Lost*. Here,
the Arch-Fiend, with a cunning that savours more
of Mephistopheles than of the ruined Archangel,
adroitly approaches the *Woman* in the first instance,
and endeavours through her to accomplish his end.
He waits until she is alone; and then, and not till
then, does he attempt her downfall.

" Behold alone
The Woman, opportune to all attempts,"—

(so muses Satan,)

> " Her husband, for I view far round, not nigh,
> Whose higher intellectual more I shun."

The opening tilt, in the deadly duel between Satan's nameless emissary and Adam, is thus told by the Anglo-Saxon poet :

> Then spake the Enemy his primal word—
> A query charged with lies :
>   " Cravest thou aught,
> O Adam, from thy God ? Hither I come
> Journeying from far to bring thee His behest.
> But little time has flown since at His side
> I sat, and then He bade me quickly hie
> To Earth with His command, that of this fruit
> Thou shouldest eat, since thus thy power and skill
> And mental grasp far greater will become,
> More radiant still thy body, and thy form
> More beauteous than before. If aught there is
> Of treasure in the World, (so spake the King),
> E'en this shall not be wanting thy desire
> When once thy ready mind hath wrought this act
> Of loyal obedience to the sovereign word
> Of Heaven's King, and thou in gratitude
> Hast served thy Master's will and made thee dear
> To thine own Lord.
>   " I heard Him as He sat
> In dazzling brightness, praise thy deeds and words
> And speak about thy life, so must thou now
> Fulfil whate'er commands His Angel brings
> To Earth.

14

" In this thy World are regions broad
And green, and thou art lord of this domain ;
But in the realm of Heaven, God rules supreme.
The Lord of Men, All-powerful on High,
Deigns not at times to visit Man, but sends
His vassals forth to speak on His behalf.
He bids thee now by me, His messenger,
True wisdom learn and zealously obey
His Angel's word.   Take then this fruit in hand
Bite it and taste ; thy mind will be enlarged
Thy form far fairer, for the Sovereign God
Thy Lord, Himself this help hath sent to thee
From Heaven's high Kingdom."

          Then Adam spake :
(The God-created Man majestic stood)
" When here I heard the mighty God, the Lord
Of Triumph, speak in strong and trenchant tones,
Bidding me keep inviolate His commands
And gave this bride, this Wife of beauteous mien,
To be the sharer of my blissful home,
He charged me to beware lest through deceit
My will should be seduced and I should taste
The Tree of Death ; since he who near his heart
Should cherish ought of sin should meet his doom
In blackest Hell.

        " I know not, (since with lies
Thou mayest come and dark designing thought),
Whether or not thou art in very deed,
A messenger from Heaven ; for to say truth,
Nought do I recognise in all thy words
Or ways or subtle hints—nought do I see
In this thy journey here, or in thy speech
To prove thy mission true.

Take then this fruit in hand

Bite it and taste.

"I know full well
What He Himself, the great Protector, said
When last I saw Him here, that all His words
Should be revered and cherished lovingly
And all His precepts strictly be obeyed.—
Unlike art thou to any of His host
That ever I have seen, nor dost thou show
E'en slightest token from our gracious Lord,
Assuring pledge of His divine command.
Thee, I will ne'er obey, so hie thee hence.
In the Almighty God, who wrought me thus
With His creative arms and placed me here
With loving hands, in Him I firmly trust.
From His high Realm, if such His sovereign Will,
He can endow His creatures with all good
Without His vassal's aid."

In this section of the narrative, the two versions
differ very widely, not only in minor points but in
the *motif* of the entire story ; and, in our opinion,
Cædmon's conception of the character assumed by
the Tempter and of his mode of attack, evinces far
greater naturalness and higher imagination than
Milton's corresponding conception. According to
the Story, the Deity is represented as wont to
descend to Earth and hold converse with Man ; and
the Angels are represented as God's " ministering
spirits,"—the " guardians of the spirits of the just."
Milton himself, represents Archangels as commis-
sioned by the Deity to perform his behests on the
Earth, and throughout the Starry Universe :

> For God will deign
> To visit oft the dwellings of just men
> Delighted, and with frequent intercourse
> Thither will send his winged messengers
> On errands of supernal grace.

What form of deception could, for one moment, compare in naturalness with the assumption by the Fiend of the character of an Angelic messenger, sent direct from the throne of God, as a celestial ambassador *ab latere* to announce the commands of the Deity, and to carry back the petitions of His lowly subjects? It was a brilliant idea, happily conceived, and carried out with all the poetic finish of genius.

Nor is this all. The Fiend, as Cædmon unquestionably imagined him, would have spurned the idea of so unchivalrous an act as a covert attack on the *Woman;* and in Cædmon's version it is not until after the Tempter has been summarily and bluntly repulsed by Adam, that he approaches the Woman as a forlorn hope of success.

Moreover, the whole *morale* of the Story is different in Cædmon's version. If the Woman really believed that the Tempter was an Angelic messenger sent by God, and bearing His command to eat of the Fruit, she may have been deceived; she may not have shown the sturdy, unquestioning obedience of her Spouse; she may have been guilty of dis-

obedience, disloyalty, treason, even sin, although
with "extenuating circumstances"; whereas in Milton's narrative, as we shall presently see, there is
nothing to relieve the dark background of the
picture; while the most unlovely and unlovable
traits in Woman's nature are depicted and empha-
sised, with no points of exculpation whatsoever, as
the cause of "all our woe."

As this incident in Cædmon's narrative finds no
counterpart in *Paradise Lost*, we shall pass on to
where the two versions once again run parallel.

The Anglo-Saxon poet, in continuation of his
story, tells how, after his discomfiture, the Fiend
turned,

> In wrathful mood, and saw, not far away,
> The Woman's perfect form, the beauteous Eve;
> And feigning deep regret expressed a fear
> Lest direst ills from henceforth should befall
> Their farthest offspring through the guilty words
> Her spouse had breathed :
> "Full well I know," said he,
> "Our Sovereign God will justly be incensed
> When, this long journey done, this tedious path
> Retraced, your stubborn message I relate ;
> That ye, His creatures, dare to disobey
> Whate'er commands He now hath hither sent
> From His far Eastern Throne. Now must He come
> In person to demand your quick response,
> Since I, His messenger, am powerless
> To carry out the task. And this, I fear,

Will draw upon yourselves the silent ire
Of mighty God. But if thyself wilt bow,
With willing mind submissive, to my word
'T were easy to devise the ready way.
Ponder within thy breast, that from you both
Thou may'st avert this dire, impending woe,
If thou wilt do as I shall now advise :
Eat of this fruit ; then will thy sight be clear
To see forthwith widely o'er all this World ;
And e'en beyond, thy sight shall pierce and see
The Throne of God Himself, and thou shalt dwell
Within the radiance of Heavenly Grace.

    If thou should'st gain the love of thy dear lord
And win his trust in all that thou dost say,
In after days *thou mayest rule thy spouse.*
Disclose to him the thoughts that burn e'en now
Within thy breast, and why thou hast performed,
By my advice, the mandate of thy God ;
Then will he quit, at once, the hateful strife
And evil answer which now rage within
The caverns of his heart. Let us forthwith
With singleness of aim approach thy lord ;
Do thou with cautious zeal urge him to heed
And follow thy advice lest ye become
Most hateful to your Lord.
                    " If thou succeed
In this thine enterprise I will conceal,
O best of Womankind, from our great King
The idle words and slanders of thy lord ;
How he accused God's messenger of lies,
Ay, and falsely said that I am eager
For the wrong, an ambassador of wrath
And not God's messenger.

> " Would that he knew
> My true celestial rank ; for I can tell
> The origin of all the Angel-tribes ;
> And on the vaulted dome of Heaven have gazed ;
> And many an æon I, with eager will
> And faithful mind, have served the mighty King,
> The Lord Himself.   Unlike indeed am I
> To Man's Arch-enemy ! "
>   Thus did he lead
> The Woman on with lies, and with his wiles
> Allured her to that wrong ; until at length
> The Serpent's counsel, deep down in her heart
> Began to rage (to her a weaker mind
> Had the Creator given), and now her mood
> Thus straitly pressed by fiendish skill, gave way,
> And from his hand she took the noxious fruit
> Culled from the Tree of Death, and thus defied
> The Lord's express command.

In the Anglo-Saxon version, which we have just given, and still more so in passages that we shall give farther on, there is an expression of all that is lovely and lovable in Woman. She tastes of the Fruit, because she believes that it is verily God's command, and to shield her loved one from any harm that might ensue from his supposed disobedience. To the Tempter's alluring promise,

> " If thou should'st gain the love of thy dear lord
> And win his trust in all that thou dost say,
> In after days *thou mayest rule thy spouse.*"

she pays no heed. It is *his* welfare, and his alone, that dominates her will. She falls, but only in the hope of saving *him.* Even if she does bring " woe " on all mankind, it is done with a noble motive, and Cædmon's Eve is the prototype of true Womanhood, selfless and self-sacrificing. If she sinned, it was a sin worthy of a beatitude rather than of a curse.

But in Milton, Eve becomes of the earth, earthy ; and the temptation is planned on a far lower moral level than in Cædmon. The Tempter is no longer an Angelic ambassador from the Empyrean, but a talking reptile :

> . . . the Enemy of Mankind, enclosed
> In serpent, inmate bad, and toward Eve
> Addressed his way—not with indented wave,
> Prone on the ground, as since, *but on his rear,**
> *Circular base of rising folds, that towered*
> *Fold above fold, a surging maze ; his head*
> *Crested aloft,* and carbuncle his eyes ;
> With burnished neck of verdant gold, erect
> Amidst his circling spires, that on the grass
> Floated redundant.

When the Serpent, adopting flattery as the surest allurement of the Miltonic Eve, ends his fulsome address by appealing to her vanity, and asks in mock surprise,

* *Vide* Note J.

And from his hand she took the noxious fruit
Culled from the Tree of Death.

" Who sees thee (and what is one ?) who shouldst be
   seen
A Goddess among Gods, adored and served
By Angels numberless, thy daily train ? "

it is no wonder that Milton's " universal dame "
should exclaim in true surprise,

" What may this mean ?   Language of Man pronounced
By tongue of brute, and human sense expressed ! "

or, that after his description of the wonderful effects
of eating of the fruit of the Tree of Knowledge, as
he professes to have done, Eve should reply in strong
amaze :

" Serpent, thy overpraising leaves in doubt
The virtue of that fruit, in thee first proved.
But say, where grows the tree ? from hence how far ?
For many are the trees of God that grow
In Paradise, and various, yet unknown
To us."

To which the Serpent replies :

" Empress, the way is ready, and not long,—
Beyond a row of myrtles, on a flat,
Fast by a fountain, one small thicket past
Of blowing myrrh and balm.   If thou accept
My conduct, I can bring thee thither soon."
" Lead then," said Eve.   He, leading, swiftly rolled
In tangles.

Having led her to the " Tree of Prohibition,"

    . . . . to thus her guide she spake :—
" Serpent, we might have spared our coming hither,
Fruitless to me, though fruit be here to excess,
The credit of whose virtue rest with thee,—
Wondrous, indeed, if cause of such effects !
But of this tree we may not taste nor touch ;
God so commanded, and left that command
Sole daughter of his voice ; the rest, we live
Law to ourselves ; our Reason is our Law."
   To whom the Tempter guilefully replied :—
" Indeed ! hath God then said that of the fruit
Of all these garden-trees ye shall not eat,
Yet lords declared of all in Earth or Air ? "
   To whom thus Eve, yet sinless :—" Of the fruit
Of each tree in the garden we may eat ;
But of the fruit of this fair tree, amidst
The Garden, God hath said, Ye shall not eat
Thereof, nor shall ye touch it, lest ye die."

Foiled in this, his first onset, the Serpent instantly
modifies his plan of attack. It would seem that the
Arch-Fiend had been proceeding on the supposition
that Eve would not recognise the Tree of Knowledge
as the " Prohibited Tree." He had already told her
that on first tasting the fruit,

    . . . " such pleasure till that hour
At feed or fountain never had I found.
Sated at length, ere long I might perceive
Strange alteration in me, to degree
Of Reason in my inward powers, and Speech
Wanted not long, though to this shape retained.

Thenceforth to speculations high or deep
I turned my thoughts, and with capacious mind
Considered all things visible in Heaven,
Or Earth, or Middle, all things fair and good."

But now that he discovers the truth, and realises
that Eve is fully on her guard against surprisal, he
returns to the attack, but not on the same lines.
Apostrophising the fruit of the Tree, as it hangs
temptingly before their eyes, he exclaims:

" O sacred, wise, and wisdom-giving Plant,
Mother of science ! now I feel thy power
Within me clear, not only to discern
Things in their causes, but to trace the ways
Of highest agents, deemed however wise."

Then, turning to Eve, he presses his temptation,
by questioning the power of the Deity to carry out
His threat of Death:

" Queen of this Universe ! do not believe
Those rigid threats of death.   Ye shall not die.
How should ye ?   By the fruit ? it gives you life
To knowledge.   By the Threatener ? look on me,
Me who have touched and tasted, yet both live,
And life more perfect have attained than Fate
Meant me, by venturing higher than my lot.
Shall that be shut to Man, which to the Beast
Is open ?

   .   .   .   .

Goddess humane, reach, then, and freely taste ! "

He ended ; and his words, replete with guile,
Into her heart too easy entrance won.
Fixed on the fruit she gazed, which to behold
Might tempt alone ; and in her ears the sound
Yet rung of his persuasive words, impregned
With reason, to her seeming, and with truth.

．　　　．　　　．　　　．　　　．　　　．　　　．

Pausing a while, thus to herself she mused :—
" Great are thy virtues, doubtless, best of fruits,
Though kept from Man, and worthy to be admired,

．　　　．　　　．　　　．　　　．　　　．　　　．

What hinders, then,
To reach, and feed at once both body and mind ? "
So saying, her rash hand in evil hour
Forth-reaching to the fruit, she plucked, she eat.
Earth felt the wound, and Nature from her seat,
Sighing through all her works, gave signs of woe
That all was lost.

．　　　．　　　．　　　．　　　．　　　．　　　．

Eve,
Intent now wholly on her taste, naught else
Regarded ; such delight till then, as seemed,
In fruit she never tasted, whether true,
Or fancied so through expectation high
Of knowledge ;

．　　　．　　　．　　　．　　　．　　　．

Thus to herself she pleasingly began :—
" O sovran, virtuous, precious of all trees
In Paradise ! of operation blest
To sapience, hitherto obscured, infamed,
And thy fair fruit let hang, as to no end
Created ! but henceforth my early care,

Not without song, each morning, and due praise,
Shall tend thee, and the fertile burden ease
Of thy full branches, offered free to all !
Till, dieted by thee, I grow mature
In knowledge, as the Gods who all things know."

The narrative of the Temptation and Fall of *Adam*, as told by Cædmon, is as distinct from that of Milton, as is the narrative of the Fall of *Eve*, and presents some most interesting points of study which we shall presently examine at length.

After Eve had eaten of the forbidden fruit, think-that thereby she was obeying God's holy will, Cædmon tells us

                    And now with vision clear,
(Usurious gift of that malignant Foe),
Her strengthened sight pierced far and wide. All things
In Heaven and Earth far fairer seemed to her,
The World more beauteous and the works of God
Grander and mightier than ere before.
'T was not by Man's device that she beheld
This wondrous change ; but that foul wretch beguiled
Her soul with studious care and deftly raised
The vision in her mind, so that she seemed
To see thus far o'er Heaven's extended realm.
Then spake the Fiend in secret hate ('T was not
Her weal he sought with these fair-sounding words) :
" I need not tell thee, since thyself canst see,
O Eve the Good, that since thou hast believed
My words to thee, and heeded my advice
No form or beauty can with thine compare.

This glorious Light, gift of a loving God,
Which I have brought, bright with the glow of Heaven,
Now shines before thee far along thy path
And bathes thy glistening form in golden mist
So thou may'st touch its rays.
                              " Go, tell thy lord
What visions thou hast seen, what wondrous powers
My coming has revealed ; and if, e'en now
With modesty of mind he will obey,
The counsel that I bring, I will bestow
On him, with generous hand, that goodly Light
Which now adorns thyself.   Nor will I e'er
Reproach him for the slanders that he spake,
Unworthy though he be of pardoning grace,
For such malicious charges as he made ;—
Thus shall thy offspring ever rule their lives ;
When they do evil then shall they repent
And working works of Love avert the curse
Of Heaven's High King and thenceforth win His Grace."

Then turned she to the spot where Adam stood,
She who was fairest of all Womankind,
Most beauteous of all who e'er were born
Into this World, the handiwork of God
Himself ;—though even then unconsciously
She was undone, misled by crafty lies.

    .   .   .   .   .   .

In her hands she bare the accursèd fruit,
Some on her bosom lay, that fruit which erst
The Lord of Lords strictly forbade her touch,
Fruit of the Tree of Death.

    .   .   .   .   .   .

Then to her spouse she spake : " This goodly fruit,
O Adam, mine own lord, is sweet indeed
And pleasant to the sense ; and sure I am
That this bright messenger in very deed
Is God's good Angel, for I clearly see,
E'en in his garb, the envoy of our Lord
The King of Heaven.· Surely 't is better far
To gain his favour than his hate.   If thou
Spake aught this day to him in bitter scorn
He will forgive thy haste, if once we show
Obedience to his word.   Will hateful strife
With God's own messenger avail thee aught ?
We need his kindly offices to bear
Our errands to the All-powerful King of Heaven.
The promise which he gave of heavenly Light
And keener vision of the Universe
He hath fulfilled.
                        " E'en now can I discern
Where the Almighty dwells, enthroned in bliss,
Creator of the world !   And I can see
The Angelic host revolve with trembling wing
Around the Throne, of all created things
The greatest and most joyous company.
Who could bestow on mortal man the gift
Of such far-seeing sense but God alone,
The Ruler of the skies ?   And I can hear
From farthest point, throughout this great wide world ;
And I can see o'er all the broad expanse
Of Earthly things.   And I can plainly hear
The music of the Spheres, as heard in Heaven.
Soon as I tasted this delicious fruit
All became sudden Light within the mind
And all without was Light.

" I have it here,
Mine own good lord, here in my hand, and fain
Would give it thee, my first most precious gift.
From all this messenger, with cautious words,
Lately unfolded to my wondering mind,
I doubt not that it comes brought here from God
With His command.   No likeness does it bear
To aught else on this Earth, but as I learn
(So saith this messenger) it comes direct
From God."

                    Oft did she speak to him and urged
Him all the livelong day to that dark deed,
To break their Lord's command.

                              Meanwhile, near by,
Hell's Envoy stood, inflaming his desires
And urging him with wiles ; and followed him
With dark intent.   The Foe was near at hand,
He who had come from far, alone to wage
That danger-fraught campaign.

                              Then to her lord
Full oft she spake, fairest of Womankind,
Until at length his mind was full of doubt
From trusting to the promises she made
Of Light and widened vision of the World.
(But all she did was done with true intent.)
As yet she knew not that so many ills
And sinful woes must follow to Mankind
Because she deemed it wise to heed the words
Of that false messenger.   For she believed
That in the revelations which she made
To Adam's listening ear she but disclosed
A token from on High and wrought the Will
Of their exalted King.

> Then in his breast
> The mind of Adam changed, and all his heart
> Went forth to do her will.   From Eve's own hand
> He took both Death and Hell ; for such it was
> Though in the form of fruit.   Beneath it lurked
> The dream of Death, the Devil's artifice,
> And loss of Eden and Eternal woe
> With ruin of Mankind.   Such was the food,
> Unholy fruit !
> Thus came the curse within
> And stained the heart !

It is almost impossible to conceive any more chaste or picturesque description of the climax of the Story of the Fall than this of Cædmon's.   In this version, Eve is represented as a model of true Womanhood, loyal at heart to her God, and staunch in her love to her Spouse.   When she urges Adam to eat of the fruit that lay on her bosom, she does so, under the full conviction that the messenger is truly an emissary from Heaven, and that Adam is disobeying God's command in opposing him ; and her chief fear is, lest he may suffer for his wilfulness.   The whole of this part of Cædmon's poem is simply an expansion of the poet's own statement that,

> All she did was done with true intent.

The same pathos and earthly charm cling around the story of *Adam's* final Fall.   There is no unmanly

15

surrender; no weak consent given to that which he
knows to be wrong; no pandering to any uxorious
instinct. It is not until,

> . . . *the mind of Adam changed*

and his reason is convinced that

> . . . *all his heart*
> *Went forth to do her will.*

If now, we compare the above passage from Cædmon with the corresponding account in Milton, we
shall find that the Anglo-Saxon poet does not suffer
by comparison.

>   Adam the while,
> Waiting desirous her return,
>
> . . . forth to meet her went, the way she took
> That morn when first they parted. By the Tree
> Of Knowledge he must pass; there he her met,
> Scarce from the tree returning; in her hand
> A bough of fairest fruit, that downy smiled,
> New gathered, and ambrosial smell diffused.
>
> "Hast thou not wondered, Adam, at my stay?
>
> . . . "strange
> Hath been the cause, and wonderful to hear.
> This tree is not, as we are told, a tree
> Of danger tasted, nor to evil unknown

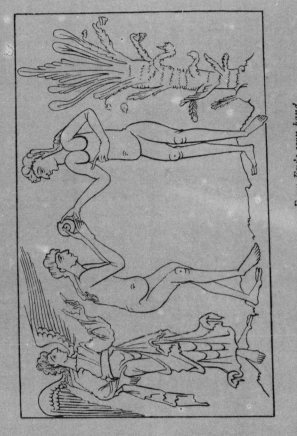

From Eve's own hand

He took both Death and Hell.

Opening the way, but of divine effect
To open eyes, and make them Gods who taste ;
And hath been tasted such.   The Serpent wise,

Hath eaten of the fruit, and is become
Not dead, as we are threatened, but thenceforth
Endued with human voice and human sense,
Reasoning to admiration, and with me
Persuasively hath so prevailed, that I
Have also tasted, and have also found
The effects to correspond—opener mine eyes,
Dim erst, dilated spirits, ampler heart,
And growing up to Godhead."

Adam, soon as he heard
The fatal trespass done by Eve, amazed,
Astonied stood and blank, while horror chill
Ran through his veins, and all his joints relaxed.

Speechless he stood and pale, till thus at length
First to himself he inward silence broke :—
" O fairest of Creation, last and best
Of all God's works, creature in whom excelled
Whatever can to sight or thought be formed,
Holy, divine, good, amiable, or sweet !
How art thou lost ! how on a sudden lost,
Defaced, deflowered, and now to death devote !

How can I live without thee ? how forego
Thy sweet converse, and love so dearly joined,
To live again in these wild woods forlorn ?

However, I with thee have fixed my lot,
Certain to undergo like doom.   If death
Consort with thee ; death is to me as life ;
So forcible within my heart I feel
The bond of Nature draw me to my own—
My own in thee ; for what thou art is mine.
Our state cannot be severed ; we are one,
One flesh ; to lose thee were to lose myself."
    So Adam, and thus Eve to him replied :—
" O glorious trial of exceeding love,
Illustrious evidence, example high !
Engaging me to emulate ; but, short
Of thy perfection, how shall I attain ?

    .   .   .   .

On my experience, Adam, freely taste,
And fear of death deliver to the winds."
    So saying, she embraced him, and for joy
Tenderly wept, much won that he his love
Had so ennobled as of choice to incur
Divine displeasure for her sake.

    .   .   .   .   .   .

       .   .   .   from the bough
She gave him of that fair enticing fruit
With liberal hand.

    .   .   .   .   .   .

Earth trembled from her entrails, as again
In pangs, and Nature gave a second groan ;
Sky loured, and, muttering thunder, some sad drops
Wept at completing of the mortal Sin
Original ; while Adam took no thought,
Eating his fill.

In this version, we are not left in doubt, any more than in Cædmon's version, as to the motive which prompts Eve to desire that Adam shall eat of the forbidden fruit. It is not womanly love; it is not anxiety for Adam's welfare; or any noble emotion of human nature. It is *jealousy* and *selfishness*, pure and simple; surely strange feelings to attribute to one who had so lately come, pure and innocent, from the hand of God: and who, from the recentness of her Fall, could have gained little, if any, knowledge of terrestrial naughtiness or have developed such loveless passions as Milton attributes to her.

> " But to Adam in what sort
> Shall I appear ?   Shall I to him make known
> As yet my change, and give him to partake
> Full happiness with me, or rather not,
> But keep the odds of knowledge in my power
> Without copartner ? so *to add what wants*
> *In female sex, the more to draw his love,*
> *And render me more equal, and perhaps,—*
> *A thing not undesirable,—sometime*
> *Superior.*

.   .   .   .   .   .

> . . . but what if God have seen,
> And death ensue ? *then I shall be no more ;*
> *And Adam, wedded to another Eve,*
> *Shall live with her enjoying, I extinct !*
> *A death to think !   Confirmed, then, I resolve,*
> *Adam shall share with me in bliss or woe.*"

But this is not all. The Miltonic Adam is scarcely, if at all, above the low moral plane of the Miltonic Eve.

> He scrupled not to eat,
> *Against his better knowledge, not deceived,*
> *But fondly overcome with female charm.*

In Cædmon, as we have seen, Adam is finally convinced that Eve's view of the character of the messenger is correct, and this, in consequence of her iterated assertion of having gained an exalted and supernatural mental state after having eaten of the Fruit. In other words, he is as completely deceived by the positive assurances of the Woman, as the Woman herself had been, by the hypnotic illusions of the Fiend.

But in Milton's hands, Adam degenerates into a mere weakling; nor is his portrait as drawn by Milton, such as to command the respect of any true man. He is not deceived. He knows full well the force of the divine warning. He understands perfectly that to eat of the forbidden Fruit will entail death,—and yet he yields,

> . . . fondly overcome with female charm.

This unedifying, uxorious phase in *Paradise Lost* will stand out in a still stronger light in the sixth section, which we have next to examine, and which relates the events immediately subsequent to the Fall.

There is, however, an incident which occurs at this point in the Epic, that may detain us for a moment, before passing on to the next section; namely, the last glimpse that we have of the Fiend after the successful termination of his adventure.

The Anglo-Saxon poet has thrown a touch of grim humour into his narrative which renders it exceedingly quaint :

> *Then gaily laughed the Fiend,*
> The bitter-purposed messenger of Hell ;
> *And making sport of his infernal deed*
> *Promised to take the grateful thanks of both*
> *To his liege Lord !*
>   His errand done, and crowned
> With fell success, his fiendish joy broke forth
> In deep soliloquy, addressed to him
> Who reigned in Hell :
>   "Now have I full discharged
> The honoured trust to me decreed by fate,
> Thy will performed ; for many a day to come
> Are men seduced, this Adam and this Eve !
> And now that through my counsel they have mocked
> The orders of their King, their certain doom
> Is the withdrawal of His love ; and hence
> No longer may they claim that heavenly Realm,
> But must perforce their darksome journey take
> To Hell's abyss.   Surely thou need'st not bear
> Deep sorrow in thy heart, though straitly bound

In chains; nor mourn that here on earth Man dwells
In highest bliss while we, wrongly deprived
Through thy great pride, of those high palaces
And goodly courts where once we dwelt, are doomed
To naught but punishment and endless woes,
A land of darkest Night.
　　　　　　　　　　"So let thy heart
Rejoice, since here on Earth both of thy dreams
Are now fulfilled, and all the sons of Man
Their heavenly heritage and fair domain
Will lose, and full of hate, will be thy slaves
In yonder flames.　Nor ends our victory here.
Much sorrow of the heart have we entailed
On God Himself.　Whate'er of misery
We must endure, is now on Adam's race
Fully avenged.　God's sovereign hate assured,
And the dire ruin of all humankind,
With pain of Death, my wounded pride is healed.
Around my heart great thoughts revolve.　The wrongs
We long have borne, fruit of relentless spite,
Are all avenged.
　　　　　　　　　" At once will I retrace
My joyous steps back to the lurid flames
And seek the spot where Satan straitly bound
With tightly-woven chains, a captive lies
In darkest Hell."
　　　　　　　　　Then swiftly downward sped
That direst messenger of woe, and passed
The Gates of Hell; thence urged his toilsome way
Though the expanse of flame and reached at length
The point where Satan lay, his lordly Chief,
With fetters bound.

Then gaily laugh'd the Fiend,
The bitter-purposed messenger of Hell.

The narrative of the return of the Arch-Fiend to Hell, as told by Milton, is more especially remarkable from the brilliant audacity of imagination which it displays ; and, next to the description of Satan's weird voyage from Hell and through Chaos up to Earth, is perhaps as grand a flight of phantasy as can be found in the whole of Milton's poem. The idea of connecting the Starry Universe and Hell

> . . . by wondrous art
> Pontifical,

is Milton's, and has no place, even as an incept, in Cædmon ;

> . . . a ridge of pendent rock,
> Over the vexed Abyss, following the track
> Of Satan to the self-same place where he
> First lighted from his wing, and landed safe
> From out of Chaos—to the outside bare
> Of this round World.

We may notice, in passing, that although Milton never loses sight of the main thread of his narrative, he is, now and again, swayed by the allegorical spirit of the age in which he lived, and introduces personifications easily recognised, to lend charm to his picture. In this instance, Sin and her offspring Death are represented as the true architects and builders who

. . . overlay
With this portentous bridge the dark Abyss ;

and these two, again, are represented as the misshapen progeny of Satan, just as they are portrayed
in the Catholic or General Epistle of St. James the
Apostle.

Sin and her son, the " meagre shadow," Death,

. . . with power (their power was great)
Hovering upon the waters, what they met
Solid or slimy, as in raging sea
Tossed up and down, together crowded drove,
From each side shoaling, towards the mouth of Hell.

.   .   .   .

The aggregated soil
Death with his mace petrific, cold and dry,
As with a trident smote, and fixed as firm
As Delos, floating once ; the rest his look
Bound with Gorgonian rigour not to move,
And with asphaltic slime ; broad as the gate,
Deep to the roots of Hell the gathered beach
They fastened, and the mole immense wrought on
Over the foaming Deep high-arched, a bridge
Of length prodigious, joining to the wall
Immovable of this now fenceless World,
Forfeit to Death—from hence a passage broad,
Smooth, easy, inoffensive, down to Hell.

.   .   .   .   .   .

With pins of adamant
And chains they made all fast, too fast they made

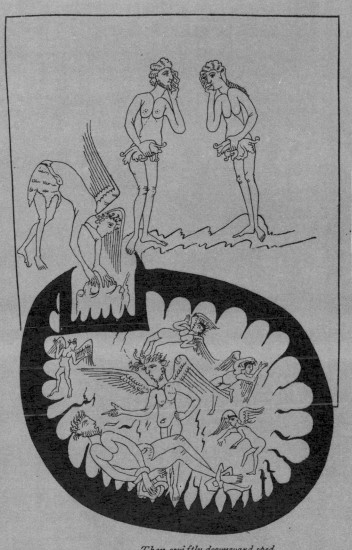

Then swiftly downward sped
That direst messenger of woe, and passed
The gates of Hell.

And durable ; and now in little space
The confines met of empyrean Heaven
And of this World, and on the left hand Hell,
With long reach interposed ; three several ways
In sight to each of these three places led.

Satan, who knows nothing of this achievement,
(as the great causey had been built during his visit
to the Earth), no sooner reaches the outermost convex of the Starry Universe, on his return journey,
than he sees the massive roadway and,

>   . . . at sight
> Of that stupendous bridge his joy increased.
> Long he admiring stood.

But at last,

>   . . . went down
> The causey to Hell-gate ; on either side
> Disparted Chaos overbuilt exclaimed,
> And with rebounding surge the bars assailed,
> That scorned his indignation.   Through the gate,
> Wide open and unguarded, Satan passed.

Having ascended, unobserved, the high throne in
Pandemonium,

>   Down a while
> He sat, and round about him saw, unseen.
> At last, as from a cloud, his fulgent head
> And shape star-bright appeared, or brighter, clad
> With what permissive glory since his fall
> Was left him.

Then Satan speaks:

" Thrones,   Dominations,   Princedoms,   Virtues,
      Powers !—
For in possession such, not only of right,
I call ye, and declare ye now, returned,
Successful beyond hope, to lead ye forth
Triumphant out of this infernal pit.

    .   .   .   .

         " Him by fraud I have seduced
From his Creator, and, the more to increase
Your wonder, with an apple !   He, thereat
Offended—worth your laughter !—hath given up
Both his beloved Man and all his World
To Sin and Death a prey, and so to us,
Without our hazard, labour, or alarm,
To range in, and to dwell, and over Man
To rule, as over all he should have ruled.

    .   .   .   .

            " Ye have the account
Of my performance."

    .   .   .   .

   So having said, a while he stood, expecting
Their universal shout and high applause
To fill his ear ; when, contrary, he hears,
On all sides, from innumerable tongues
A dismal universal hiss, the sound
Of public scorn.   He wondered, but not long
Had leisure, wondering at himself now more.
His visage drawn he felt to sharp and spare,
His arms clung to his ribs, his legs entwining
Each other, till, supplanted, down he fell,

A monstrous serpent on his belly prone,
Reluctant, but in vain ; a greater power
Now ruled him, punished in the shape he sinned,
According to his doom.   He would have spoke,
But hiss for hiss returned with forked tongue
To forked tongue ; for now were all transformed
Alike, to serpents all.

The next section of the Epic, which has to do with
the conduct of the guilty pair, after the Fall and before their banishment from Eden, is exquisitely told
in Cædmon :

     Meanwhile, great sorrow filled
The guilty heart of Adam and his Spouse,
And oft between them words of sadness passed,
For much they feared the anger of their Lord
And Heaven's avenging wrath.   And oftentimes
They sat deep-brooding o'er their sin, and oft
In bitter anguish chided their own selves
For listening to the Fiend's delusive words.
Great was the Woman's grief ; for well she knew
That through seductive arts they both had lost
The love of Heaven.   And penitent in mind
She wept, for now she saw that Light depart
Which he who counselled them to do the crime
Had showed to her—false and illusive sign
Of his pretended claim.   Deep sorrow burned
Within their breasts as dark remorse displayed
The unnumbered ills and ghastly punishment
Their sin entailed.   At times on bended knee,
These guilty partners in a common sin,
In heartfelt prayer, invoked their heavenly King

The Lord of Victory, the source of Good,
Beseeching Him that they alone might bear
And expiate the deadly penalty
Due to their guilty act, since they alone
Had broken His command.

       Many a word of sadness
Passed between the two, for each shared deeply
In the other's woe.
      " O Eve, my helpmate,"
(Thus spake the Man) " in evil hour indeed
Didst thou mark out our future path. E'en now
Seest thou not the dark abyss of Hell
With open gates wide-yawning at our feet ?
The raging of its fires I plainly hear
E'en from this distant spot. And how unlike
The beauteous realm of Heaven are yonder flames !
But now no fairer land than this our Earth
May we anticipate, nor can we ask
Such favour of our Lord, since thou didst heed
The evil counsellor who planned our woe
And urged disloyalty to Heaven's dread King,
The Ruler of the World. Naught now remains
Save that we mourn in deepest penitence
The visit of that Fiend, since God Himself
Bade us beware that greatest of all ills,
Unending torment. E'en at this moment
Hunger and burning thirst, warring within
Like deadly foes, already rend in twain
This mortal flesh ! And how shall we protect
Our fragile life or find subsistence here
When piercing winds from heaven's four quarters blow
And mists arise or showers of hail descend ?

When biting frost and winter's cruel cold
Bind fast the Earth in iron bands? or when
The Solar Sphere sends forth its glowing beams
And radiant heat?   How can we then withstand,
In our defenceless state, each sudden change
Of Nature's fickle mood, devoid alike
Of shelter from the storm and present store
Of needful food?   In truth, possessing naught
Unless it be the dread hostility
Of an offended and All-puissant God?
Deeply I grieve, (since now thou hast beguiled
My loving trust and hast subjected both
To God's just ire,) that ever I invoked
The great Creator's might, bone of my bone,
To frame thy beauteous form and place thee here
To share with me the joys of this fair World.
Yea, and it may repent me all my days
That e'er I gazed upon thee with mine eyes."

Then answered Eve, fairest of Womankind,
Most beautiful of wives, the handiwork
Of God e'en though undone through subtle craft :
" Well mayest thou upbraid me as thou dost,
O Adam, my belovèd spouse, and yet
Believe me, that thyself canst not bewail
More bitterly the outcome of this deed
Than I do in my heart."

                    Then Adam spake :
" If I but knew the Almighty's sovereign Will,
What penalty awaits this fearful crime,
None couldst thou find more ready to perform
That Will than I ; e'en though by Heaven's decree

I had to plunge beneath the surging flood
And seek the Ocean's deep and sunken caves.
No depth could terrify or rapid stream
Could keep me from the abyss, if thus I might
Perform God's holy Will.

                     " No heart have I
For worship, now that I have forfeited,
Beyond retrieve, the favour of our King.
But let us hasten into yonder wold
And sit within the grove's protecting shade,
For naked as we are it is not meet
To tarry longer here."

                    Departing thence
They sought the shelter of the grateful wold
With deepest grief oppressed, and sat apart,
Awaiting now whatever righteous doom
Heaven might inflict for guilty faithlessness
To that high trust which God had erst imposed.
Then sheltered by the forest's inmost shade
They plucked the leaves and clothed themselves
     therewith,
(For they were destitute of other garb) ;
And every morn they knelt in solemn prayer
That God, the Mighty, Ruler of the World
Would not forget them in their great distress
But graciously reveal how they thenceforth
Should live their ruined lives.

Some years before Milton had composed the epic
of *Paradise Lost*, he had taken the public into his
confidence, and in a pamphlet published in 1641, he

Naked as we are it is not meet
To tarry longer here.

had spoken of his future poem as "being a work not to be raised from the heat of youth, or the vapours of wine, like that which flows at waste from the pen of some vulgar amorist, or the trencher-fury of a riming parasite, nor to be obtained by the invocation of Dame Memory and her Siren daughters, but by devout prayer to that Eternal Spirit who can enrich with all utterance and knowledge, and sends out his Seraphim with the hallowed fire of his altar to touch and purify the lips of whom he pleases."

As we read Milton's narrative of the conduct of Adam and his Spouse after the departure of the Arch-Enemy from the Garden, we fail to see any evidence of the purifying touch of the "Eternal Spirit," or of any Seraphic fire; on the contrary, many passages in this part of his epic savour too much of the "vulgar amorist" to be pleasant or even agreeable reading. Who can read without a feeling of repugnance such a passage as that beginning,

> 　　　　　．　．　．　that false fruit
> Far other operation first displayed,
> Carnal desire inflaming.　He on Eve
> Began to cast lascivious eyes ; she him
> As wantonly repaid ; in lust they burn,
> Till Adam thus 'gan Eve to dalliance move.—
>
> 　．　　．　　．　　．　　．　　．　　．　　．

16

Milton's version of this section of the narrative is
as coarse and repulsive as that of Cædmon is chaste
and refined.

Passing by, then, this unsavoury side of *Paradise
Lost*, we emerge into a purer atmosphere where
Milton once again approaches, although he cannot
reach, the higher moral level of the Anglo-Saxon
monk.

Soon as the force of that fallacious fruit,
That with exhilarating vapour bland
About their spirits had played, and inmost powers
Made err, was now exhaled, and grosser sleep,
Bred of unkindly fumes, with conscious dreams
Encumbered, now had left them, up they rose
As from unrest,

  .   .   .   .

                      destitute and bare
Of all their virtue.   Silent, and in face
Confounded, long they sat, as strucken mute ;
Till Adam, though not less than Eve abashed,
At length gave utterance to these words constrained :—
  " O Eve, in evil hour thou didst give ear
To that false Worm, of whomsoever taught
To counterfeit Man's voice—true in our fall,
False in our promised rising ; since our eyes
Opened we find indeed, and find we know
Both good and evil, good lost and evil got ;
Bad fruit of knowledge, if this be to know,
Which leaves us naked thus, of honour void,
Of innocence, of faith, of purity,
Our wonted ornaments now soiled and stained,

*Departing thence
They sought the shelter of the grateful wold
With deepest grief oppressed, and sat apart.*

And in our faces evident the signs
Of foul concupiscence.

.   .   .   .

                    "Oh, might I here
In solitude live savage, in some glade
Obscured, where highest woods, impenetrable
To star or sun-light, spread their umbrage broad,
And brown as evening : Cover me, ye pines !
Ye cedars, with innumerable boughs
Hide me !"

.   .   .   .

                    .   .   .   both together went
Into the thickest wood.

.   .   .   .

                    From thus distempered breast
Adam, estranged in look and altered style,
Speech intermitted thus to Eve renewed :—
"Would thou hadst hearkened to my words, and stayed
With me, as I besought thee, when that strange
Desire of wandering this unhappy morn,
I know not whence possessed thee !   We had then
Remained still happy—not, as now, despoiled
Of all our good, shamed, naked, miserable !"

.   .   .   .

To whom, soon moved with touch of blame, thus
       Eve :—
"What words have passed thy lips, Adam severe ?
Imput'st thou that to my default, or will
Of wandering, as thou call'st it, which who knows
But might as ill have happened thou being by,
Or to thyself perhaps ?   Hadst thou been there
Or here the attempt, thou couldst not have discerned

Fraud in the Serpent, speaking as he spake ;
No ground of enmity between us known
Why he should mean me ill or seek to harm.
Was I to have never parted from thy side ?
As good have grown there still, a lifeless rib.
Being as I am, why didst not thou, the head,
Command me absolutely not to go,
Going into such danger as thou saidst ?
Too facile then, thou didst not much gainsay,
Nay, didst permit, approve, and fair dismiss.
Hadst thou been firm and fixed in thy dissent,
Neither had I transgressed, nor thou with me."

   To whom, then first incensed, Adam replied :—
" Is this the love, is this the recompense
Of mine to thee, ingrateful Eve, expressed
Immutable when thou wert lost, not I,—
Who might have lived and joyed immortal bliss,
Yet willingly chose rather death with thee ?
And am I now upbraided as the cause
Of thy transgressing ? not enough severe,
It seems, in thy restraint ! What could I more ?
I warned thee, I admonished thee, foretold
The danger, and the lurking enemy
That lay in wait ;

    .   .   .   .   .   .

            . . . and perhaps
I also erred in overmuch admiring
What seemed in thee so perfect that I thought
No evil durst attempt thee. But I rue
That error now, which is become my crime,
And thou the accuser. Thus it shall befall
Him who, to worth in woman overtrusting,
Lets her will rule ; restraint she will not brook ;

And, left to herself, if evil thence ensue,
She first his weak indulgence will accuse."
  Thus they in mutual accusation spent
The fruitless hours, but neither self-condemning;
And of their vain contest appeared no end.

According to Milton, no sooner is it known in Heaven that Satan has triumphed, and has accomplished the ruin of Man, than the Deity, in the Person of the Son, descends to Earth to pronounce sentence.

        . . . from his radiant seat he rose
Of high collateral glory.   Him Thrones and Powers,
Princedoms, and Dominations ministrant,
Accompanied to Heaven-gate, from whence
Eden and all the coast in prospect lay.
Down he descended straight.

This, as we have already seen, does not occur in Cædmon until after the heart-felt contrition of Adam and his Spouse, and their daily striving for a renewal of that Communion with their Maker, the loss of which, had entailed a sense of utter solitude, well-nigh unbearable.

After the return of the dread Judge to the Empyrean, Milton describes a scene of earthly, madding passions which it is almost impossible to picture to the mind as the sequel of the visit of the King Immortal.   It is a continuation of the wild battling of hell-born feelings when,

                            Nor only tears
Rained at their eyes, but high winds worse within
Began to rise, high passions—anger, hate,
Mistrust, suspicion, discord—and shook sore
Their inward state of mind, calm region once
And full of peace, now tossed and turbulent.

An extract will show the sullen, felon-mood which
Milton attributes to his conception of Paradisaic
" Old Mortality."

          . . . in a troubled sea of passion tost,
    .   .   .   .   .   .
        Adam to himself lamented loud
Through the still night,—not now, as ere Man fell,
Wholesome and cool and mild, but with black air
Accompanied, with damps and dreadful gloom ;
Which to his evil conscience represented
All things with double terror.   On the ground
Outstretched he lay, on the cold ground, and oft
Cursed his creation ; Death as oft accused
Of tardy execution.
    .   .   .   .
        Whom thus afflicted when sad Eve beheld,
Desolate where she sat, approaching nigh,
Soft words to his fierce passion she assayed :
But her, with stern regard, he thus repelled :—
    " Out of my sight, thou serpent ! that name best
Befits thee, with him leagued, thyself as false
And hateful ; nothing wants, but that thy shape
Like his, and colour serpentine, may show
Thy inward fraud, to warn all creatures from thee
Henceforth, lest that too heavenly form, pretended

To hellish falsehood, snare them.   But for thee
I had persisted happy.

.　　.　　.　　.　　　.　　.　　.

"Oh, why did God
Creator wise, that peopled highest Heaven
With Spirits masculine, create at last
This novelty on Earth, this fair defect
Of Nature, and not fill the World at once
With men as Angels, without feminine ;
Or find some other way to generate
Mankind ?"

This unbridled outburst of senseless passion, (for
Milton himself tells us that Adam was

.　.　.　*not deceived*
But fondly overcome with female charm),—

this unjust crimination, and unmanly subterfuge, are
peculiar to Milton, and as foreign to Cædmon's version, as they would be to the nature of any true gen-
tleman, whose uxuriousness had led him into a gross
indiscretion.

The Almighty, being cognisant of the events
which were transpiring in Paradise, called forth by
name,

His mighty Angels, gave them several charge,
As sorted best with present things.   The Sun
Had first his precept so to move, so shine,
As might affect the Earth with cold and heat

Scarce tolerable, and from the north to call
Decrepit winter, from the south to bring
Solstitial summer's heat.

.   .   .   .

                         To the winds they set
Their corners, when with bluster to confound
Sea, air, and shore ; the thunder when to roll
With terror through the dark aerial hall.

.   .   .   .

                         At that tasted fruit,
The Sun, as from Thyestean banquet, turned
His course intended ; else how had the world
Inhabited, though sinless, more than now
Avoided pinching cold and scorching heat ?
These changes in the heavens, though slow, produced
Like change on sea and land—sideral blast,
Vapour, and mist, and exhalation hot,
Corrupt and pestilent.

.   .   .   .

                         These were from without
The growing miseries ; which Adam saw
Already in part, though hid in gloomiest shade,
To sorrow abandoned.

This, it will be seen, is the same thought that
Cædmon attributes to Adam, although, in Milton's
more elaborate narrative, we find a great deal of
astronomical pedantry from which the Anglo-Saxon
poem is fortunately free.   It is a curious point, that
in both versions, the poet seems to take it for
granted that, but for the Fall, there would have been

the monotony of an eternal *Summer* in Paradise.
Milton tells us that, "some say" the Deity, after the
Fall, made grand solar changes so as to allow,

> Of seasons to each clime.   Else had the spring
> Perpetual smiled on Earth with vernant flowers,
> Equal in days and nights.

In the scenes which follow, the two versions, bar-
ring only the *order* of the narrative, run virtually in
parallel lines, although the palm for simplicity and
delicacy of treatment, still rests with the elder poet.
Eve,

> . . . with tears that ceased not flowing,
> And tresses all disordered, at his feet
> Fell humble, and, embracing them, besought
> His peace, and thus proceeded in her plaint :—
>   "Forsake me not thus, Adam ! witness Heaven
> What love sincere and reverence in my heart
> I bear thee, and unweeting have offended,
> Unhappily deceived ! Thy suppliant
> I beg, and clasp thy knees ; bereave me not
> Whereon I live, thy gentle looks, thy aid,
> Thy counsel in this uttermost distress.
>
> .   .   .   .
>
> Between us two let there be peace ; both joining,
> As joined in injuries, one enmity
> Against a foe by doom express assigned us,
> That cruel Serpent.   On me exercise not
> Thy hatred for this misery befallen,—
> On me already lost, me than thyself

More miserable. Both have sinned ; but thou
Against God only ; I against God and thee,
And to the place of judgment will return,
There with my cries importune Heaven, that all
The sentence, from thy head removed, may light
On me, sole cause to thee of all this woe,
Me, me only, just object of His ire."

    She ended, weeping ; and her lowly plight,
Immovable till peace obtained from fault
Acknowledged and deplored, in Adam wrought
Commiseration. Soon his heart relented
Towards her, his life so late, and sole delight,
Now at his feet submissive in distress,—
Creature so fair his reconcilement seeking,
His counsel whom she had displeased, his aid.
As one disarmed, his anger all he lost.

His anger thus subdued by the Woman's passion-
ful love, Adam forecasts the probable future of their
earthly life, dark and shrouded though that future
seems to be, and, finally, suggests that they sue for
mercy at the hands of an offended Deity.

    " What better can we do than,
                       . . . prostrate fall
Before him reverent, and there confess
Humbly our faults, and pardon beg, with tears
Watering the ground, and with our sighs the air
Frequenting, sent from hearts contrite, in sign
Of sorrow unfeigned and humiliation meek ?
Undoubtedly he will relent, and turn

From his displeasure, in whose look serene,
When angry most he seemed and most severe,
What else but favour, grace, and mercy shone?"
    So spake our Father penitent; nor Eve
Felt less remorse.   They, forthwith to the place
Repairing where he judged them, prostrate fell
Before him reverent, and both confessed
Humbly their faults, and pardon begged, with tears
Watering the ground, and with their sighs the air
Frequenting, sent from hearts contrite, in sign
Of sorrow unfeigned and humiliation meek.
Thus they, in lowliest plight, repentant stood
Praying.

The narrative of the sentence of the doom and
banishment of the guilty Pair, which forms the con-
cluding section of this sacred Epic, follows strictly
the simple artistic lines of the Hebrew story.
    Cædmon tells us how,

                              When many days
Had come and gone, the mighty God at length
Revealed Himself, walking at eventide
Amid the glories of that Earthly realm.
The King All-merciful, in pity stooped
To learn His children's need, and how they bare
Their ruined state, bereft of all the Grace
Which at the first adorned their mortal state.
Soon as they heard the voice of Holy God
They sought, with saddened mind and shorn of joy,
The shelter of the thickest grove, and seized
With sudden dread concealed themselves within
The rocky portals of a cave.

Straightway,
The Heavenly Chief, the mighty Lord of Hosts,
Summoned the Warden of this Eartly sphere
And bade His son approach.
               Then Adam cried
In deep humility :
           " Lord of my life,
Devoid of raiment, I conceal me here
And cover me with leaves.   Great is my guilt
And this foul sin of mine fills me with pain
And weighs upon my soul.   I do not dare,
All naked as I am, to leave this shade
And meet Thee face to face."
             Then spake the King :
" Tell me, my son, why seekest thou in shame
The shelter of the grove ?   Dost thou conceive
That I have sense of shame ?   Whence does it come,
That 'mid surrounding joy thou knowest aught
Of woe ? and wouldst conceal thy naked form
With clothing from the trees ?   Whence knowest thou
This earthly sorrow, for thou say'st, thy life
Is full of care and thou thyself full sad
With downcast mind ?   Why dost thou feel the need
Of clothing thus thy form, unless thou hast
Been faithless to thy trust and touched the fruit
Of yon forbidden Tree ? "
             Then in reply
The man confessed :
            " This beauteous bride of mine,
This virgin Wife, did place within my hand
The baleful fruit and I, O mine own Lord,
Forgetful of Thy Love, did eat, and now,
Within myself plain token do I bear

Of this my sin, since day by day, I see
Fresh sorrows teeming in upon my path."

Then thus the Almighty spake, close-questioning
The guilty Wife :

        " Didst thou have need of aught,
O daughter Eve, here 'midst the ample joys,
The new creations and the bounteous gifts
Of Paradise, that thou didst set thine heart
To taste the Tree of Death, and in disdain
Of My esteem, didst pluck and eat its fruit
To thy great harm ? ay, and didst give thereof
To Adam, though I straitly charged you both
To shun that deadly fruit ? "
                  The virgin Wife
In deepest shame replied :
                  " With artful words
Of fairest import was I sore beguiled.
Most urgently the serpent prompted me
To this foul crime, this daring act of Sin,
Till overcome by specious argument
I basely gave the victory to the Fiend
And to my shame I seized the tempting tree
And ate the fruit."

So, in Milton we read,

    The voice of God they heard
Now walking in the Garden, by soft winds
Brought to their ears, while day declined ; they heard,
And from his presence hid themselves among
The thickest trees, both man and wife, till God
Approaching, thus to Adam called aloud :—

" Where art thou, Adam, wont with joy to meet
My coming, seen far off?   I miss thee here,
Not pleased, thus entertained with solitude,
Where obvious duty erewhile appeared unsought.
Or come I less conspicuous, or what change
Absents thee, or what chance detains?   Come forth! "
  He came, and with him Eve, more loth, though first
To offend, discountenanced both, and discomposed.
Love was not in their looks, either to God
Or to each other, but apparent guilt,
And shame, and perturbation, and despair,
Anger, and obstinacy, and hate, and guile.
Whence Adam, faltering long, thus answered brief :—
  " I heard thee in the Garden, and, of thy voice
Afraid, being naked, hid myself."   To whom
The gracious Judge, without revile, replied :—
  " My voice thou oft hast heard, and hast not feared,
But still rejoiced ; how is it now become
So dreadful to thee ?   That thou art naked who
Hath told thee ?   Hast thou eaten of the tree
Whereof I gave thee charge thou shouldst not eat ? "
  To whom thus Adam, sore beset, replied :—
  .   .   .   .
  .   .   .   " should I hold my peace, yet thou
Wouldst easily detect what I conceal.
This woman, whom thou mad'st to be my help,
And gav'st me as thy perfect gift, so good,
So fit, so acceptable, so divine,
That from her hand I could suspect no ill,
And what she did, whatever in itself,
Her doing seemed to justify the deed—
She gave me of the tree, and I did eat."
  To whom the Sovran Presence thus replied :—

"Was she thy God, that her thou didst obey
Before his voice? or was she made thy guide,
Superior, or but equal, that to her
Thou didst resign thy manhood, and the place
Wherein God set thee above her, made of thee
And for thee, whose perfection far excelled
Hers in all real dignity?   Adorned
She was indeed, and lovely, to attract
Thy love, not thy subjection; and her gifts
Were such as under government well seemed,—
Unseemly to bear rule; which was thy part
And person, hadst thou known thyself aright."

The sentiment expressed in the last twelve lines of the extract just given, and the harsh and undignified tone of the passage, belong to Milton alone, and find no parallel either in the solemn utterances of the Deity as related by the Hebrew chronicler, or in the exquisite narrative of the inspired peasant of Whitby.

In Eve's confession, Milton once again, follows the simplicity of the ancient story:

So having said, he thus to Eve in few :—
"Say, Woman, what is this which thou hast done?"
To whom sad Eve, with shame nigh overwhelmed,
Confessing soon, yet not before her Judge
Bold or loquacious, thus abashed replied :—
"The Serpent me beguiled, and I did eat."

The sentence pronounced by the Deity, on these guilty ones, is thus described by Cædmon:

Forthwith the mighty God,
Protector of Mankind, proclaimed His will
That thenceforth should the serpent be condemned
To wander far and wide :
    " Thy livelong life,"
For thus He spake, " shalt thou accursèd be ;
And on thy breast shalt drag thy footless form
O'er the fair face of Earth ; and dust shalt eat
The remnant of thy days, and long as life
And breath remain—just meed of this great crime,
Thy malice hath inspired.
    " And there shall burn
Within the Woman's breast, a mortal Hate
And quenchless enmity, and she shall tread
Thy hostile head beneath her feet, while thou
May'st strive, with deep and crafty plans, to snare
The offspring of this new-born race.   As long
As this fair World shall stand, a deadly feud
Shall last 'twixt her and thee.
    " Now dost thou know
Thy doom, fell Scourge of Man, and canst discern
The future of thy life."
    The Holy God
To Eve in anger spake :
    " Take thyself hence
Far from these scenes of joy.   From this day forth
Obedience shalt thou yield to Adam's will,
And in the fear of him shalt expiate
The error of thy deeds, humbled and vext
By keen remorse, till Death ensue.   Meanwhile,
With weeping and with moans and bitter pains
Shalt thou bring forth thy daughters and thy sons
To people Earth's domain."

The Heavenly Chief, the mighty Lord of Hosts,
Summoned the Warden of this Earthly sphere
And bade His son approach.

Then to the Man

The Eternal King, Lord of the Light of Life,
Announced His dire decree :

" Now must thou seek

Another home, a realm more joyless far,
And into exile go, in nakedness
And want, shorn of the bliss which thou hast known
In Paradise.   And since with evil mind
Thou didst commit this crime, I do decree
That Death, at last, shall break the golden bond
Which now unites thy body and thy soul.
Henceforth thy days shall pass in arduous toil
And from the ground shalt thou thyself now seek
Thy sustenance, and eat thy daily bread
By sweat of brow so long as thou dost live,
And until fell Disease, of which, alas,
Thou didst partake in the forbidden fruit,
Doth strike thee at the heart.   Then shalt thou die."

Thus did our writ of Evil take its rise
In righteous wrath, entailing World-wide woe.
The Lord of glory, Guardian of Mankind,
In goodly raiment robed the guilty pair
And bade them hide their nudeness from the gaze
Of mortal eyes.

Milton makes few and unimportant changes in
this part of the narrative ; but here shows himself
more of a Bible " paraphrast " than even Cædmon
himself :

Which when the Lord God heard, without delay
To judgment he proceeded on the accused
Serpent :

.   .   .   .

" Because thou hast done this, thou art accursed
Above all cattle, each beast of the field ;
Upon thy belly grovelling thou shalt go,
And dust shalt eat all the days of thy life.
Between thee and the Woman I will put
Enmity, and between thine and her seed ;
Her seed shall bruise thy head, thou bruise his heel."

.   .   .   .

And to the Woman thus his sentence turned :—
  " Thy sorrow I will greatly multiply
By thy conception ; children thou shalt bring
In sorrow forth, and to thy husband's will
Thine shall submit ; he over thee shall rule."
  On Adam last this judgment he pronounced :—
" Because thou hast hearkened to the voice of thy wife,
And eaten of the tree concerning which
I charged thee, saying, *Thou shalt not eat thereof*,
Curs'd is the ground for thy sake ; thou in sorrow
Shalt eat thereof all the days of thy life ;
Thorns also and thistles it shall bring thee forth
Unbid ; and thou shalt eat the herb of the field ;
In the sweat of thy face shalt thou eat bread
Till thou return unto the ground : for thou
Out of the ground wast taken : know thy birth,
For dust thou art, and shalt to dust return."
  So judged he Man, both Judge and Saviour sent,
And the instant stroke of death, denounced that day,
Removed far off ; then, pitying how they stood
Before him naked to the air, that now
Must suffer change, disdained not to begin
Thenceforth the form of servant to assume.
As when he washed his servants' feet, so now,

The Eternal King, Lord of the Light of Life,
Announced His dire decree.

As father of his family, he clad
Their nakedness with skins of beasts.

The *finale* in Cædmon's " Fall of Man," although
quite brief, possesses the same charm of chaste simplicity that characterises the whole of his poem :

> Their sentence once pronounced
> They bent their mournful steps from Paradise
> To seek a narrower sphere.
> Behind them closed
> The glistening gates of their once joyous home,
> Its comforts and delights forever lost !
> And at the Lord's behest, one of His host
> Of holy Angels, armed with fiery sword,
> Kept constant guard to hinder their return.
>
> .   .   .   .   .   .
>
> Nor even then, would mighty God, at once
> Despoil the guilty pair of all their joys,
> E'en though His presence He had now withdrawn ;
> But for their comfort, still he let shine forth
> The vault of heaven adorned with radiant stars,
> And of the treasures of the Earth, He gave
> With open hand ; and for their use He bade
> The denizens of Earth and Sea increase
> And multiply, and trees bring forth their fruit.
> Sin-stained, they henceforth sojourned in a land
> More sorrowful, a region and a home
> More barren far of every earthly Good
> Than were those blissful Seats from which, alas,
> By Sin they were expelled.

This final scene in Milton's epic is more elaborate

than the above, and more strangely embroidered
with ideas foreign to Oriental modes of thought.
The mode is excellent, but it is the mode of the
classic Hellenist, and not of the ancient Eastern
bard.

> The Archangel soon drew nigh,
> Not in his shape celestial, but as man
> *Clad to meet man.*   Over his lucid arms
> A military vest of purple flowed.
>
> .   .   .   .   .
>
> His starry helm unbuckled showed him prime
> In manhood where youth ended ; by his side,
> As in a glistering zodiac, hung the sword,
> Satan's dire dread, and in his hand the spear.
> Adam bowed low ; he, kingly, from his state
> Inclined not, but his coming thus declared : —
>   " Adam, Heaven's high behest no preface needs,
>
> .   .   .   .   .   .
>
> But longer in this Paradise to dwell
> Permits not.   To remove thee I am come,
> And send thee from the Garden forth, to till
> The ground whence thou wast taken, fitter soil."
>   He added not ; for Adam, at the news
> Heart-strook, with chilling gripe of sorrow stood,
> That all his senses bound ; Eve, who unseen
> Yet all had heard, with audible lament
> Discovered soon the place of her retire :—
>   " O unexpected stroke, worse than of Death !
> Must I thus leave thee, Paradise ? thus leave
> Thee, native soil ? these happy walks and shades,
> Fit haunt of Gods, where I had hoped to spend,
> Quiet, though sad, the respite of that day

Now must thou seek
Another home, a realm more joyless far,
And into exile go.

That must be mortal to us both ?   O flowers,
That never will in other climate grow,
My early visitation, and my last
At even, which I bred up with tender hand
From the first opening bud, and gave ye names,
Who now shall rear ye to the Sun, or rank
Your tribes, and water from the ambrosial fount ? "

The Archangel and Adam descend together the hill, where the emissary of the Empyrean had announced the object of his mission ; then

          Adam to the bower where Eve
Lay sleeping ran before, but found her waked ;
And thus with words not sad she him received :—
" Whence thou return'st, and wither went'st, I know ;
For God is also in sleep, and dreams advise,
Which he hath sent propitious, some great good
Presaging, since, with sorrow and heart's distress
Wearied, I fell asleep.   But now lead on ;
In me is no delay ; with thee to go
Is to stay here ; without thee here to stay
Is to go hence unwilling ; thou to me
Art all things under Heaven, all places thou,
Who for my wilful crime art banished hence.
This further consolation yet secure
I carry hence : though all by me is lost,
Such favour I unworthy am voutsafed,
By me the Promised Seed shall all restore."
So spake our mother Eve ; and Adam heard
Well pleased, but answered not ; for now too nigh
The Archangel stood.

    .   .   .   .   .   .

In either hand the hastening Angel caught
Our lingering parents, and to the eastern gate
Led them direct, and down the cliff as fast
To the subjected plain—then disappeared.
They, looking back, all the eastern side beheld
Of Paradise, so late their happy seat,
Waved over by that flaming brand ; the gate
With dreadful faces thronged and fiery arms.
Some natural tears they dropped, but wiped them soon ;
The world was all before them, where to choose
Their place of rest, and Providence their guide.
They, hand in hand, with wandering steps and slow,
Through Eden took their solitary way.

And so the " Commedia " of the Creation ends
with the " Tragedia " of the Fall.

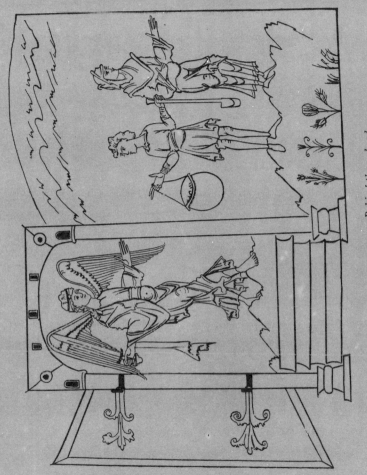

Behind them closed

The glistening gates of their once joyous home.

CHAPTER VII.

The Angel of Presumption and Other Devils.

THE two grandest poetic conceptions of the Spirit of Evil to be found in the whole of English literature are, without doubt, Satan, the " Angel of Presumption " of Cædmon (se engel ofermódes), and Satan, the fallen " Archangel " of Milton.

In the present chapter we propose to compare the respective characteristics of these two colossal beings ;—or rather, these two conceptions of the same colossal being,—both before and after the expulsion of the rebel hosts from the Empyrean ; and, if we introduce the Serpent of the Hebrew story, or any modern personification of the Spirit of Evil, we shall do so simply to bring out, in still bolder relief, the salient points in the main study.

It is scarcely necessary to premise, that with any philosophical or theological speculations on the " Origin of Evil," or the existence of a " Personal Devil," we have no concern in the present work. We shall treat of Satan, the subject of this special study, as a character in *literature*, pure and simple ; the creation of poetic phantasy, whether in Cædmon's poem, in Milton's epic, or in the Hebrew story ; and to be studied, irrespective of any religious or theological considerations, just as we might study the character of Hamlet or of Don Quixote.

In saying this, we do not, for one moment, mean to imply that either Cædmon, or Milton, or the historian of the Hebrew cosmogony, regarded his personification of the Spirit of Evil as a mere poetic creation. As a pupil of the Lady Hilda, it is more than presumable that Cædmon held the tradition of the Catholic Church on this question. Milton, we know from authentic sources, was as firm, although a less fantastic, believer in a real, personal Devil, as Luther was. And whoever wrote the so-called Mosaic account of the Fall, believed, (according to Rabbinical tradition), as fully in the existence of a Satan as did the writer of the prose introduction to the Book of *Job*.

Both Cædmon's poem, and Milton's epic, are founded on the proposition of the treason and expulsion from Heaven of a great Archangel, who determines to drag down in his Fall, a favoured race of terrestrial beings, less than angelic both in form and intellect, yet the beloved ones of the Omnipotent King, who had hurled the Arch-Traitor from his princedom in the Empyrean, down to deepest Hell.

Both poets, moreover, adopt, as the groundwork of their narrative, the main features of the Hebrew story; incorporating, besides, certain straggling Bible hints, Rabbinical comments and fancies, and early Catholic traditions. But the brilliant phantasy of the Anglo-Saxon monk, and the still more brilliant imagination of the erudite Milton, have overlaid the original, simple, Hebrew narrative with such a wealth of invention and imagery, that it is scarcely recognisable as it appears in their writings. To such an extent has the *poetic* version taken possession of the non-Catholic mind of both England and America, that to-day it is the *Epic* of the fall, and not the *Bible* narrative, that is regarded as the authorised version.

But further. Both poets borrow, not only the groundwork of their narrative as a whole, but also the elements of their conception of the nameless Archangel, from the sources just above mentioned; and here again, as we shall now see, the genius of the poet has transformed a very ordinary, and not particularly prepossessing supernatural personage, into a transcendent figure of colossal proportions.

In the Hebraic or Biblical narrative of the Fall, there is no account of the previous history of the

Serpent; no description of what his celestial rank or intellectual pre-eminence may have been before the fatal crisis of the Temptation; no hint that he had ever been an Archangel; no suggestion that his high estate had ever been forfeited for *lèse majesté;* no account of any wars in Heaven; no tale of expulsion; and no mention of any fiery dungeon of Hell to which he had been consigned forever. On the contrary, the first glimpse that we get of the Arch-Enemy of Man in the Hebrew story, occurs immediately after the second account of the Creation, when, as yet, there were but two human beings on the face of the newly created Earth. At this point in the narrative, the Serpent is introduced abruptly upon the scene, and with no intimation as to his true personality; as though the narrator took it for granted that his antecedents and present avocation were too well known to require any comment whatsoever.

"Now the serpent was more subtle than any of the beasts of the earth which the Lord God had made. And he said to the woman: 'Why hath God commanded you, that you should not eat of every tree of paradise'? And the woman answered him, 'Of the fruit of the trees that are in paradise we do eat: but of the fruit of the tree which is in the midst of paradise, God hath commanded us that we

should not eat; and that we should not touch it,
lest perhaps we die.'   And the serpent said to the
woman : 'No, you shall not die the death.   For God
doth know that in what day soever you shall eat
thereof, your eyes shall be opened : and you shall be
as Gods, knowing good and evil.'   And the woman
.   .   .   took of the fruit thereof and did eat, and
gave to her husband who did eat."

This brief statement comprises, absolutely, all the
information which the author of the Hebrew narrative vouchsafes, with reference to the " Serpent " of
his story ; but, short as the statement is, and faint
as are the outlines of the portrait, we can, nevertheless, recognise the distinguishing features which re-
appear in every subsequent poetic delineation of the
character of the Satan—traits, which stand out in
greater prominence as the *Epic of the Fall* develops
under the fashioning hand of subsequent poets.
The groundwork of the character, here, as in every
version, is *the innate love of doing evil for its own
sake, and of tempting others to do evil* to gratify a
passion for relentless revenge; and the deadly
weapons which the " Serpent" employs, in the accomplishment of his devilish life-aim, are the same
in every version, namely, *subtlety* or devil-craft in
the choice of a point of approach ; *flattery* or an
appeal to intellectual pride as an inducement to

sin; and a brilliant lie, or an apparently innocent query charged with lies, as an *argumentum ad hominem*.

Before passing on to later developments in the Story, we may notice another Hebrew type of the Spirit of Evil as depicted in the two introductory chapters to the Book of *Job;* and we make this digression for reasons that will presently appear. In this poem, Satan is the personification of the Spirit of Evil in a somewhat later stage in the civilisation of the world. He is not only perfectly aware that such a planet as the Earth exists; he knows, with the exactitude of an old explorer, its astronomcal position in the Universe, and that he has freedom of access to both Earth and the Empyrean. He is represented as appearing before the Deity, on a grand day in Heaven's year, when the sons of God come to present themselves before the Lord, and sneeringly accusing Job, a prominent denizen of the Earth, of covert disloyalty to his God.

But here, again, as in the Mosaic narrative, the writer furnishes us with no details as to the past history of his Satan.

At the same time, it is to be noted that the conception of the character of the Satan, in the story of *Job*, is generically different from that of the "Serpent" in *Genesis*. The Satan of the Book of *Job* is

one of the characters in a *drama*, and represents the
Spirit of Evil after the experience of centuries; no
longer planning the ruin of an entire race, but
adopting the far more ignoble, the meaner, the
smaller tactics of scheming for the ruin of a single
soul.

" Now there was a day when the sons of God
came to present themselves before the Lord, and
Satan came also among them. And the Lord said
unto Satan, ' Whence comest thou '? Then Satan
answered the Lord, and said, ' From going to and fro
in the earth, and from walking up and down in it.'
And the Lord said unto Satan, ' Hast thou considered my servant Job, that there is none like him in
the earth, a perfect and an upright man, one that feareth God, and escheweth evil '? Then Satan answered
the Lord, and said, ' Doth Job fear God for naught?
Hast thou not made an hedge about him, and about
his house, and about all that he hath on every side?
Thou hast blessed the work of his hands, and his
substance is increased in the land. But put forth
thine hand now, and touch all that he hath, and he
will curse thee to thy face.' "

.   .   .   .

" Again there was a day when the sons of God
came to present themselves before the Lord, and

Satan came also among them to present himself before the Lord. . . . And the Lord said unto Satan, 'Hast thou considered my servant Job, that there is none like him in the earth, a perfect and an upright man, one that feareth God and escheweth evil? and still he holdeth fast his integrity, although thou movedst me against him, to destroy him without cause.' And Satan answered the Lord, and said, 'Skin for skin, yea, all that a man hath will he give for his life. But put forth thine hand now, and touch his bone and his flesh, and he will curse thee to thy face.'"

It is impossible to read this passage from the highly philosophical drama of Job, without recalling to mind the "Prologue in Heaven" in Goethe's grand drama of *Faust*. Here the angelic hosts, the sons of God, are represented as assembled around the throne of the Deity, and the three Archangels Raphael, Gabriel, and Michael appear before the Lord. The theme of their song is the grandeur of the Creation. Raphael sings of the Sun, as rolling in thunder through the heavens in harmonic symphony with the kindred planets. Gabriel sings of the supreme beauty of the Earth, as she revolves on her axis, one hemisphere glittering in the dazzling light, while the other is dipped in darkest shadow. Michael sings of the storms, darting forth lightning

and, glorying in their strength, sweeping in awful
majesty over land and sea.   Then, the three burst
forth in unison, exulting in the blessedness of their
being, magnifying and lauding all the works of God
as even grander and more glorious than on the day
of their creation.   Suddenly, while the whole of
Heaven is thrilling with the dying echoes of the
Archangelic anthem, Mephistopheles breaks in, with
harsh discordant tones of mock servility and sarcas-
tic bantering, the very sounds that he utters, no less
than the jarring metre that he employs, making discordant harmony in strange contrast to the pæans
of the Archangels.   He tells the Deity, that he has
no thought of trying to emulate the magniloquent
strains that he has just heard ; and, with the splen-
did audacity of an Aristotelian μεγαλόψωχος, declares that he has no wish to rank himself with
the three Archangels who have just sung of the
perfect working of suns and planets; but, he has
just a word to say, as to how poor humanity is doing
down on the Earth ; and, accordingly, he flats and
sharps out the dismal anthem that the queer little
Godkin, Man, is just as odd as on the day he was
made, and, with a sublime impudence, tells, that on
the tiny planet, everything is in inextricable muddle
and confusion, and that, in his opinion, human nature
is a magnificent *fiasco*.

" Since thou, O Lord, approaches us once more,
And askest how affairs with us are going,
And oftentimes hast seen me here before,
To this my presence 'mid the rest is owing.
Excuse my plainness ; I 'm no hand at chaffing ;
I can't talk fine, though all around should scorn ;
My pathos, certainly would set thee laughing,
Had'st thou not laughter long ago forborne.
Of Suns and Worlds, deuce one word can I gabble ;
I only know how men grow miserable.
The little god of Earth is still the same old clay,
And is as odd this hour as on Creation's day.
Better somewhat his situation
Had'st thou not given him that light of inspiration ;
Reason, he calls it, and uses it so that he
Grows but more beastly than the beasts to be ;
He seems to me, begging your Grace's pardon,
Like one of those long-legged things in a garden
That fly about and hop and spring,
And in the grass the same old chirrup sing.
Would I could say that here the story closes !
But in each filthy mess they poke their noses."

The author of the Book of *Job* and the author of
Faust, both, depict the modern Spirit of Evil in the
civilisation of their own day.   In neither case is the
portrait that of the fallen Archangel as Cædmon or
as Milton conceived him ; but a being far more
cunning, far more clever than either of these, and
rendered so by ages of constant touch with the
littlenesses of fallen humanity. The " Satan " of *Job*

and the " Mephistopheles " of *Faust* are portraits of the modernised Satan plying his unhallowed vocation, now in the seclusion of a rich Hebrew ranche or now in the streets and by-ways of the crowded city. The "Serpent" of the Hebrew narrative is the prototype of the " Satan " of Cædmon and Milton ; while the " Satan " of *Job* is the prototype of the " Mephistopheles " of Goethe.

So far as we have gone in this comparative study, we have found little more than the *germ* of the elaborate portrait of the Satan of later poems. In the writings of the early ages of Christianity, however, the authors of the Gospels, and of other canonical writings, were doubtless familiar with the traditional Hebrew views, Biblical, Apocryphal, Talmudic, and poetical, on the subject of the Serpent and of the Fall; and so we find occasional references, in their writings, to such well known traditions. These, together with other germs, subsequently gave rise to the fully developed portraits of Satan that we have in Cædmon and Milton, and to the fully developed history of our hero as we find it in the modern, highly finished versions of the *Epic of the Fall.*

Two or three illustrations of our meaning will suffice. In the *Apocalypse* we read : " And there was war in heaven : Michael and his angels fought
18

against the dragon ; and the dragon fought and his angels: And they prevailed not, neither was their place found any more in heaven. And that great dragon was cast out, that old Serpent who is called the Devil and Satan, who seduceth the whole world : and he was cast unto the earth, and his angels were thrown down with him."

.   .   .   .

" And I saw an Angel coming down from heaven, having the key of the bottomless pit, and a great chain in his hand. And he laid hold on the dragon the old Serpent, which is the Devil and Satan, and bound him for a thousand years. And he cast him into the bottomless pit and shut him up and set a seal upon him that he should no more seduce the nations."

.   .   .   .

" And the Devil who seduced them was cast into the pool of fire and brimstone."

In these passages, we have the *germ* of the first part of the Epic, which narrates the Treason, Rebellion and Expulsion of *Satan ;* just as in the so-styled Mosaic account, we have the *germ* of the remaining part of the Epic, which narrates the story of the Temptation, Fall, and Expulsion of *Man.*

It will be noted, that although the statements in the *Apocalypse* leave the impression upon the mind that Satan's rank in Heaven must have been among the highest, if not *the* highest of the Angelic hierarchy, still, nothing definite is stated on this point; and we are left to surmise, from the rank of his antagonist, the Warrior-Archangel Michael, the rank that Satan must doubtless have held in the Empyrean.

On another point intimately connected with the perfection of the Epic, namely, the motive which led Satan to rebel against the Almighty, we have more direct information. Speaking of the qualifications of a bishop of the Church, St. Timothy disapproves of the appointment of a neophite or novice, *" lest being puffed up with pride he fall into the judgment of the Devil."* It was evidently an early Christian tradition that *Pride* was the cause of Satan's ruin. When, in the Gospel narrative, the seventy were elated, because, " even the devils," were subject unto them, the Master checked their incipient pride with the characteristic remark, " I saw Satan like lightning fall from Heaven."

We are now in a position to enter upon a comparison of the two poetic Satans; the hero of Cædmon's poem, and the hero of Milton's epic.

Satan, as conceived by Cædmon, is not only a magnificent portrait, it is a colossal figure. Originally, and before his mind had become tainted by treasonous thought, he was the Archangel peerless. His Angel-form eclipsed, in its brilliant perfection, that of the brightest and most beauteous of the Heavenly hosts. In Angel-strength he had no rival. His proud intellect towered above that of all Angelic intelligences. Exalted, by the sovereign will of the Supreme, he held the highest rank,

> Above all Principalities and Powers
> That next to God Omnipotent he stood,
> O'er all created things, lone and supreme.

The illumination or drawing which accompanies this part of the Junian manuscript, however, gives a far more accurate idea of the exalted position which the lone Archangel held in Heaven, than any verbal description could possibly give. Here, in our opinion, the artist of the *Scriptorium* has caught the true spirit of the poem. The Archangel's transcendent physical proportions, his high-born features, and his regal bearing, plainly show his exalted rank, and contrast strikingly with the corresponding characteristics of his followers, who, both by their plebeian looks and servile bearing, clearly disclose their inferior celestial status.

This Archangel is represented in the poem as *the one* especially beloved by the Deity—the God who made him ; and, at first sight, it may seem remarka-

Around me, even now, are strong allies.

ble, almost improbable, that a being who stood so high in favour at Heaven's court,— a *persona grata* in the Empyrean,—should have been willing, for any consideration whatsoever, to chance the forfeiture of his high estate. And it is here that Cædmon's keen knowledge of the springs of action, intellectual and physical, becomes apparent. The Archangel's life or existence, as the Vicegerent or Executive of the Almighty, was one of *action* as contradistinguished from one of *adoration*. What an eminent writer has said of Milton's " Satan," can with far greater truth be applied to Cædmon's " Angel of Presumption " : " Rejoicing in his strength, walking colossal through Heaven, gigantic in his conceptions, incessant in his working, ever scheming, ever imagining new enterprises, Satan was in his very nature the most active of God's Archangels. He was ever doing some great thing, and ever longing for some greater thing to do. But he was not a contemplative spirit ; and his feeling of derived existence grew weak in the glow and excitement of constant occupation. As the feeling of enjoyment in action grew strong, the feeling of being an Angel grew weak. Thus, the mere duration of his existence had undermined his strength and prepared him for sin. Although the greatest Angel in Heaven—nay, just because he was such—he was the readiest to fall."

The exhilaration of the constant, unimpeded exercise of his powers, naturally induced pride of conscious strength, and impatience of being dependent; until, finally, it led to the conviction that he could do without a Superior.

       " Why should I toil
Who stand in need of no Superior ?
Marvels as great, ay, greater in renown,
Can I perform than our Omnific Chief ;
A Godlier throne than His and more sublime
Can I unaided rear. Why, as a slave
Dependent on his lord for worthless gifts,
Should I His will obey and bow the head
In abject vassalage as to a King ?
I, too erelong may be a God as He !

 .   .   .   .   .   .

      " Such power is mine,
Such goodly fellowship, I well believe
'T is greater e'en than God's own following."

With a passion for action that only Almightiness could satisfy, and a pride as inordinate as his love of power, the Archangel turns rebel at heart, and, as a consequence, his very capability for adoration and worship deserts him.

     Then silent stood
The great Archangel 'mid the Heavenly choir.
No grateful anthem rose in meet return
For gifts divine. No joyful antiphon
Burst forth responsive from his guilty lips.

At length, impelled by his stupendous pride, the Archangel takes the cardinal step of his existence:

> " No longer I,
> With radiant form endowed and heavenly mien,
> Will brook subjection to a tyrant God ;
>
> .   .   .   .   .   .
>
> I am resolved,
> No longer will I be His vassal slave."

Cædmon, in thus making *Pride* the cause of the great Archangel's fall, simply voices the consentient sentiment of early Christian tradition.

The Lucifer of Milton's epic, like the Archangel of Cædmon's poem, is a colossal figure. It is true that the features of the hero of *Paradise Lost* may be wanting in some of the more delicate touches which we notice in the delineation of the hero of the Anglo-Saxon poem ; but, even though this may be the case, the *heroic* lines in Milton's gigantic Archangel are strikingly prominent.

By what name this celestial Intelligence may have been known before his treason and expulsion is an eternal secret since,

> .   .   .   his former name
> Is heard no more in Heaven.

But Milton adopts the symbolical name of Lucifer,

> . . . by allusion called,
> Of that bright star to Satan paragoned ;

> . . . brighter once amidst the host
> Of Angels than that star the stars among ;

> . . . for great indeed
> His name, and high was his degree in Heaven ;
> His countenance, as the morning-star ;

and he describes him more particularly as *one*

> . . . of the first,
> *If not the first Archangel*, great in power,
> In favour and pre-eminence,

who, in the " limits of the North," possessed

> . . . his royal seat
> High on a hill, far-blazing, as a mount
> Raised on a mount, with pyramids and towers
> From diamond quarries hewn and rocks of gold—
> The palace of great Lucifer.

So great was the fame of this peerless Spirit, that even after his banishment from Heaven, when he was beginning his upward flight from the Gates of Hell in search of the newly created Universe, " Chaos and ancient Night " recognise him at once :

> . . . the Anarch old,
> With faltering speech and visage incomposed,

Answered :—" I know thee, stranger, who thou art—
That mighty leading Angel, who of late
Made head against Heaven's King, though overthrown."

Subsequently, when Ithuriel and Zephon discover
Satan in Paradise, and the former asks,

" Which of those rebel Spirits adjudged to Hell
Com'st thou, escaped thy prison ? "

the Arch-Fiend replies, with indignant sarcasm,

" Know ye not, then," said Satan, filled with scorn,
" Know ye not me ?   Ye knew me once no mate
For you, there sitting where ye durst not soar !
Not to know me argues yourselves unknown,
The lowest of your throng."

In Cædmon, the Archangel is not only, " of the
first if not the first," but he is the highest of all
created beings, " sole and supreme."   He not only
holds the precedence over the other Archangels by
virtue of conventional custom, but by the divine
right of superiority.   He is not only *primus inter
pares ;* he is *princeps inter inferiores.*   And it is this
proud distinction, viz., that there is no other created
being on his own high level of merited rank, and no
being between him and the Great Uncreated, that
confers a distinctive character upon Cædmon's poem
and lends a grandeur to the fall of the Archangel
unknown to Milton's epic.

We have here the explanation of the difference in
motive which causes the " Angel of Presumption " of
Cædmon, and the Archangel of Milton, respectively,
to rebel and foment treason in Heaven. In the
Anglo-Saxon version, the poet takes the more pronounced monotheistic view of the Trinity, and represents his Archangel as the sole created existence
standing between the Archangelic hierarchy and the
Deity ; and thus precludes the possibility of any
such motive of rebellion as envy or jealousy.

Milton, on the other hand, taking a *quasi* Arian
view of the Trinity, and virtually making the Son
an inferior Person in the blessed Trinity, describes
the Father as having proclaimed His Only Begotten
Son His sole Vicegerent.

>   .   .   .   on such day
> As Heaven's great year brings forth, the empyreal host
> Of Angels, by imperial summons called,
> Innumerable before the Almighty's throne
> Forthwith from all the ends of Heaven appeared
> Under their hierarchs in orders bright.
> Ten thousand thousand ensigns high advanced.

Then the Almighty Father,

>   .   .   .   as from a flaming mount, whose top
> Brightness had made invisible, thus spake :—
>   .   .   .   .   .   .

" Hear my decree, which unrevoked shall stand !

This day I have begot whom I declare
My only Son, and on this holy hill
Him have anointed, whom ye now behold
At my right hand. *Your head I him appoint,*
And by myself have sworn to him shall bow
All knees in Heaven, and shall confess him Lord.
Under his great vicegerent reign abide,
United as one individual soul,
For ever happy.   Him who disobeys
Me disobeys, breaks union, and, that day,
Cast out from God and blessed vision, falls
Into utter darkness, deep ingulfed, his place
Ordained without redemption, without end."

The great Archangel, (according to Milton's version), not having had an orthodox notion of the character of the blessed Trinity instilled into him in early archangelhood, demurs at the thought of having any one, however exalted his rank, made his superior, refuses to bow the knee to any one less than God, becomes jealous,

> .   .   . fraught
> With envy against the Son of God, that day
> Honoured by his great Father, and proclaimed
> Messiah, King Anointed,

and, unable to brook the appointment of any Vicegerent, created or begotten, he frowns, turns rebel, and whispers to his most trusted retainer:

> " New laws thou seest imposed ;
> New laws from him who reigns, new minds may raise

In us who serve—new counsels, to debate
What doubtful may ensue.   More in this place
To utter is not safe."

In the Anglo-Saxon poem, moreover, Cædmon tells us that even after it was known to the Deity that His Archangel had begun to entertain presumptuous thoughts, yet,

> Deore wæs he dryhtne úrum
> Ne mihte him bedyrned wyrthan
> Thæt his engyl ongan
> Ofermód weran.

> Nor was it hid from God's omniscient eye
> That his Archangel, though *belovèd* still,
> Began to harbour dark, presumptuous thoughts.

Cædmon's hero is depicted not only as

> . . . great in power,
> In *favour* and pre-eminence ;

he has all of these prerogatives; but "favour" does not necessarily imply "affection," and the Anglo-Saxon poet, by describing the Archangel as *beloved*, or more literally, as still "dear to our Lord," has given a touch of pathos to the narrative that lends an especial charm to the Anglo-Saxon version.

But the Archangel, stained and ruined,—the Satan of both poem and epic,—is as grand a conception as

the Archangel pure and beloved,—perhaps grander.
It has been said by one who loved epigram better
than dogma, that the Fall of Man was a grand
stride in the advancement of the human race ; and
this, because it opened up an illimitable field for the
exercise of every power in man.   Be this as it may,
the Satan of literature, ever striving, scheming,
daring, suffering, is a far grander being than the
spotless Archangels who

> . . . in Heaven above the Starry Sphere,
> Their happy hours in joy and hymning spent,

" stupidly good."

The Anglo-Saxon poet does not give us any
especial portraiture of his Satan, but leaves to
imagination the appearance of the great Archangel
in his fallen estate, noting simply his change of
name :

> Then the Lord
>
> . . . . . .
>
> . . . gave the Fiend a name by which thenceforth
> Throughout all ages he should e'er be known—
> *Satan,* the enemy of God and Man.

Milton, on the contrary, presents a full length
portrait of his Satan as the ruined Archangel:

> . . . the Arch-Enemy,
> And thence in Heaven called Satan.
>
> . . . . . .

> Satan,—so call him now ; his former name
> Is heard no more in Heaven.

And the poet's aim, in depicting his hero, seems to
have been to give an idea of *immensity*, coupled
with Oriental splendour. Thus, in the first glimpse
that we have of Satan, in the very opening of the
epic, Milton describes him as,

> With head uplift above the wave, and eyes
> That sparkling blazed ; his other parts besides
> Prone on the flood, extended long and large,
> Lay floating many a rood, in bulk as huge
> As whom the fables name of monstrous size,
>
> .   .   .   .
>
> So stretched out huge in length the Arch-Fiend lay,
> Chained on the burning lake.

Satan was the first to awake out of stupor, while
the rebel host lay rolling unconscious in Hell, the
pool of liquid fire beneath Chaos.

> Forthwith upright he rears from off the pool
> His mighty stature ; on each hand the flames
> Driven backward slope their pointing spires, and, rolled
> In billows, leave i' the midst a horrid vale.
> Then with expanded wings he steers his flight
> Aloft, incumbent on the dusky air,
> That felt unusual weight.
>
> .   .   .   .   .   .
> . . . the Superior Fiend
> Was moving toward the shore ; his ponderous shield,

Ethereal temper, massy, large, and round,
Behind him cast.   The broad circumference
Hung on his shoulders like the moon.

In order to arouse his stupefied hosts,

> He called so loud that all the hollow deep
> Of Hell resounded.

Then the standard-bearer of Hell,

> .   .   . forthwith from the glittering staff unfurled
> The imperial ensign ; which, full high advanced,
> Shone like a meteor streaming to the wind,
> With gems and golden lustre rich emblazed,
> Seraphic arms and trophies ; all the while
> Sonorous metal blowing martial sounds :
> At which the universal host up-sent
> A shout, that tore Hell's concave, and beyond
> Frighted the reign of Chaos and old Night.
> All in a moment through the gloom were seen
> Ten thousand banners rise into the air,
> With orient colours waving : with them rose
> A forest huge of spears ; and thronging helms
> Appeared, and serried shields in thick array
> Of depth immeasurable.

At the council in Pandemonium Satan,

> .   .   . above the rest
> In shape and gesture proudly eminent,
> Stood like a tower ;
>
> .   .   . whom now transcendent glory raised
> Above his fellows, with monarchal pride

Conscious of highest worth, unmoved.
              Darkened so, yet shone
Above them all the Archangel : but his face
Deep scars of thunder had entrenched, and care
Sat on his faded cheek, but under brows
Of dauntless courage, and considerate pride
Waiting revenge.

On the opening of the council, Milton tells us that,

High on a throne of royal state, which far
Outshone the wealth of Ormus and of Ind,
Or where the gorgeous East with richest hand
Showers on her kings barbaric pearl and gold,
Satan exalted sat,

together with,

A thousand demi-gods on golden seats.

At length, the Stygian council dissolved,

                    . . .   forth
In order came the grand Infernal Peers :
Midst came their mighty Paramount, and seemed
Alone the antagonist of Heaven, nor less
Than Hell's dread Emperor, with pomp supreme,
And God-like imitated state : him round
A globe of fiery Seraphim inclosed
With bright emblazonry, and horrent arms.

On the commencement of the wars in Heaven,

Satan, with vast and haughty strides advanced,
Came towering, armed in adamant and gold.

And finally, during the scene of the Temptation, when Satan is brought by Ithuriel and Zephon before the Archangel Gabriel, Milton tells us that,

> . . . Satan, alarmed,
> Collecting all his might, dilated stood,
> Like Teneriff or Atlas, unremoved :
> His stature reached the sky, and on his crest
> Sat Horror plumed.

It would be possible to extend this list of quotations, but enough has been adduced to show the means that Milton employs in order to convey an adequate idea of his own colossal conception of Satan.

The *punishment* of the rebellious Archangel is essentially different in the two versions, and leads to the widest divergence that exists, at this point, between the two narratives.

The Satan of Cædmon, by his rebellion, not only forfeits the Beatific Vision of the Deity, but he is *manicled* and *fettered*, and so loses the gratification of his *passion for action:*

> Oh ! that my hands were free ! that I might hence
> But for a moment, for a winter's day ;
> Then with this host would I—but now these chains
> Press on me and these iron bands embrace !
> Oh ! I am kingdomless !   Hell's fetters cling
> Hard on each limb.   Above, beneath, the flame

19

Fierce rages.   Sight more horrible mine eyes,
Ne'er yet have witnessed.   O'er these scorching deeps
The fire no respite knows.   The strong forged chain
With ever-biting links forbids my flight.
My feet are bound, my hands are manacled ;
Around my neck is forged this lattice-belt
Of iron strangely wrought by Angel-skill.

It is a deadly punishment, cleverly conceived by
the poet, and skilfully described.

The Satan of Milton, like the " Angel of Presumption," forfeits the Beatific Vision but although he is
described as,

> Chained in the burning lake

and,

> Hurled headlong flaming from the ethereal sky
>
> .   .   .   .   .   .
>
> To bottomless perdition, there to dwell
> In adamantine chains and penal fire,

yet, in some unexplained way, he contrives to escape
his doom and give vent to his insatiable passion for
action, by taking the adventurous journey to Earth,
and effecting the Fall of Man ; which in the Anglo-
Saxon poem, are accomplished not by Hell's " dread
Emperor " in person, but by an Ambassador, duly
chosen by his infernal peers.

It does not seem that either Cædmon or Milton
imagined that the apostate Archangel forfeited, by

his fall, any of his purely angelic or intellectual gifts.
He forfeited, it is true, the Beatific Vision, *i.e.*, the
beatific view of the immediate Presence of the Deity.
He was a rebel, and all that term implies morally
and spiritually.   But he was still a colossal being,
with a transcendent intellect, an indomitable will,
full of gigantic schemes, and possessed of untiring
energy.   He was the same Archangel as of old, but
the foe, and no longer the beloved one, of Heaven:

> His form had yet not lost
> All her original brightness, nor appeared
> Less than Archangel ruined.

The delineation of the change in character from
the Archangel of Cædmon, and the Lucifer of Milton, to the Angel of Presumption and the Satan, is
one of the most telling features in the Anglo-Saxon
poem, as it is in *Paradise Lost*.

In each case, Satan, at the very outset of his
demon career, formulates the leading postulate of
his future life; and by so doing, has the bad distinction of devising the dark, though gigantic scheme
of becoming a Devil.

Cædmon's Angel of Presumption tells his followers:

> Naught now remains
> But to devise a scheme by which to thwart

The Victor's known intent and deftly strive
That Man possess not our escheated realm,
But urged by subtle craft to disobey
The stern command of his despotic God,
Forfeit celestial Grace.   Then will He cast
These faithless creatures from His fickle heart,
And in one moment hurl them from their height
Of stainless bliss, down to this dark abode
To share our bitter torment and become
Our vassal slaves.
                    Here then lies
Our only hope of adequate revenge ;—
To ruin, if we may, this new-born Man
And on his race, eternal woe entail.

Similarly, in *Paradise Lost*, from the first dialogue
that takes place between Satan and Beëlzebub, on
their awakening from stupor, it is evident that thus
early in his new career, Satan had decided what his
exact function was to be for the future, and how he
proposed to accomplish his idea :—

>   .   .   .   *" Of this be sure—*
> *To do aught good never will be our task,*
> *But ever to do evil our sole delight,*
> As being the contrary to His high will
> Whom we resist."

And subsequently, in the Garden, after he has recovered from his momentary spasm of feeling
" stupidly good," the devil in him reasserts itself,
and he exclaims :

" So farewell hope, and with hope, farewell fear,
Farewell remorse !   All good to me is lost ;
Evil, be thou my Good."

In neither Cædmon nor Milton, does it appear
that the bare fact of the Archangel being ruined,
necessitated his being a *Devil*.   On the contrary,
during the debate in Pandemonium, the leading
Spirits, such as Beëlzebub, could see in the future
nothing but the prospect of continued suffering;
while others, like Mammon, suggest various means
by which to retrieve their fallen condition.   The
idea of forgetting suffering in *revengeful action* was
Satan's.

Having thus marked out for himself his future
course of life as a Devil, he at once began to fall to
his own ideal of badness.   To reach it at once was
impossible.   There was too much of the nobility of
the Archangel still clinging to him to allow of this.
It took six thousand years for Satan to develop into
a Mephistopheles.   The Archangel, newly ruined
and but just starting out on his self-chosen career,
had not as yet reached the insensibility of the hard-
ened criminal.   He could still feel remorse ; he had
a sympathetic knowledge of good ; he adopts evil as
his profession, but he has sublime moral conceptions ;
he is often " inly racked," or racked with deep
despair ; he has compunctions of conscience ; and,

at times, seems to be on the verge even of contrition. He is no longer an Archangel, but he is
not as yet a Devil. But the first step in his endless
descent had been taken. The unendurableness of
the Beatific Vision, which is the unfailing precursor
of apostasy, had been reached.

"Is this the region, this the soil, the clime,"
Said then the lost Archangel, "this the seat
That we must change for Heaven?—this mournful gloom
For that celestial light? Be it so, since He
Who now is sovran can dispose and bid
What shall be right: *farthest from Him is best.*"

Apart from this, he had not reached any of the
further depths of devildom.

Cædmon tells us that,

> . . . deep remorse and envious thought
> Made willing captive each rebellious heart;
> For while the false Archangel and his band
> Lay prone in liquid fire,
>
> . . . .
>
> . . . the Angelic host
> Who fell not from their love, still held far off
> The empyreal battlements of Heaven.
> This, then perceived the traitorous fiends in Hell,
> And in one moment stood their folly bare.

This idea of *remorse*, so foreign to the currently accepted notion of devil-life, is only one of the delicate

artistic touches that we find in both Cædmon and Milton, in their delineation of the early history of the Satan.

We find the same idea in *Paradise Lost*. Satan shows,

> Signs of remorse and passion, to behold
> The fellows of his crime, the followers rather
> (Far other once beheld in bliss), condemned
> For ever now to have their lot in pain,—
> Millions of Spirits for his fault amerced
> Of Heaven, and from eternal splendours flung
> For his revolt—yet faithful how they stood,
> Their glory withered.

This is not the devil-mood. It is the Archangel on the first step of his fearful descent ; not yet a Devil, but bound erelong to become one. So, shortly after, when the ruined Archangel attempts to address his followers for the first time since their expulsion from the Empyrean, Cædmon's simple line,

> *Then Satan sorrowing spake :*

is beautifully expanded in the epic, when Satan throws around,

> . . . his baleful eyes,
> That witnessed huge affliction and dismay,
> Mixed with obdurate pride and steadfast hate.
>
> .   .   .   .   .   .
> Thrice he assayed, and thrice, in spite of scorn,

> Tears, such as Angels weep, burst forth : at last
> Words interwove with sighs found out their way :—

This is not only one of the most pathetic touches in the *Epic of the Fall*, it is, moreover, ideally natural ; and, as affording an insight into the mind of the fallen Archangel, is not surpassed by any similar touch in English literature.

The last point in this character-study that we shall notice, is the conduct of Satan immediately before and during the Temptation in Paradise. This scene is peculiar to Milton, as the "Angel of Presumption" of Cædmon is so straitly fettered that he is unable to leave the dread Abyss even

> For a moment, for a winter's day.

One remark before passing on. The whole scene of the Temptation and Fall, is conceived by Cædmon with a power of imagination far above that which marks the corresponding scene in Milton, and the Fiend who undertakes the expedition, on Satan's behalf, conducts the enterprise with far more statesmanship and diplomatic ability than does the Satan of Milton. At the same time, there is no indication in Cædmon's delineation of the character of the emissary, that the inferior Fiend was ever troubled by any scruples of conscience or was ever "inly racked," or knew,

How awful goodness is

or indeed, was anything but a devil, pure and simple.

Milton's Satan, on the other hand, though not evincing the same dash and brilliancy of manœuvre in the conduct of the campaign, still retains some of the lineaments of the great Archangel; some of the moral traits of the Archangel; some of the Archangelic greatness of the original Being. He is not, as yet, a vulgar Devil, though he may end in becoming so; and it is this fact that he *does* still possess so much of his original splendour, even after his ruin, that gives to Milton's Satan his especial charm of grandeur.

It is in the opening of the Fourth Book of *Paradise Lost*, that we find, at its highest point of development, Milton's delineation of the warring thoughts and passions which so terribly racked the whole being of the Apostate, as he alights on the top of Niphates:

Now conscience wakes despair
That slumbered ; wakes the bitter memory
Of what he was, what is, and what must be
Worse ; of worse deeds worse sufferings must ensue !
Sometimes towards Eden, which now in his view
Lay pleasant, his grieved look he fixes sad ;
Sometimes towards Heaven and the full-blazing Sun,
Which now sat high in his meridian tower :
Then, much revolving, thus in sighs began :—

"O thou that, with surpassing glory crowned,
Look'st from thy sole dominion like the god
Of this new World—at whose sight all the stars
Hide their diminished heads—to thee I call,
But with no friendly voice, and add thy name,
O Sun, to tell thee how I hate thy beams,
That bring to my remembrance from what state
I fell, *how glorious once above thy Sphere*,
Till pride and worse ambition threw me down,
Warring in Heaven against Heaven's matchless King!
Ah, wherefore? He deserved no such return
From me, whom he created what I was
In that bright eminence, and with his good
Upbraided none ; nor was his service hard.
What could be less than to afford him praise,
The easiest recompense, and pay him thanks,
How due? *yet all his good proved ill in me*,
And wrought but malice.   Lifted up so high,
I 'sdained subjection, and thought one step higher
Would set me highest, and in a moment quit
The debt immense of endless gratitude.

　　　　．　　　．　　　．　　　．　　　．　　　．

Oh, had his powerful destiny ordained
Me some inferior Angel, I had stood
Then happy ; no unbounded hope had raised
Ambition.   Yet why not?   Some other power
As great might have aspired, and me, though mean,
Drawn to his part.   But other Powers as great
Fell not, but stand unshaken, from within
Or from without to all temptations armed!
Hadst thou the same free will and power to stand?
Thou hadst.   Whom hast thou then, or what to accuse,
But Heaven's free love dealt equally to all?

Be then his love accursed, since love or hate,
To me alike it deals eternal woe.
Nay, cursed be thou ; since against his thy will
Chose freely what it now so justly rues.
Me miserable ! which way shall I fly
Infinite wrath and infinite despair ?
Which way I fly is Hell ; myself am Hell ;
And, in the lowest deep, a lower deep
Still threatening to devour me opens wide,
To which the Hell I suffer seems a Heaven.
*O, then, at last relent ! Is there no place
Left for repentance, none for pardon left ?*
None left but by submission ; and that word
Disdain forbids me, and my dread of shame
Among the Spirits beneath, whom I seduced
With other promises and other vaunts
Than to submit, boasting I could subdue
The Omnipotent.   Ay me ! they little know
How dearly I abide that boast so vain,
Under what torments inwardly I groan.
While they adore me on the throne of Hell,
With diadem and sceptre high advanced,
The lower still I fall, *only supreme*
In misery ; such joy ambition finds !
But say I could repent, and could obtain,
By act of grace, my former state ; how soon
Would highth recal high thoughts, how soon unsay
What feigned submission swore ! Ease would recant
Vows made in pain, as violent and void
(For never can true reconcilement grow
Where wounds of deadly hate have pierced so deep) ;
Which would but lead me to a worse relapse
And heavier fall."

This grand soliloquy, (of which we have given
only an extract), which Satan utters as he strolls,
magnificent, towards the garden of Eden, discloses
far more of the ruined Archangel than of the future
Devil. It is a retrospect tinged with the deepest
remorse. The devilish object of his journey seems,
for the moment, to be forgotten, or eclipsed under
weightier thoughts. There is a gleam of his infinite
obligation for an infinite favour; a passing sense that
his rebellion is an ignoble act; a momentary flash of
his weakness of will compared with that of those who
had kept their high estate; and finally, a thought, as
quickly abandoned as expressed, of the bare possibility of penance and pardon. But the Archangel
had taken an irretrievable step;—the first step in an
infinite descent;—and so, in spite of his noble reason-
ings, in spite of his sublime conceptions and compunctions of conscience, despair resumes its throne
in his mind and he exclaims:

> ". . . farewell hope, and with hope, farewell fear,
> Farewell remorse! *All good to me is lost;*
> *Evil, be thou my Good:* by thee at least
> Divided empire with Heaven's King I hold,
> By thee, and more than half perhaps will reign;
> As Man, ere long, and this new World, shall know."
> Thus while he spake, each passion dimmed his face.
> Thrice changed with pale—ire, envy, and despair.

Subsequently, after he has entered the Garden

and sees the Man and the Woman in their primeval
home,

> . . . Satan, still in gaze as first he stood,
> Scarce thus at length failed speech recovered sad :—
> "O Hell ! what do mine eyes with grief behold ?
> Into our room of bliss thus high advanced
> Creatures of other mould—Earth-born, perhaps,
> Not Spirits, yet to Heavenly Spirits bright
> Little inferior—whom my thoughts pursue
> With wonder, *and could love ; so lively shines*
> *In them divine resemblance,* and such grace
> The hand that formed them on their shape hath poured."

Yet here again, Satan's bad actions are preceded
by noble thoughts, for he is forced to acknowledge,

> "Melt, as I do, yet public reason just—
> Honour and empire, with revenge enlarged
> By conquering this new World—compels me now
> To do what else, though damned, I should abhor."

One of the deepest, truest touches, in this connection, in Milton's epic, is where Ithuriel and Zephon
discover Satan, "squat like a toad," and trying to
hypnotise Eve during sleep. Compelled, by the
point of Ithuriel's spear, to assume his true personality and listen to their withering rebuke,

> Abashed the Devil stood,
> And felt how awful goodness is, and saw
> Virtue in her shape how lovely—saw, and pined
> His loss.

Even at this point, Satan had not sunk so low but that he could discern the supreme charm of goodness and virtue, and see down into the depths of his own loss.

But one step further, and the Archangel becomes the Devil. As he approaches Eve, on the day of the great Temptation, he sees,

> Her heavenly form
> Angelic, but more soft and feminine,
> Her graceful innocence, her every air
> Of gesture or least action, overawed
> His malice, and with rapine sweet bereaved
> His fierceness of the fierce intent it brought.
> That space the Evil One abstracted stood
> From his own evil, and for the time remained
> *Stupidly good, of enmity disarmed,*
> Of guile, of hate, of envy, of revenge.

It is but for a moment that he hesitates,

> . . . the hot hell that always in him burns,
> Though in mid Heaven, soon ended his delight,
> And tortures him now more, the more he sees
> Of pleasure not for him ordained. Then soon
> Fierce hate he recollects, and all his thoughts
> Of mischief, gratulating, thus excites :—
> " Thoughts, whither have ye led me ? with what sweet
> Compulsion thus transported to forget
> What hither brought us ? hate, not love, nor hope
> Of Paradise for Hell, hope here to taste
> Of pleasure, *but all pleasure to destroy,*
> *Save what is in destroying ; other joy*
> *To me is lost.*"

Satan is now a Devil,—irretrievably and irrevocably.

In the future history of the world, he may sink to the level of the Hebrew Satan in the Book of *Job*, or of the Mephistopheles in *Faust*, or of the mediæval Devil of legend, or of the Arch-Fool of Luther; but the Archangel of the *Epic of the Fall of Man* is an essentially grand creation, of whose after career we know nothing. He had accomplished his part as the hero of an Epic, and the dazzling glamour which had distinguished him, as the prince of Archangels in the Empyrean, still surrounds him in his fall, although lurid clouds may partially obscure him, whether as the Angel of Presumption of Cædmon or as the Satan of *Paradise Lost*.

CHAPTER VIII.

Three Poetic Hells: The Torture-house of Cædmon, the Inferno of Dante, and the Hell of Milton.

HITHERTO, we have omitted all mention of the *Divina Commedia* of Dante, since this great work cannot be regarded, except in a very general way, as forming any essential part, or indeed any part whatsoever, of the *Epic of the Fall of Man.* As we shall presently see, the action of this sublime Allegory opens some five thousand years *after* the supposed era of the Fall; but, nevertheless, it is so intimately connected with the Epic, and offers so many interesting topics of contrast, if not of comparison, that we propose, in the present chapter, to consider a few of the points of similarity or dissimilarity between the Allegory and the Epic; more especially, with regard to the early legendary Hell of Cædmon, the mediæval, philosophical Hell of Dante, and the modern, traditional Hell of Milton.

It is well known that Lord Macaulay assigns to

Dante the *third* place among the six greatest poets of the world; allowing to Shakespeare and Homer alone, the distinction of superior poetic merit, and relegating Milton to the *fifth* place in this *suum cuique* list.

Whether we agree with Lord Macaulay or not, in this *dictum* of his, it is beyond dispute that the *Divina Commedia* is the grandest and most profound religious allegory of which Europe can boast; while *Paradise Lost* is the grandest and most learned sacred epic, in verse, of which England can boast.

Moreover, there are several striking marks of resemblance between these two great poets and thinkers.

Both were men of remarkable talents and erudition. As Mr. Eliot Norton very truly says, " Dante was a born student as he was a born poet, and had he never written a single poem, he would still have been famous as the most profound scholar of his times. Far, as he surpassed his contemporaries in poetry, he was no less their superior in the depth and extent of his knowledge."

It has been estimated that, so far as concerns the Classical authors alone, and not including the wide field of Scholastic theology and philosophy, over one thousand passages may be found in Dante's works, as direct citations, obvious references, or evident

20

allusions, showing the wide range of his research and reading in this branch of learning. Aristotle is quoted or referred to, three hundred times; and there is scarcely an important work of Aristotle which is not represented, and often very fully represented, in the pages of Dante. With Virgil's works, especially with the *Æneid*, he shows himself to be thoroughly acquainted, and introduces at least two hundred quotations from or references to the Mantuan poet. Ovid, Cicero, Horace, Livy, Juvenal, and Seneca are often quoted or referred to, and, besides all this, we have scattering references to Homer, Plato, and others. Our admiration of Dante's acquirements becomes indefinitely increased when we remember the difficulties under which this surprising amount of learning was amassed; when we reflect that it was in the days before the invention of printing, when books existed only in manuscript, and were consequently very rare and difficult of access; when there were no helps for study in the way of notes and dictionaries, no conveniences for reference, such as divisions of chapters, sections, paragraphs; above all, no indexes or concordances to help the fallible memory; when, finally, we add to all this the consideration of the circumstances of Dante's own life, a turbulent, wandering, unsettled life, a life of which we may truly say, " without were fightings, within were fears "; one intensely preoccupied, with fierce political struggles and anxieties. The varied and extensive reading of which Dante's works give evidence would be admirable if it had been exhibited under the most favourable conditions of what we call " learned leisure," and with the help of modern appliances, but under the circumstances under which Dante accomplished it it is nothing less than amazing.

To speak of the vast erudition of Milton, would be superfluous. His classical learning was, perhaps, more profound and varied than that of Dante. He was, also, Hellenist, Hebraist, and modern linguist of no mean order. But we must not forget the wide gulf that divided the literary conditions of the thirteenth from those of the seventeenth century ; and if, genius consists in a " continued attention," or in a " protracted patience," then, taking everything into consideration, we should be inclined to accord the palm of genius to the Italian poet rather than to Milton.

Perhaps, it may be matter of surprise to some readers, to know that very few writers, mediæval or modern, have had as thorough a knowledge of the Christian Scriptures as Dante had. The whole of the *Vulgate*, seems to have been perfectly familiar to him ; and judging, not only from the number of his direct quotations (nearly five hundred), but from the frequent interweaving of Scriptural allusion and phraseology into the fabric of his works, and especially of his *Divina Commedia*, he shows himself to have been as deeply versed, if not more deeply so, in the *Vulgate*, than Milton was in the Hebrew and Greek Testaments.

In one direction, however, Dante was unquestionably the superior of Milton, namely, in his mastery of mediæval Scholastic learning. The influence of the writings of Peter Lombard, Bonaventura, Hugh and Richard of St. Victor, and, above all, of St. Thomas Aquinas, and Albertus Magnus, is apparent throughout the *Divina Commedia ;* indeed, the Scholastic theology of the age forms the very atmosphere of the Allegory. But in Milton, there is no trace of any knowledge of mediæval scholastic thought, except in such passages or allusions as are evidently borrowed from Dante.

The last mark of resemblance between these two great men, which we shall notice, but which we cannot stay to describe at length, is as curious as it is interesting. Dante was not only a born student, and a born poet, he was a born *politician*, in the nobler sense of the term ; taking the deepest interest in public affairs, and active in all that he considered to be for the good of his native Florence. But it was an age when the conduct of public affairs was but too often a question of life and death to those who engaged in them; and defeat meant, as in Dante's own case, exile, confiscation, ruin.

We have but scant data for determining when or where the *Divina Commedia* was written. We know the era of the poem from the author's own statement in Canto twenty-one, where he makes the Fiend, Malacoda, say to Virgil,

> " Yesterday, later by five hours than now,
> Twelve hundred threescore years and six had filled
> The circuit of their course, since here the way
> Was broken."

This passage fixes the era of Dante's descent, at Good Friday in the year 1300 and at the thirty-fifth year of the Poet's age; but it does not help us in fixing the exact years spent by the Poet in the composition of his immortal work. From internal evidence, however, it is certain that Dante did not enter seriously upon the composition of his great Allegory until after his banishment; and, perhaps, not until all hope of ever regaining his full status as a citizen of Florence, had passed for ever from his mind.

Similarly, Milton was not only a born student, and a born poet, but, like Dante, he was deeply inter-

ested in all the public questions of his day. He was
an ardent admirer of Cromwell; became his Latin
Secretary; and was in sympathy with all that the
name of Cromwell implies. But he was not on the
winning side in politics, and with the death of Cromwell, the ex-Secretary of the Commonwealth was
buried in as deep a political oblivion, as was Dante,
after the issue of the edict of his banishment from
Florence.

But more than this. Although the first drafts of
the scheme of a possible poem on the subject of
Paradise Lost, were written out by Milton as early
as between the years 1639 and 1642, or between his
thirty-first and thirty-fourth years, yet it is more than
probable, that Milton, like Dante, did not begin, in
earnest, to turn his attention to the realisation of his
life-dream—the writting of his sacred epic—until
after his forced retirement from public life. The
year when Milton began *Paradise Lost* [1658], was
the year of Cromwell's death.

Dante's conception of the divisions of infinite
space is somewhat different from that of either
Cædmon or Milton. It will be remembered, that
both of the latter poets, depict infinite space as a
tripartite kingdom, consisting of the Empyrean,
Chaos, and Hell; and subsequently, introduce a
fourth kingdom, comprising the Starry Universe,

with the Earth at its centre as a fixed immovable
orb or globe.

According to Dante's scheme, however, as developed in the *Divina Commedia*, the Empyrean and
Infinite space are interchangeable terms for one and
the same idea ; and, if we may be allowed to venture
an expression of the unthinkable, Dante's Empyrean may be imagined as a sphere of infinite radius,
just as Infinite space is represented by both Cædmon
and Milton. Hanging at the centre of this infinite
globe, is the Starry Universe, surrounded on all
sides by the Empyrean.

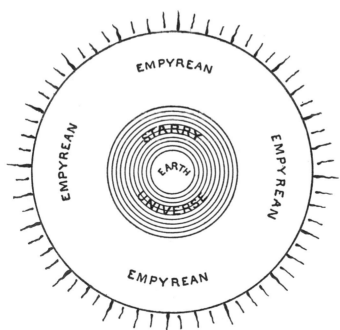

This Starry Universe of the Allegory, is a repro-
duction of the Ptolemaic or rather the Alphonsine
system of Moon and Planets revolving, each in its
own concentric Sphere, around the Earth as a fixed
immovable centre ; the same astronomical system
that Milton adopted in his epic three hundred and
fifty years later, though with different intent.

THE STARRY UNIVERSE
ACCORDING TO THE ALPHONSINE SYSTEM

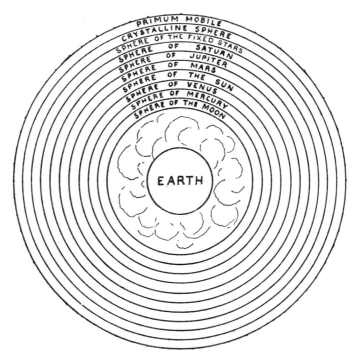

PRIMUM MOBILE
CRYSTALLINE SPHERE
SPHERE OF THE FIXED STARS
SPHERE OF SATURN
SPHERE OF JUPITER
SPHERE OF MARS
SPHERE OF THE SUN
SPHERE OF VENUS
SPHERE OF MERCURY
SPHERE OF THE MOON

EARTH

There is no Chaos in Dante's scheme of Infinite
space, as in Cædmon's and Milton's ; no " concave

of Hell," below the Starry Universe, in some deep-seated region. Dante, following classical models, places his Inferno or Hell within the crust of the Earth. It is an immense hollow cone, with a base or opening on the circumference or surface of the Earth, four thousand miles in breadth ; and with its apex at the centre of the globe, four thousand miles deep.

Such is Dante's conception of the divisions of Universal Space ; and on this conception, as a basis, is erected the whole fabric of the *Divina Commedia*.

We shall now see the exquisite skill with which the poet has made use of this framework in the construction and elaboration of the three kingdoms of his Allegory,—*Inferno*, *Purgatorio*, and *Paradiso*,— which, (to quote the words of Carlyle), "look out on one another like compartments of a great edifice, a great supernatural world-cathedral, piled up stern, solemn, awful." *

[1] *Vide* Note K.

It must be borne in mind that Dante's allegorical poem presupposes the *Epic of the Fall of Man*. In the dark background of the Allegory, is the gigantic figure of Lucifer, falling, like a sudden flash of serpentine lightning on a black sky, from the Empyrean, down through the Starry Spheres. As he strikes the Earth, he makes a wide-gaping chasm, which gradually contracts as the fallen Archangel plunges downwards towards the centre of the globe, where his fall is stayed, and he remains for ever wedged in transparent ice.

Moreover the era of the poem is fixed, by the poet himself, at thirteen hundred years after the Incarnation, when the divine forecast regarding the Serpent, as narrated in the Hebrew version of the Fall, was already being fulfilled :

" She shall crush thy head, and thou shalt lie in wait for her heel,"

so that, when Dante visits, in his Vision, the great tripartite kingdom of his imagination, he finds Hell, Purgatory, and Paradise thickly peopled with the shades of a hundred and fifty generations.

The huge cone or chasm of Dante's Hell, formed by the fall of the Archangel, is represented as the " torture-house " of the lost, and as consisting of a number of circles or zones in which the torments

gradually increase in severity as the zones decrease
in circumference, until, at the apex or centre of the
Earth the Arch-Traitor stands, wedged in a lake of
everlasting ice, the punishment of an Archangel,
traitor to his God.

INFERNO.

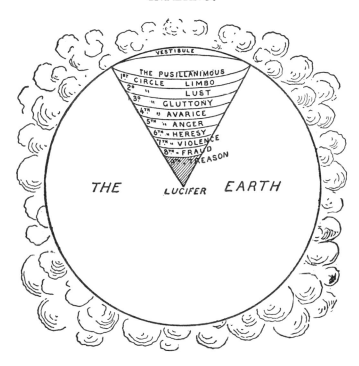

These various zones of Dante's Inferno, through
which the poet and his guardian Virgil pass on their
way to Purgatorio or "the intermediate state," we
shall presently notice more at length, when we

come to compare Dante's Inferno with the Hell of
Cædmon and Milton.

Purgatorio, as imagined by Dante, is an immense
conic mountain with its base on the Earth, and

PURGATORIO.

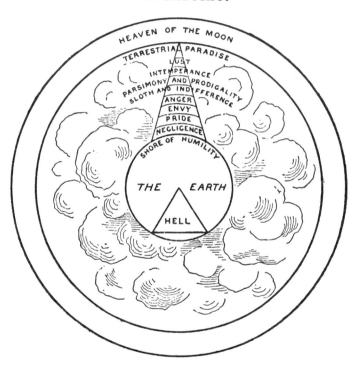

its apex piercing the Sphere of the Moon. In
its design, it is the inverse of Inferno, the circles
or zones of which, symbolic of ever-deepening
spiritual deformity, narrow as they *descend;* while
the terraces of the cone of Purgatorio, symbolic

of ever-increasing purity of soul, narrow as they *ascend*, till, at length, they land the purified spirit within the precincts of the first Heaven, the Heaven of the Moon.

There is a contrast, and a very marked one, at this point between the Epic and the Allegory. In *Paradise Lost*, it will be remembered, Milton draws, in strong lines, the picture of an adamantine causey built by Sin and Death, through the darkness and howling of Chaos, to render easier the communication between Earth and *Hell*. Here, on the contrary the poet depicts a mountain of Light, the sides of which are terraced to facilitate communication between Earth and *Heaven*.

In the construction of the *Paradiso*,—the climax of the Allegory,—the brilliant imagination of the poet reaches its grandest flight of phantasy. The prosaic system of the Alphonsine Spheres becomes, under the enchanting touch of the Italian, a series of Heavens, leading up, Sphere by Sphere, to the Empyrean—the Heaven of Heavens.

The pathway through the Starry Spheres, by which the ruined Archangel was hurled from the Empyrean to Hell, becomes, in Dante, the golden stairway of Cædmon, connecting the just with the throne of the Eternal, and making possible, once again, the realisation of the Beatific Vision. At the very pinnacle of Paradiso is the Deity, clothed in Light and Majesty ineffable; shrouded, yet visible; the symbol of perfection, absolute, infinite; the

PARADISO.

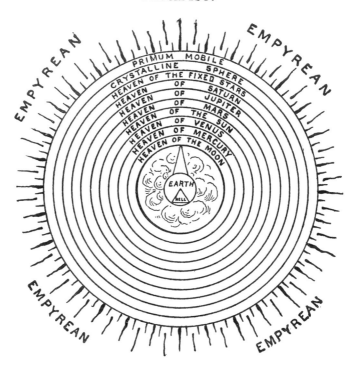

symbol of the Highest Good. Beneath, in the lowest depths of Inferno, separated from the Deity by the whole diameter of moral and spiritual being, is Satan, colossal and monstrous in form, imbedded in eternal ice, the symbol of treason, of death, and of every kind of moral and spiritual depravity.

Such is a brief outline of the construction of the *Divina Commedia.*

With the *Purgatorio* and *Paradiso* we have no concern in the present study, but the *Inferno* is especially interesting, inasmuch as it offers many marked contrasts both to the torture-house of Cædmon and to the Hell of Milton.

In the simple narrative of the Anglo-Saxon poet, Hell is the legendary place of punishment after death for those who, like the rebel angels, are traitors to their God; traitors to themselves; and traitors to Society at large. This idea of punishment hereafter, pervades every national literature in some form or another; and seems to be the poetic expression of a world-thought, that, whatever militates against the Highest Good, whether of the individual or of Society, entails punishment. In Cædmon, this thought finds expression in its simplest and most natural form of bodily pain, as represented by the two mightiest forces in nature, for evil as well as for good, namely, fire and ice.

In the prologue to his poem, Cædmon depicts the Deity as creating,

A place of banishment, an exile-house,
Filled with deep anguish and with hellish groans
And direful punishments; a fell retreat
For those who faithless proved to their high trust.

Deep was the torture-house and void of joys ;
Home of perpetual Night, with sulphur charged,
With fire and cold intense, with lurid flame
And black Tartarean smoke. The cold, He bade,
And direful flames increase a thousand-fold
That by alternate tortures Hell itself
Might be henceforth doubly unbearable.

Later on in the poem we are told that,

   . . . on the approach of each returning eve
The fires, rekindled, fiercely rage anew,
And Night appears immeasurably long.
Then ere the dawn leads back the joyless light,
Sharp biting cold and glacial blasts attack
Their fervid forms, and evermore they writhe
In lurid torture or deep, piercing cold.

In addition to all this physical suffering,

      . . . ceaseless woe,
Deep racking pain, grief unassuageable
And hydra-headed torture, all around,
Enthroned in blackest darkness, mocked their cries.

For a long time after their terrific fall through
Chaos,

    . . . the false Archangel and his band
Lay prone in liquid fire, scarce visible
Amid the surging clouds of rolling smoke
And deep infernal gloom.

At length, however, the Angel of Presumption on

awakening from his shock inveighs in bitter terms
against Heaven's Tyrant, who, he tells his followers,

> . . . in ire
> Pours the dread flames of this infernal gulf
> In full upon us and denies us Heaven !

and in the course of the speech in which he advocates eternal revenge he exclaims:

> . . . " Above, beneath, the flame
> Fierce rages. Sight more horrible mine eyes
> Ne'er yet have witnessed. O'er these scorching deeps
> The fire no respite knows. The strong forged chain
> With ever-biting links forbids my flight.
> My feet are bound, my hands are manacled ;
> Around my neck is forged this lattice-belt
> Of iron strangely wrought by Angel-skill ;
> And e'en the pathway to the Gates of Hell
> Lies thick beset with foul and horrid Shapes
> That bar all exit. In this loathsome den
> We, princes once, chained by a Tyrant's whim
> Now suffer chastisement for fancied wrong."

This idea of the necessity of a torture-house, as a
punishment for wrong-doing, is evidently the poet's
own idea of Hell; as he himself styles it,

> Just *retribution* for the unholy war
> They thought to wage against Almighty God.

Dante's conception of the punishment of sin or
wrong-doing, as developed in the *Inferno*, is totally

21

different from that of Cædmon. It is more logical,
more thinkable, more spiritual, and more philosophical. The poem, as a whole, embodies and illustrates
the Catholic view of life; and presents an exhaustive
picture of the moral relation between the individual
and his deeds. The *free-will* of man, involving as it
does human responsibility, is the very atmosphere
of the poem. If we might venture to express an
opinion as to the spiritual meaning of so profound
an Allegory as the *Divina Commedia*, we should say,
that in Dante's philosophy, each human being is
regarded, at any given moment, as the resultant of
all that he has been or done in the past years of his
life,—physically, morally, spiritually; and that so-
called punishments and rewards hereafter, are simply the logical results of the character which the
individual stamps upon *himself*, by obedience or
disobedience to law,—physical, moral, spiritual. In
the *Inferno*, the punishments, (which are evidently
intended to be allegorical), are all symbolical of the
states of mind experienced by the individual when
under the influence of the passion for which he is
being punished. The poet has collected together,
and has classified, all manner of wrong-doing, and
all guilty mind-states, antecedent to and conse-
quent upon, wrong-doing. The machinery of the
poem, and the description of the invisible regions,

especially that of the *Inferno*, while they embody
the little that the Catholic Faith reveals on the subject, and while they are enriched with the chaste
creations of Grecian and Roman imagination, scraps
of current Italian history, and the grim fantastic
myths of the North and the East, still, evince, in
every Canto, the central thought of the poem as a
soul-picture, of which the current of philosophic and
scholastic thought is apparent under every shifting
phase of the poet's fancy.

We shall now pass to the examination of the poem
itself.

When Dante, with Virgil as his guardian-guide,
comes to the portal of Hell with its dread inscription, Virgíl tells the poet:

> " We are come
> Where I have told thee we shall see the souls
> To misery doom'd, who intellectual good
> Have lost."

and, on entering the dark chasm, he gains his first
impression of the mental atmosphere that pervades
the whole of Inferno:

> . . . sighs, with lamentations and loud moans,
> Resounded through the air pierced by no star,
> That e'en I wept at entering. Various tongues,
> Horrible languages, outcries of woe,
> Accents of anger, voices deep and hoarse.

On a dark plain, within the Vestibule of Hell, the poet sees, behind a whirling flag, a vast train of spirits, running furiously around and sorely stung by wasps and hornets.

"O master! what is this I hear? what race
Are these, who seem so overcome with woe?"
    He thus to me: "This miserable fate
Suffer the wretched souls of those, who lived
Without or praise or blame, with *that ill band
Of angels mix'd, who nor rebellious proved,
Nor yet were true to God, but for themselves
Were only.* From his bounds Heaven drove them forth
Not to impair his lustre; nor the depth
Of Hell receives them, lest the accursed tribe
Should glory thence with exultation vain."
    I then: "Master! what doth aggrieve them thus,
That they lament so loud?" He straight replied:
"That will I tell thee briefly. These of death
No hope may entertain: and their blind life
So meanly passes, that all other lots
They envy."

This outside circle, so to speak, is the Circle of the "Pusillanimous," consisting of angels and men, too weak in will-power to be the architects of their own character, the environing circumstances of the moment impelling or progging them on to follow the flag of some senseless cause.

Here, at the very opening of the poem, we are met by an instance of the subtile genius of Dante.

In neither Cædmon nor in Milton, is there the recognition of any *degrees* of guilt among the rebel
Angels. It is true, that in Cædmon, Satan is supposed to be hopelessly fettered, while his followers
are free to move at pleasure; but the punishment
of fire and ice is the same for *all* of the fallen. In
Milton, there does not exist even this slight distinction between guilt and guilt, but all are indiscrimi-
nately hurled to one common Hell, and to one
common level of torture. In Dante, on the contrary, the inferior Angels, who allowed themselves to
be made the dupes of the great Archangel, are punished as human souls of a similar caste are punished,
viz., by the absence of either pain or bliss; their
eternal future being as colourless as their finite past.

On the approach of Dante and Virgil to the river
Acheron they see,

> A throng upon the shore of a great stream
>   . . . and lo ! in a bark
> Comes on an old man, hoary white with eld,
> Crying, "Woe to you, wicked spirits ! hope not
> Ever to see the sky again. I come
> To take you to the other shore across,
> Into eternal darkness, there to dwell
> In fierce heat and in ice."

This idea of darkness, heat, and ice, as we have
already seen is, in Cædmon, the legendary symbol

of punishment.   So in Milton, beyond the flood of
Lethe,

> . . . *a frozen continent*
> Lies dark and wild, beat with perpetual storms
> Of whirlwind and dire hail, which on firm land
> Thaws not, but gathers heap, and ruin seems
> Of ancient pile ; all else deep snow and ice,
>
> .   .   .   .
>
> . . . the parching air
> Burns frore, and cold performs the effect of fire.
> Thither, by harpy-footed Furies haled,
> At certain revolutions all the damned
> Are brought ; and feel by turns the bitter change
> Of fierce extremes, extremes by change more fierce,
> From beds of raging fire to starve in ice
> Their soft ethereal warmth, and there to pine,
> Immovable, infixed, and frozen round
> Periods of time,—thence hurried back to fire.

This symbolic attempt at expressing a subjective
state, by the means of physical phenomena, is common to the three poets.

In the Circle of Limbo, the first that girds the
abyss of Dante's Hell,

> . . . no plaint was heard
> Except of sighs, that made the eternal air
> Tremble, not caused by tortures, but from grief
> Felt by those multitudes, many and vast,
> Of men, women, and infants.   Then to me
> The gentle guide : " Inquirest thou not what spirits

Are these which thou beholdest ?   Ere thou pass
Farther, I would thou know, that *these of sin*
Were blameless ; and if aught they merited,
It profits not, *since baptism was not theirs,*
The portal to thy faith.   If they before
The Gospel lived, they served not God aright ;
And among such am I.   For these defects,
And for no other evil, we are lost ;
Only so far afflicted, that we live
Desiring without hope."

Here again, the punishment is purely subjective.

We now come to the second Circle of Inferno,
the first Circle of Hell proper, the Hell of the rebellious, beyond the court Minos, where sins of lust,
intemperance, and incontinence are punished, and
where,

     . . . carnal sinners are condemn'd, in whom
Reason by lust is sway'd.

The description, by the poet, of this Circle is
especially vivid :

                Into a place I came
Where light was silent all.   Bellowing there groan'd
A noise, as of a sea and tempest torn
By warring winds.   The stormy blast of hell
With restless fury drives the spirits on,
Whirl'd round and dash'd amain with sore annoy.
When they arrive before the ruinous sweep,
There shrieks are heard, there lamentations, moans,
And blasphemies.

This Canto we have referred to in another work, as exemplifying the strong hold which the Arthurian Epic * has ever exercised over the greatest minds of mediæval Europe. As the two shades, embracing each other, are borne by the whirlwind past the poet he exclaims :

> . . . " Bard ! willingly
> I would address those two together coming,
> Which seem so light before the wind." He thus :
> "Note thou, when nearer they to us approach.
> Then by that love which carries them along,
> Entreat ; and they will come." Soon as the wind
> Sway'd them towards us, I thus framed my speech :
> "O wearied spirits ! come, and hold discourse
> With us, if by none else restrain'd."
>
> .   .   .   .
>
> My cry prevail'd, by strong affection urged.

Francesca answers,

> " O gracious creature and benign ! who go'st
> Visiting, through this element obscure,
> Us, who the world with bloody stain imbrued ;
> If, for a friend, the King of all, we own'd,
> Our prayer to him should for thy peace arise,
> Since thou hast pity on our evil plight.
>
> .   .   .   .   .   .
>
> " Love, that in gentle heart is quickly learnt,
> Entangled him by that fair form, from me
> Ta'en in such cruel sort, as grieves me still :

* *Vide The Arthurian Epic*, p. 11, etc.

Love, that denial takes from none beloved,
Caught me with pleasing him so passing well,
That, as thou seest, he yet deserts me not.
Love brought us to one death "

Then turning, I to them my speech address'd,
And thus began : " Francesca ! your sad fate
Even to tears my grief and pity moves.
But tell me ; in the time of your sweet sighs,
By what, and how Love granted, that ye knew
Your yet uncertain wishes ? " She replied :

.   .   .   .   .   .

                                    " One day,
For our delight we read of Lancelot,
How him love thralled.   Alone we were, and no
Suspicion near us.   Oft-times by that reading
Our eyes were drawn together, and the hue
Fled from our altered cheek.   But at one point
Alone we fell.   When of that smile we read,
The wishèd smile, so rapturously kissed
By one so deep in love, then he, who ne'er
From me shall separate, at once my lips
All trembling kissed.   The book and writer both
Were love's purveyors.   In its leaves that day
We read no more." While thus one spirit spake,
The other wailed so sorely, that heart-struck
I, through compassion fainting, seemed not far
From death, and like a corse fell to the ground.

The punishment of the Lustful in this Circle, is a
fine illustration of Dante's emblematic method.
The "stormy blast" which,

With restless fury drives the spirits on,
Whirl'd round and dash'd amain with sore annoy,

or the " tyrannous gust " that tosses,

                 . . . those evil souls.
On this side and on that, above, below,

is an exact image—a realistic symbol—of the state
of mind of those who allow themselves to be swept,
hither and thither, by the whirlwind of violent carnal passions. The Canto brings out, in a strong
light, the exquisite skill with which Dante's powerful imagination pictures dramatically the subjective
state of the sinner,—the Hell within him.

    The next Circle in the descent, is that of Gluttons
and Dipsomaniacs; the intemperate in eating and
drinking.

In the third circle I arrive, of showers
Ceaseless, accursed, heavy and cold, unchanged
For ever, both in kind and in degree.
Large hail, discolour'd water, sleety flaw
Through the dun midnight air stream'd down amain :
Stank all the land whereon that tempest fell.
    Cerberus, cruel monster, fierce and strange,
Through his wide threefold throat, barks as a dog
Over the multitude immersed beneath.
His eyes glare crimson, black his unctuous beard,
His belly large, and claw'd the hands, with which
He tears the spirits, flays them, and their limbs
Piecemeal disparts. Howling there spread, as curs,

Under the rainy deluge, with one side
The other screening, oft they roll them round,
A wretched, godless crew.

The description here given of Cerberus, the devourer, who reigns over this Circle, with his blood-shot eyes, his threefold throat, and his horrid paunch, presents a vivid picture of the diseases induced by the deadly sin of Gluttony, which transforms the divine symmetry of the human body into the ugliness of a formless, misshapen mass. The ceaseless rains of turbid water; the putrid smell, ever arising from the ground; the nervous twitchings, and constant rolling from side to side, of the sufferers;— these, are but an allegory of the effects of a vice which dulls and deadens, which both chills and inflames, the intellectual and moral powers in man.

Descending to the fourth Circle, the Circle of the Miser and the Spendthrift; the avaricious and the prodigal; the ill-keeping and the ill-giving, the poet encounters Plutus, the god of Avarice, who guards this sub-kingdom; who, being awed into silence, the two poets proceed on their way through this region which Dante thus describes:

E'en as a billow, on Charybdis rising,
Against encounter'd billow dashing breaks;
Such is the dance this wretched race must lead,
Whom more than elsewhere numerous here I found.

From one side and the other, with loud voice,
Both roll'd on weights, by main force of their breasts,
Then smote together, and each one forthwith
Roll'd them back voluble, turning again ;
Exclaiming these, " Why holdest thou so fast ? "
Those answering, " And why castest thou away ? "
So, still repeating their despiteful song,
They to the opposite point, on either hand,
Traversed the horrid circle ; then arrived,
Both turn'd them round, and through the middle space
Conflicting met again.

The imagery here employed, although not peculiar
to Dante, sufficiently expresses the uniform mind-
mood of the man who is dominated by a propensity
for hoarding ; and that of the man whose propensity
is to squander for the gratification of passing appe-
tites.   In both cases, the vice is essentially the same,
namely, intemperance in the holding, or intemperance
in the dispensing, of property ; the accumulation of
wealth for its own sake, or the accumulation of
wealth for self-gratification.   The one passion of the
avaricious is to " roll up " wealth ; the one passion
of the prodigal is to dissipate it.   In neither case is
wealth viewed in its true relation to life, as the means
of supplying, rationally, the innocent needs of one-
self and others.

The poets now come to the fifth Circle of Inferno, and reach a boiling well whose dusky waters

expand into the Stygian lake; the place of punishment of the Wrathful and the Sullen.

> We the circle cross'd
> To the next steep, arriving at a well,
> That boiling pours itself down to a foss
> Sluiced from its source.   Far murkier was the wave
> Than sablest grain : and we in company
> Of the inky waters, journeying by their side,
> Enter'd, though by a different track, beneath.
> Into a lake, the Stygian named, expands
> The dismal stream, when it hath reach'd the foot
> Of the grey wither'd cliffs.   Intent I stood
> To gaze, and in the marish sunk descried
> A miry tribe, all naked, and with looks
> Betokening rage.   They with their hands alone
> Struck not, but with the head, the breast, the feet,
> Cutting each other piecemeal with their fangs.
>   The good instructor spake : " Now seest thou, son !
> The souls of those, whom anger overcame.
> This too for certain know, that underneath
> The water dwells a multitude, whose sighs
> Into these bubbles make the surface heave,
> As thine eye tells thee wheresoe'er it turn.
> Fix'd in the slime, they say : ' Sad once were we,
> ' In the sweet air made gladsome by the sun,
> ' Carrying a foul and lazy mist within :
> ' Now in these murky settlings are we sad.'
> Such dolorous strain they gurgle in their throats,
> But word distinct can utter none."

It would be difficult to imagine any more fitting
emblems of the state of mind of a person in fierce

angry mood, than that of being immersed in a boiling surge, and in muddy water. Or, what could
express the impotence of *rage* more accurately than
the closing words of the above quotation:

> . . . they gurgle in their throats,
> But word distinct can utter none.

Equally fine, is the poet's description of those
who are the victims of silent, smouldering anger,
whom he compares to souls "fixed in the slime,"
and carrying within their hearts a "lazy smoke"
which obscures the true perspective of things, and
leads to distorted views of life and society.

As Dante and his guide are passing over the
Stygian lake, a remarkable sight presents itself. On
the opposite shore they see the city of Dis [Pluto,]
which forms the entrance to the deeper Hell; its
towers and wall, red with the eternal fires that burn
within.

> I thus: "The minarets already, Sir!
> There, certes, in the valley I descry,
> Gleaming vermilion, as if they from fire
> Had issued." He replied: "Eternal fire,
> That inward burns, shows them with ruddy flame
> Illumed; as in this nether hell thou seest."

Their entrance to the city is opposed by myriads
of demons, who guard the gate of the fortress; but

an angel from Paradise is sent to their assistance, who throws wide open the gates of the city, and they enter unharmed.

> To the gate
> He came, and with his wand touch'd it, whereat
> Open without impediment it flew.
>
> .   .   .   .
>
> We, unopposed,
> There enter'd ; and my mind eager to learn
> What state a fortress like to that might hold,
> I, soon as enter'd, throw mine eye around,
> And see, on every part, wide-stretching space,
> Replete with bitter pain and torment ill.
> As where Rhone stagnates on the plains of Arles,
> Or as at Pola, near Quarnaro's gulf,
> That closes Italy and laves her bounds,
> The place is all thick spread with sepulchres ;
> So was it here, save what in horror here
> Excell'd : for 'midst the graves were scatter'd flames,
> Wherewith intensely all throughout they burn'd,
> That iron for no craft there hotter needs.
> Their lids all hung suspended ; and beneath,
> From them forth issued lamentable moans,
> Such as the sad and tortured well might raise.
> I thus : "Master ! say who are these, interr'd
> Within these vaults, of whom distinct we hear
> The dolorous sighs." He answer thus return'd :
> "The arch-heretics are here, accompanied
> By every sect their followers ; and much more,
> Than thou believest, the tombs are freighted : like
> With like is buried ; and the monuments
> Are different in degrees of heat."

Virgil informs Dante that

> The cemetery on this part obtain,
> With Epicurus, all his followers,
> Who with the body make the spirit die.

This sixth Circle is the Circle of Arch-heretics and Materialists. From the picture which the poet himself draws of the burning tombs with the lids raised, and from his placing Arch-heretics and Epicurus in the same Circle of punishment, it is more than probable that Dante was referring, not to heretics in general, but more especially, to those who denied the twin crucial doctrines of Christianity, the resurrection of the body, and the immortality of the soul.

The poets now descend a rocky precipice to the seventh Circle, and reach a river of blood, in which those are punished who, by Violence, have injured their fellowmen. Accompanied by one of the host of Centaurs who guard the bank of the river, Dante relates:

> 　　　　　　　Onward we moved,
> The faithful escort by our side, along
> The border of the crimson-seething flood,
> Whence, from those steep'd within, loud shrieks arose.
> 　Some there I mark'd, as high as to their brow
> Immersed, of whom the mighty Centaur thus:
> "These are the souls of tyrants, who were given
> To blood and rapine. Here they wail aloud
> Their merciless wrongs."

. . . . . .

                      Then further on a space
The Centaur paused, near some, who at the throat
Were extant from the wave.

    . . . . . .

  A race I next espied who held the head,
And even all the bust, above the stream.

     . . . . .

Thus shallow more and more the blood became,
So that at last it but imbrued the feet ;
And there our passage lay athwart the foss.
  " As ever on this side the boiling wave
Thou seest diminishing," the Centaur said,
  "So on the other, be thou well assured,
It lower still and lower sinks its bed,
Till in that part it re-uniting join,
Where 't is the lot of tyranny to mourn."

The Circle of Violence comprises, however, two
gulfs or regions: the place of punishment of those
who have laid violent hands upon themselves; and
the region where those are tormented who have
been guilty of violence against God or against
Nature.

After passing the river, they come to a forest,
overhung with dark foliage.

  The kind instructor in these words began :
" Ere further thou proceed, know thou art now
I' th' second round, and shalt be, till thou come
Upon the horrid sand : look therefore well

22

Around thee, and such things thou shalt behold,
As would my speech discredit." On all sides
I heard sad plainings breathe, and none could see
From whom they might have issued. In amaze
Fast bound I stood. He, as it seem'd, believed
That I had thought so many voices came
From some amid those thickets close conceal'd,
And thus his speech resumed : "If thou lop off
A single twig from one of those ill plants,
The thought thou hast conceived shall vanish quite."
 Thereat a little stretching forth my hand,
From a great wilding gather'd I a branch,
And straight the trunk exclaim'd : "Why pluck'st thou
   me ?"
Then, as the dark blood trickled down its side,
These words it added : " Wherefore tear'st me thus ?
Is there no touch of mercy in thy breast ?
Men once were we, that now are rooted here.
Thy hand might well have spared us, had we been
The souls of serpents."

With striking poetic justice, those who destroy
their bodies by suicide, are denied a human body
hereafter.

The poets then arrive at the third region :

A plain we reach'd, that from its steril bed
Each plant repell'd. The mournful wood waves round
Its garland on all sides, as round the wood
Spreads the sad foss. There, on the very edge,
Our steps we stay'd. It was an area wide
Of arid sand and thick.

  . . . . . .

Of naked spirits many a flock I saw,
All weeping piteously, to different laws
Subjected ; for on the earth some lay supine,
Some crouching close were seated, others paced
Incessantly around ; the latter tribe
More numerous, those fewer who beneath
The torment lay, but louder in their grief.
    O'er all the sand fell slowly wafting down
Dilated flakes of fire, as flakes of snow
On Alpine summit, when the wind is hush'd.

.   .   .   .   .   .

Unceasing was the play of wretched hands,
Now this, now that way glancing, to shake off
The heat, still falling fresh.

Seeing a spirit of immense proportions, lying
haughty on the burning sand, Dante enquires,

                    . . . " who
Is yon huge spirit, that, as seems, heeds not
The burning, but lies writhen in proud scorn,
As by the sultry tempest immatured ?"

Virgil, in reply, tells him,

             " This of the seven kings was one,
Who girt the Theban walls with siege, and held,
As still he seems to hold, God in disdain,
And sets his high omnipotence at nought.
But, as I told him, his despiteful mood
Is ornament well suits the breast that wears it.
Follow me now ; and look thou set not yet

Thy foot in the hot sand, but to the wood
Keep ever close."

. . . . . .

Silently on we pass'd
To where there gushes from the forest's bound
A little brook, whose crimson'd wave yet lifts
My hair with horror.   As the rill, that runs
From Bulicame, to be portion'd out
Among the sinful women, so ran this
Down through the sand ; its bottom and each bank
Stone-built, and either margin at its side,
Whereon I straight perceived our passage lay.

Along this stream of living blood, Dante meets
and recognises, although " smirched with fire," his
old instructor Brunetto.

I not the less still on my way proceed,
Discoursing with Brunetto, and inquire
Who are most known and chief among his tribe.
" To know of some is well ; " he thus replied,
" But of the rest silence may best beseem.
Time would not serve us for report so long.
In brief I tell thee, that all these were clerks,
Men of great learning and no less renown,
By one same sin polluted in the world."

After parting from Brunetto they come,

. . . where the water's din was heard,
As down it fell into the other round,
Resounding like the hum of swarming bees :

. . . .

> Straight my guide
> Pursued his track. I follow'd : and small space
> Had we passed onward, when the water's sound
> Was now so near at hand, that we had scarce
> Heard one another's speech for the loud din.

> .   .   .   .   .   .

> .   .   .   downward from a craggy steep we found
> That this dark wave resounded, roaring loud,
> So that the ear its clamour soon had stunn'd.

While waiting for the monster, Geryon, to carry them down to the next Circle, the poet, at Virgil's suggestion, proceeds to the farthest boundary of the seventh Circle, where those are being punished who had been guilty of violence against the rights of property: usurers, extortioners, arch-speculators, and others who accumulate wealth by illegitimate or nefarious means.

> Thus alone,
> Yet forward on the extremity I paced
> Of that seventh circle, where the mournful tribe
> Were seated.   At the eyes forth gush'd their pangs.
> Against the vapours and the torrid soil
> Alternately their shifting hands they plied.
> Thus use the dogs in summer still to ply
> Their jaws and feet by turns, when bitten sore
> By gnats, or flies, or gadflies swarming round.
>   Noting the visages of some, who lay
> Beneath the pelting of that dolorous fire,
> One of them all I knew not ; but perceived,

That pendent from his neck each bore a pouch
With colours and with emblems various mark'd,
On which it seemed as if their eye did feed.

These, sitting crouched on the burning sand and beneath the fiery flakes, keep their eyes fixed, each on his bag of pilfered wealth, with its tell-tale armorial bearings.

On the return of Dante to rejoin his guide,

    . . . that image vile of Fraud appear'd,
His head and upper part exposed on land,
But laid not on the shore his bestial train.
His face the semblance of a just man's wore,
So kind and gracious was its outward cheer ;
The rest was serpent all : two shaggy claws
Reach'd to the arm-pits ; and the back and breast,
And either side, were painted o'er with nodes
And orbits.

   .   .   .   .

  My guide already seated on the haunch
Of the fierce animal I found ; and thus
He me encouraged. "Be thou stout : be bold.
Down such a steep flight must we now descend."

   .   .   .   .   .   .

    . . . and thus he spake :
"Geryon ! now move thee : be thy wheeling gyres
Of ample circuit, easy thy descent.
Think on the unusual burden thou sustain'st."

   .   .   .   .   .   .

        He, slowly sailing, wheels
His downward motion, unobserved of me,

But that the wind, arising to my face,
Breathes on me from below.   Now on our right
I heard the cataract beneath us leap
With hideous crash ; whence bending down to explore,
New terror I conceived at the steep plunge ;
For flames I saw, and wailings smote mine ear :
So that, all trembling, close I crouch'd my limbs,
And then distinguish'd, unperceived before,
By the dread torments that on every side
Drew nearer, how our downward course we wound.

    ·   ·   ·   ·   ·   ·   ·

        Geryon lighting places us on foot
Low down at base of the deep-furrow'd rock,
And, of his burden there discharged, forthwith
Sprang forward, like an arrow from the string.

This eighth Circle, the circle of Fraud or *Malebolge*, consists of *ten* consecutive gulfs, hollowed out of dark rock, each successive gulf becoming deeper and more contracted as the centre of the Earth is gradually approached.

There is a place within the depth of hell
Call'd Malebolge, all of rock dark-stain'd
With hue ferruginous, e'en as the steep
That round it circling winds.   Right in the midst
Of that abominable region yawns
A spacious gulf profound, whereof the frame
Due time shall tell.   The circle, that remains,
Throughout its round, between the gulf and base
Of the high craggy banks, successive forms
Ten bastions, in its hollow bottom raised.

The first chasm contains the Seducers of women, who are pursued and unmercifully tormented by horned demons.

After recognising some few among the spirits inhabiting this region, the poets pass to the next bridge, whence they see, in the gulf below, the ghosts of Flatterers immersed in horrid filth.

Hence, in the second chasm we heard the ghosts,
Who gibber in low melancholy sounds,
With wide-stretch'd nostrils snort, and on themselves
Smite with their palms.　Upon the banks a scurf,
From the foul steam condensed, encrusting hung,
That held sharp combat with the sight and smell.

　　.　　　.　　　.　　　.　　　.　　　.

And thence I saw, within the foss below,
A crowd immersed in ordure, that appeared
Draff of the human body.　There beneath
Searching with eye inquisitive, I mark'd
One with his head so grimed, 't were hard to deem
If he were clerk or layman.　Loud he cried:
"Why greedily thus bendest more on me,
Than on these other filthy ones, thy ken?"
　"Because, if true my memory," I replied,
"I heretofore have seen thee with dry locks;

　　.　　　.　　　.　　　.　　　.　　　.

Therefore than all the rest I scan thee more."
　Then beating on his brain, these words he spake:
"Me thus low down my flatteries have sunk,
Wherewith I ne'er enough could glut my tongue."

Passing from this loathsome scene, Dante and his

guide reach the gulf of the Simoniacs, who barter
the sanctities of the Church for pelf.

> Woe to thee, Simon Magus ! woe to you,
> His wretched followers ! who the things of God,
> Which should be wedded unto goodness, them,
> Rapacious as ye are, do prostitute
> For gold and silver in adultery.
> Now must the trumpet sound for you, since yours
> Is the third chasm.

Thus sings the poet, apostrophising the Arch-fiend
of Simony and his followers, and then, tells of their
awful punishment :

> I saw the livid stone, throughout the sides
> And in its bottom full of apertures,
> All equal in their width, and circular each.
>
> .   .   .   .   .
>
>   From out the mouth
> Of every one emerged a sinner's feet,
> And of the legs high upward as the calf.
> The rest beneath was hid.   On either foot
> The soles were burning ; whence the flexile joints
> Glanced with such violent motion, as had snapt
> Asunder cords or twisted withes.   As flame,
> Feeding on unctuous matter, glides along
> The surface, scarcely touching where it moves ;
> So here, from heel to point, glided the flames.

These men invert the true order of things spiritual
and things material, and, accordingly, are buried in

inverted position in the ardent rock, their feet only being visible ;—emblem of the impossibility of entirely concealing their crime.

Ascending a path,

> Not easy for the clambering goat to mount,
> . . . another vale appear'd,

the rounding valley where those are punished who presume to predict future events, and amass lucre by the profession of a knowledge of futurity ; Astrologers, Fortune-tellers, and Diviners of every class :

> Ernest I look'd
> Into the depth, that open'd to my view,
> Moisten'd with tears of anguish, and beheld
> A tribe, that came along the hollow vale,
> In silence weeping : such their step as walk
> Quires, chanting solemn litanies, on earth.
> As on them more direct mine eye descends,
> Each wonderously seem'd to be reversed
> At the neck-bone, so that the countenance
> Was from the reins averted ; and because
> None might before him look, they were compell'd
> To advance with backward gait.

The meaning of this punishment is apparent on the surface. A future event, if it could possibly be known, would be, to him who knows it, virtually a *past* event. With the revelation or disclosure of the future, both present and future virtually cease to exist, and only the weird sister of the Past is a

reality.   Dante, accordingly, depicts diviners with
the face twisted around to the back of the body,
indicative of the effect of their supposed supernatural powers.

From the next bridge, the poets look into a
chasm, where those are plunged who barter public
office or justice for money.   They are represented
as wallowing in pitch or tar;—a fit emblem of the
infamy which clings to the soul of him who, for
selfish ends, diverts the course of justice and moral
order.

> Marvellous darkness shadow'd o'er the place.
>   In the Venetians' arsenal as boils
> Through wintry months tenacious pitch, to smear
> Their unsound vessels ; for the inclement time
> Sea-faring men restrains, and in that while
> His bark one builds anew, another stops
> The ribs of his that hath made many a voyage,
> One hammers at the prow, one at the poop,
> This shapeth oars, that other cables twirls,
> The mizen one repairs, and main-sail rent ;
> So, not by force of fire but art divine,
> Boil'd here a glutinous thick mass, that round
> Limed all the shore beneath.

In the sixth chasm are plunged the Hypocrites,
whose punishment of everlasting weariness at being
doomed to bear the terrible weight of an assumed
character, is graphically symbolised :

There in the depth we saw a painted tribe,
Who paced with tardy steps around, and wept,
Faint in appearance and o'ercome with toil.
Caps had they on, with hoods that fell low down
Before their eyes, in fashion like to those
Worn by the monks in Cologne. Their outside
Was overlaid with gold, dazzling to view,
But leaden all within, and of such weight,
That Frederick's compared to these were straw.
Oh, everlasting wearisome attire !

From this gulf the poets climb, by a rugged and precipitous path, to the next bridge, where the seventh chasm bursts upon their view. Here, they see a gulf filled with the forms of men and serpents, the men being continually changed into serpents, and the serpents, in turn, transformed into men. This is the torture-house of Thieves :

We from the bridge's head descended, where
To the eighth mound it joins ; and then, the chasm
Opening to view, I saw a crowd within
Of serpents terrible, so strange of shape
And hideous, that remembrance in my veins
Yet shrinks the vital current. Of her sands
Let Libya vaunt no more : if Jaculus,
Pareas and Chelyder be her brood,
Cenchris and Amphisbæna, plagues so dire
Or in such numbers swarming ne'er she show'd,
Not with all Ethiopia, and whate'er
Above the Erythræan sea is spawn'd.

Amid this dread exuberance of woe
Ran naked spirits wing'd with horrid fear,
Nor hope had they of crevice where to hide,
Or heliotrope to charm them out of view.
With serpents were their hands behind them bound,
Which through their reins infix'd the tail and head,
Twisted in folds before. And lo ! on one
Near to our side, darted an adder up,
And, where the neck is on the shoulders tied,
Transpierced him. Far more quickly than e'er pen
Wrote O or I, he kindled, burn'd, and changed
To ashes all, pour'd out upon the earth.
When there dissolved he lay, the dust again
Uproll'd spontaneous, and the self-same form
Instant resumed.

One of the robber-spirits, confined in this dismal chasm, confesses to Dante,

" It grieves me more to have been caught by thee
In this sad plight, which thou beholdest, than
When I was taken from the other life.
I have no power permitted to deny
What thou inquirest. I am doom'd thus low
To dwell, for that the sacristy by me
Was rifled of its goodly ornaments,
And with the guilt another falsely charged.

In the following description of the weird transformation of men to serpents, we have a fine illustration of the wonderful imagination of the poet :

If, O reader ! now
Thou be not apt to credit what I tell,
No marvel ; for myself do scarce allow
The witness of mine eyes.   But as I look'd
Toward them, lo ! a serpent with six feet
Springs forth on one, and fastens full upon him :
His midmost grasp'd the belly, a forefoot
Seized on each arm (while deep in either cheek
He flesh'd his fangs) ; the hinder on the thighs
Were spread, 'twixt which the tail inserted curl'd
Upon the reins behind.   Ivy ne'er clasp'd
A dodder'd oak, as round the other's limbs
The hideous monster intertwined his own.
Then, as they both had been of burning wax,
Each melted into other, mingling hues,
That which was either now was seen no more.
Thus up the shrinking paper, ere it burns,
A brown tint glides, not turning yet to black,
And the clean white expires.   The other two
Look'd on, exclaiming, " Ah ! how dost thou change,
Agnello !   See !   Thou art nor double now,
Nor only one."   The two heads now became
One, and two figures blended in one form
Appear'd, where both were lost.   Of the four lengths
Two arms were made : the belly and the chest,
The thighs and legs, into such members changed
As never eye hath seen.   Of former shape
All trace was vanish'd.   Two, yet neither, seem'd
That image miscreate, and so pass'd on
With tardy steps.   As underneath the scourge
Of the fierce dog-star that lays bare the fields,
Shifting from brake to brake the lizard seems
A flash of lightning, if he thwart the road ;

So towards the entrails of the other two
Approaching seem'd an adder all on fire,
As the dark pepper-grain livid and swart.
In that part, whence our life is nourish'd first,
One he transpierced ; then down before him fell
Stretch'd out.   The pierced spirit look'd on him,
But spake not ; yea, stood motionless and yawn'd,
As if by sleep or feverous fit assail'd.
He eyed the serpent, and the serpent him.
One from the wound, the other from the mouth
Breathed a thick smoke, whose vapoury columns join'd.

.   .   .   .

. . . They in mutual guise
So answer'd, that the serpent split his train
Divided to a fork, and the pierced spirit
Drew close his steps together, legs and thighs
Compacted, that no sign of juncture soon
Was visible : the tail, disparted, took
The figure which the spirit lost ; its skin
Softening, his indurated to a rind.
The shoulders next I mark'd, that entering join'd
The monster's arm-pits, whose two shorter feet
So lengthen'd, as the others dwindling shrunk.
The feet behind them twisting up became
That part that man conceals, which in the wretch
Was cleft in twain.   While both the shadowy smoke
With a new colour veils, and generates
The excrescent pile on one, peeling it off
From the other body, lo ! upon his feet
One upright rose, and prone the other fell.
Nor yet their glaring and malignant lamps
Were shifted, though each feature changed beneath.

Of him who stood erect, the mounting face
Retreated towards the temples, and what there
Superfluous matter came, shot out in ears
From the smooth cheeks ; the rest, not backward
    dragg'd,
Of its excess did shape the nose ; and swell'd
Into due size protuberant the lips.
He, on the earth who lay, meanwhile extends
His sharpen'd visage, and draws down the ears
Into the head, as doth the slug his horns.
His tongue, continuous before and apt
For utterance, severs ; and the other's fork
Closing unites.   That done, the smoke was laid.
The soul, transform'd into the brute, glides off,
Hissing along the vale, and after him
The other talking sputters.

We have quoted this passage at length for a double reason. The emblematical character of the punishment is striking; the fear of capture; the fear of loss of freedom of action; the robbery of their physical form as they have robbed others; the serpentine disguise which they constantly exchange for their proper lineaments and garb ;—all, are strikingly symbolical of the state of soul of the thief.

But over and above this, there can be little doubt that Milton had these passages in mind when he wrote his description of the effect of Satan's speech in Pandemonium, in which he relates to his rebel

followers the incidents of the Fall of Man.   As he
concludes, he tells them :

>   "Ye have the account
> Of my performance ; what remains, ye Gods,
> But up and enter now into full bliss ? "
>   So having said, a while he stood, expecting
> Their universal shout and high applause
> To fill his ear ; when, contrary, he hears
> On all sides, from innumerable tongues
> A dismal universal hiss, the sound
> Of public scorn.   He wondered, but not long
> Had leisure, wondering at himself now more.
> His visage drawn he felt to sharp and spare,
> His arms clung to his ribs, his legs entwining
> Each other, till, supplanted, down he fell,
> A monstrous serpent on his belly prone,
> Reluctant, but in vain ; a greater power
> Now ruled him, punished in the shape he sinned,
> According to his doom.   He would have spoke,
> But hiss for hiss returned with forked tongue
> To forked tongue ; for now were all transformed
> Alike, to serpents all, as accessories
> To his bold riot.   Dreadful was the din
> Of hissing through the hall, thick-swarming now
> With complicated monsters, head and tail—
>
> .   .   .   .
>
>   .   .   .   greatest he the midst,
> Now Dragon grown, larger than whom the Sun
> Engendered in the Pythian vale on slime,
> Huge Python ; and his power no less he seemed
> Above the rest still to retain.   They all
> Him followed, issuing forth to the open field,

23

Where all yet left of that revolted rout,
Heaven-fallen, in station stood or just array,
Sublime with expectation, when to see
In triumph issuing forth their glorious Chief.
They saw, but other sight instead—a crowd
Of ugly serpents ! Horror on them fell,
And horrid sympathy ; for what they saw
They felt themselves now changing. Down their arms,
Down fell both spear and shield ; down they as fast,
And the dire hiss renewed, and the dire form
Catched by contagion, like in punishment
As in their crime. Thus was the applause they meant
Turned to exploding hiss, triumph to shame
Cast on themselves from their own mouths. There stood
A grove hard by, sprung up with this their change,
His will who reigns above, to aggravate
Their penance, laden with fair fruit, like that
Which grew in Paradise, the bait of Eve
Used by the Tempter. On that prospect strange
Their earnest eyes they fixed, imagining
For one forbidden tree a multitude
Now risen, to work them further woe or shame ;
Yet, parched with scalding thirst and hunger fierce,
Though to delude them sent, could not abstain,
But on they rolled in heaps, and, up the trees
Climbing, sat thicker than the snaky locks
That curled Megæra. Greedily they plucked
The fruitage fair to sight, like that which grew
Near that bituminous lake where Sodom flamed ;
This, more delusive, not the touch, but taste
Deceived ; they, fondly thinking to allay
Their appetite with gust, instead of fruit
Chewed bitter ashes, which the offended taste

With spattering noise rejected.   Oft they assayed,
Hunger and thirst constraining ; drugged as oft,
With hatefulest disrclish writhed their jaws
With soot and cinders filled ; so oft they fell
Into the same illusion, not as Man
Whom they triumphed once lapsed.   Thus were they
      plagued,
And, worn with famine, long and ceaseless hiss,
Till their lost shape, permitted, they resumed—
Yearly enjoined, some say, to undergo
This annual humbling certain numbered days,
To dash their pride, and joy for Man seduced.

But to return.

The poets now climb to the arch that overhangs
the eighth gulf, and from this point, see numberless
tongues of flame, wherein are punished all sorts of
Evil Counsellors, each flame encircling one wrong-
doer and symbolical of the evil tongue which is a
fire "set on fire by hell."

As in that season, when the sun least veils
His face that lightens all, what time the fly
Gives way to the shrill gnat, the peasant then,
Upon some cliff reclined, beneath him sees
Fire-flies innumerous spangling o'er the vale,
Vineyard or tilth, where his day-labour lies ;
With flames so numberless throughout its space
Shone the eighth chasm, apparent, when the depth
Was to my view exposed.   As he, whose wrongs
The bears avenged, at its departure saw
Elijah's chariot, when the steeds erect

Raised their steep flight for heaven ; his eyes, meanwhile,
Straining pursued them, till the flame alone,
Upsoaring like a misty speck, he kenn'd :
E'en thus along the gulf moves every flame,
A sinner so enfolded close in each,
That none exhibits token of the theft.

   ·   ·   ·   ·   ·   ·   ·

                   The guide, who mark'd
How I did gaze attentive, thus began :
"Within these ardours are the spirits, each
Swathed in confining fire."

In the next chasm, those are punished who have
started or fostered Schism in the Church, the State,
or the Family, represented by the rending of the
body by the religious schismatic; the dismember-
ment of the body by the political schismatic; and
the decapitation of the body by the schismatic of
kindred.

     Who, e'en in words unfetter'd, might at full
     Tell of the wounds and blood that now I saw,
     Though he repeated oft the tale ?   No tongue
     So vast a theme could equal, speech and thought
     Both impotent alike.

   ·   ·   ·   ·   ·   ·   ·

                A rundlet, that hath lost
     Its middle or side stave, gapes not so wide
     As one I mark'd, torn from the chin throughout
     Down to the hinder passage : 'twixt the legs
     Dangling his entrails hung, the midriff lay

Open to view, and wretched ventricle,
That turns the englutted aliment to dross.
    Whilst eagerly I fix on him my gaze,
He eyed me, with his hands laid his breast bare,
And cried, " Now mark how I do rip me : lo !
How is Mohammed mangled : before me
Walks Ali weeping, from the chin his face

        .   .   .   .   .   .

Cleft to the forelock ; and the others all,
Whom here thou seest, while they lived, did sow
Scandal and schism, and therefore thus are rent.
A fiend is here behind, who with his sword
Hacks us thus cruelly, slivering again
Each of this ream, when we have compast round
The dismal way ; for first our gashes close
Ere we repass before him.

        .   .   .   .   .   .

                        Another shade,
Pierced in the throat, his nostrils mutilate
E'en from beneath the eyebrows, and one ear
Lopt off, who, with the rest, through wonder stood
Gazing, before the rest advanced, and bared
His wind-pipe, that without was all o'ersmear'd
With crimson stain. " O thou ! " said he, " whom sin
Condemns not, and whom erst (unless too near
Resemblance do deceive me) I aloft
Have seen on Latian ground, call thou to mind
Piero of Medicina.

        .   .   .   .   .   .

I saw, and yet it seems to pass before me,
A headless trunk, that even as the rest
Of the sad flock paced onward. By the hair

It bore the sever'd member, lantern-wise
Pendent in hand, which look'd at us, and said,
"Woe's me!"   The spirit lighted thus himself;
And two there were in one, and one in two.
How that may be, he knows who ordereth so.
When at the bridge's foot direct he stood,
His arm aloft he rear'd, thrusting the head
Full in our view, that nearer we might hear
The words, which thus it utter'd : "Now behold
This grievous torment, thou, who breathing go'st
To spy the dead : behold, if any else
Be terrible as this.   And, that on earth
Thou mayst bear tidings of me, know that I
Am Bertrand, he of Born, who gave king John
The counsel mischievous.   Father and son
I set at mutual war.

The two poets now arrive at the bridge that
crosses the tenth, and last bolgia or chasm, where
Forgers and Falsifiers of every kind are suffering for
their misdeeds.   So loathsome is the sight, so dire
the stench, so loud the bitter wailing, that Dante has
"many a dart of sore lament" at the sight of this
lazar-house

We on the utmost shore of the long rock
Descended still to leftward.   Then my sight
Was livelier to explore the depth, wherein

.   .   .   .   .   .

All-searching Justice, dooms to punishment
The forgers noted on her dread record.

Here they

>   . . . languished through the murky vale,
> Up-piled on many a stack.   Confused they lay,
> One o'er the belly, o'er the shoulders one
> Roll'd of another ; sideling crawl'd a third
> Along the dismal pathway.   Step by step
> We journey'd on, in silence looking round,
> And listening those diseased, who strove in vain
> To lift their forms.

One of the horde of Alchemists, who is suffering from the foulest form of leprosy, symbolical of the superficial and polluting effect of his so-called art, tells the poet :

> "I am Capocchio's ghost,
> Who forged transmuted metals by the power
> Of alchemy ; and if I scan thee right,
> Thou needs must well remember how I aped
> Creative nature by my subtle art."

Adamo, a noted counterfeiter of Florence, whose body is swollen into a hideous mass by dropsy, the alloy of water in the blood being emblematical of his nefarious craft, exclaims, as the poets pass by,

>   "I falsified
> The metal with the Baptist's form imprest,
> For which on earth I left my body burnt.
>
>   .   .   .   .   .   .
>
>   I stamp'd
> The florens with three carats of alloy."

Elsewhere, those who have fraudulently person-
ated others are engaged in a never-ending and brutal
fight, symbolical of the violence done to personality
by counterfeiting it; while liars and false witnesses
for ever burn and rage with fever and delirium,
emblem of the hallucinations and despondent depths
that invariably accompany this species of Fraud.

Leaving this Circle, the poets, with the aid of
the giant Antæus, come to the ninth and last Circle
of Inferno, the Circle of *Treason*. In this, the
lowest Circle of deepest Hell, Traitors are eternally
imprisoned in ice, symbolic of the coldness and
deadness of feeling which is the characteristic of the
state of mind of those who are guilty of this transcendent crime. Dante tells us, that he saw before
and underneath his feet,

> A lake whose frozen surface liker seem'd
> To glass than water. Not so thick a veil
> In winter e'er hath Austrian Danube spread
> O'er his still course, nor Tanais far remote
> Under the chilling sky.
>
> .　　.　　.　　.　　.　　.
>
> Blue pinch'd and shrined in ice the spirits stood,
> Moving their teeth in shrill note like the stork.

In the first chasm of this Circle, Caïna (so named
from Cain), is punished treason or treachery towards
one's Family.

Two murderers, brothers and fratricides, especially attract the attention of Dante:

His face each downward held ; their mouth the cold,
Their eyes express'd the dolour of their heart.
    A space I look'd around, then at my feet
Saw two so strictly join'd, that of their head
The very hairs were mangled.   "Tell me ye,
Whose bosoms thus together press," said I,
"Who are ye?"   At that sound their necks they bent ;
And when their looks were lifted up to me,
Straightway their eyes, before all moist within,
Distill'd upon their lips, and the frost bound
The tears betwixt those orbs and held them there.

    They reply,

    " Not him, whose breast and shadow Arthur's hand
    At that one blow dissever'd ; "

i. e., not Modred, but two brothers who had murdered each other.

    As the poet is passing through the second chasm of ice, or valley of Antenora, where traitors to their Country are punished, he tells us,

                    A thousand visages
Then mark'd I, which the keen and eager cold
Had shaped into a doggish grin ; whence creeps
A shivering horror o'er me, at the thought
Of those frore shallows.   While we journey'd on
Towards the middle, at whose point unites

All heavy substance, and I trembling went
Through that eternal chilness, I know not
If will it were, or destiny, or chance,
But, passing 'midst the heads, my foot did strike
With violent blow against the face of one.

This shade and others are shown to have been guilty
of treachery to their native State or native land, and
to be suffering condign punishment.

Leaving the valley of Antenora, the two poets
pass to the next chasm, called Ptolemea, (perhaps
from Ptolemy the betrayer of Pompey), the region
where those are incarcerated who are guilty of
treachery under the mask of friendship and hospitality.

                    Onward we pass'd,
Where others, skarf'd in rugged folds of ice,
Not on their feet were turn'd, but each reversed.
   There, very weeping suffers not to weep ;
For, at their eyes, grief, seeking passage, finds
Impediment, and rolling inward turns
For increase of sharp anguish : the first tears
Hang cluster'd, and like crystal vizors show,
Under the socket brimming all the cup.
   Now though the cold had from my face dislodged
Each feeling, as 't were callous, yet me seem'd
Some breath of wind I felt. " Whence cometh this,"
Said I, " my Master ? Is not here below
All vapour quench'd ? "—" Thou shalt be speedily,"
He answer'd, " where thine eyes shall tell thee whence,
The cause descrying of this airy shower."

Friar Alberigo, whose soul is being punished in this chasm, asks Dante to help him open his frozen eyelids and tells him,

> .   .   . "that thou mayst wipe out more willingly
> The glazed tear-drops that o'erlay mine eyes,
> Know that the soul, that moment she betrays
> As I did, yields her body to a fiend
> Who after moves and governs it at will,
> Till all its time be rounded : headlong she
> Falls to this cistern."

At length, Dante and Virgil arrive at the fourth and last chasm, named Giudecca, so called from Judas Iscariot. In this region of eternal ice are imbedded those who are traitors to their benefactors, their monarch, or their God.

> Now came I (and with fear I bid my strain
> Record the marvel) where the souls were all
> Whelm'd underneath, transparent, as through glass
> Pellucid the frail stem.   Some prone were laid ;
> Others stood upright, this upon the soles,
> That on his head, a third with face to feet
> Arch'd like a bow.

At the bottom of this chasm,—at the very centre of Earth, or apex of the cone of Inferno,—wedged in eternal ice is Lucifer, the Arch-Traitor of the Empyrean.

            When to the point we came,
Whereat my guide was pleased that I should see
The creature eminent in beauty once,
He from before me stepp'd and made me pause.
     " Lo ! " he exclaim'd, " lo *Dis ;* and lo the place,
Where thou hast need to arm thy heart with strength."
     How frozen and how faint I then became,
Ask me not, reader ! for I write it not ;
Since words would fail to tell thee of my state.
I was not dead nor living.   Think thyself,
If quick conception work in thee at all,
How I did feel.   That emperor, who sways
The realm of sorrow, at mid breast from the ice
Stood forth ; and I in stature am more like
A giant, than the giants are his arms.
     Mark now how great that whole must be, which suits
With such a part.   If he were beautiful
As he is hideous now, and yet did dare
To scowl upon his Maker, well from him
May all our misery flow.   Oh what a sight !
How passing strange it seem'd, when I did spy
Upon his head three faces : one in front
Of hue vermilion, the other two with this
Midway each shoulder join'd and at the crest ;
The right 'twixt wan and yellow seem'd ; the left
To look on, such as come from whence old Nile
Stoops to the lowlands.   Under each shot forth
Two mighty wings, enormous as became
A bird so vast.   Sails never such I saw
Outstretch'd on the wide sea.   No plumes had they,
But were in texture like a bat ; and these
He flapp'd i' th' air, that from him issued still
Three winds, wherewith Cocytus to its depth

Was frozen. At six eyes he wept ; the tears
Adown three chins distill'd with bloody foam.
At every mouth his teeth a sinner champ'd,
Bruised as with ponderous engine ; so that three
Were in this guise tormented. But far more
Than from that gnawing, was the foremost pang'd
By the fierce rending, whence oft-times the back
Was stript of all its skin. " That upper spirit,
Who hath worst punishment," so spake my guide,
" Is Judas, he that hath his head within
And plies the feet without. Of th' other two,
Whose heads are under, from the murky jaw
Who hangs, is Brutus : lo ! how he doth writhe
And speaks not. The other, Cassius, that appears
So large of limb. But night now re-ascends."

Seeing the portal of a

                     . . . hidden way
My guide and I did enter, to return
To the fair world : and heedless of repose
We climb'd, he first, I following his steps,
Till on our view the beautiful lights of heaven
Dawn'd through a circular opening in the cave ;
Thence issuing we again beheld the stars.

The Satan of Milton is not only the fallen Archangel, he is the Prince of devils, presiding at the
Council of his infernal peers, defying the Almighty,
and devising schemes of warfare and "adequate
revenge" against his Sovereign's supreme authority.
The Lucifer of Dante, colossal as the foundation-

stone of Inferno, is powerless, speechless, hopeless; doomed to be so for all eternity, as the archetype of the deadly, unpardonable crime of high treason against his Maker, from whom he thought to wrench the sceptre of the Universe. Bereft of his pride, his ambition, and his former power, fettered and harmless, he stands the symbol of degradation and impotent hate.

Moreover, in Dante's description of Lucifer, he tell us:

> . . . Oh, what a sight!
> How passing strange it seemed, when I did spy
> Upon his head three faces: one in front
> Of hue vermilion, the other two with this
> Midway each shoulder joined and at the crest;
> The right 'twixt wan and yellow seemed; the left
> To look on, such as come from whence old Nile
> Stoops to the lowlands.

What a contrast! the anger, the envy, and the despair, emblematical of the threefold personality of Lucifer; and the love of the Father, the self-sacrifice of the Son, and the grace of the Holy Ghost, One God, whom the Arch-Traitor, in his haughty insolence, had defied!

CHAPTER IX.

Three Poetic Hells.

Conclusion.

THE modern traditional Hell of Milton has very little in common with the mediæval, philosophical Inferno of Dante.

As we pointed out in the last chapter, Dante collects and classifies all manner of wrong-doing, and all manner of states of the human soul before and after a guilty deed, and then paints a grand panorama of the punishments which follow those who are guilty of these evil deeds. But the poet, being Italian, adopts as the basis of his classification, the fundamental principle of Roman jurisprudence, namely, that the punishment inflicted for wrong-doing should be proportioned, not to its effects on the individual who commits it, or to the crime *per se*, but to its effects on Society at large. Hence, in the *Inferno*, treason against God or Universal order, meets with the direst punishment which the poet's imagination can depict. Treachery, Fraud,

and Violence are punished more severely than Anger
and Sullen Rage; and these, again, are more severely
punished than Avarice, Prodigality, Gluttony, and
Lust.

But Dante himself explains most fully this principle of punishment which characterises the *Inferno*.
Before passing to the seventh Circle, the two poets
rest behind a huge tomb,—the tomb of one of the
Popes,—in order to become accustomed to the fetid
exhalations rising from the abyss below. While
here, Virgil explains the principle or law of punishment which Dante adopts in his poem.

> Upon the utmost verge of a high bank,
> By craggy rocks environ'd round, we came,
> Where woes beneath, more cruel yet, were stow'd.
> And here, to shun the horrible excess
> Of fetid exhalation upward cast
> From the profound abyss, behind the lid
> Of a great monument we stood retired.
>
> .   .   .   .
>
> "My son! within these rocks," he thus began,
> "Are three close circles in gradation placed,
> As these which now thou leavest. Each one is full
> Of spirits accurst; but that the sight alone
> Hereafter may suffice thee, listen how
> And for what cause in durance they abide.
>   "*Of all malicious act abhorr'd in heaven,*
> *The end is injury;* and all such end
> Either by force or fraud works other's woe.

But fraud, because of man peculiar evil,
To God is more displeasing ; and beneath,
The fraudulent are therefore doom'd to endure
Severer pang.   The violent occupy
All the first circle ; and because, to force,
Three persons are obnoxious, in three rounds,
Each within other separate, is it framed.
To God, his neighbour, and himself, by man
Force may be offer'd ; to himself I say,
And his possessions, as thou soon shalt hear
At full.   Death, violent death, and painful wounds
Upon his neighbour he inflicts ; and wastes,
By devastation, pillage, and the flames,
His substance.   Slayers, and each one that smites
In malice, plunderers, and all robbers, hence
The torment undergo of the first round,
In different herds.   Man can do violence
To himself and his own blessings : and for this,
He, in the second round must aye deplore
With unavailing penitence his crime,
Whoe'er deprives himself of life and light,
In reckless lavishment his talent wastes,
And sorrows there where he should dwell in joy.
To God may force be offer'd, in the heart
Denying and blaspheming his high power,
And Nature with her kindly law contemning.
And thence the inmost round marks with its seal
Sodom, and Cahors, and all such as speak
Contemptuously of the Godhead in their hearts.
  "Fraud, that in every conscience leaves a sting
May be by man employ'd on one, whose trust
He wins, or on another who withholds
Strict confidence.   Seems as the latter way
24

Broke but the bond of love which Nature makes.
Whence in the second circle have their nest,
Dissimulation, witchcraft, flatteries,
Theft, falsehood, simony, all who seduce
To lust, or set their honesty at pawn,
With such vile scum as these.   The other way
Forgets both Nature's general love, and that
Which thereto added afterward gives birth
To special faith.   Whence in the lesser circle,
Point of the universe, dread seat of Dis,
The traitor is eternally consumed."

But there is another feature of Dante's philosophy to be noticed, before we shall be in a position to form an estimate of the relative grandeur of imagination, and depth of thought, of Dante and Milton.

According to Dante's philosophy, or rather his scholastic theology, a person's free-will may act in any one of three directions.   It may act in harmony with wrong-doing, which is the mental and spiritual state of Inferno; the deed itself producing the subjective environment of punishment.   Or, it may act in uniform opposition to wrong-doing, which is the mental and spiritual state of Paradiso; the deed itself producing a subjective environment of happiness.   Or, it may recoil from wrong-doing, when it sees the injurious effects upon Self and Society, which is the mental and spiritual state of

Purgatorio; when the free-will which has previously given a wrong bent to the character, strives, once again, to restore it to a normal state of rectitude.

In this way each created intelligence, by virtue of the possession of the gift of free-will, creates its own environment, through, and by means of, its social relations. Apart from the existence of free-will, Hell, Purgatory, and Paradise would be a Divine Comedy in a far different sense from that in which Dante uses the term.

Milton, as we have before pointed out, describes the punishment of Hell, only at the era of the fall of the great Archangel and of the Fall of Man; and before ever one of the human race had descended to his doom along the causey of Sin and Death. All that Milton professes to describe is the ultimate fate of *Satan*, and of the one rebellious third of the angelic host who joined him in his arch-treason.

The first strain in which Milton introduces, what he terms, "the deep tract of Hell," occurs in the opening of *Paradise Lost*, where the poet describes the expulsion of Satan from the Empyrean:

> Him the Almighty Power
> Hurled headlong flaming from the ethereal sky,
> With hideous ruin and combustion, down
> To bottomless perdition, there to dwell
> In adamantine chains and penal fire.

.   .   .   .   .   .

                    Hell at last,
Yawning, received them whole, and on them closed—
Hell, their fit habitation, fraught with fire
Unquenchable, the house of woe and pain.

.   .   .   .   .   .

            . . . o'erwhelmed
With floods and whirlwinds of tempestuous fire.

.   .   .   .   .   .

At once, as far as Angel's ken, he views
The dismal situation waste and wild.
A dungeon horrible, on all sides round,
As one great furnace flamed ; yet from those flames
No light ; but rather darkness visible
Served only to discover sights of woe,
Regions of sorrow, doleful shades, where peace
And rest can never dwell, *hope never comes*
That comes to all, but torture without end
Still urges, and a fiery deluge, fed
With ever-burning sulphur unconsumed.
Such place Eternal Justice had prepared
For those rebellious ; here their prison ordained
In utter darkness, and their portion set,
As far removed from God and light of Heaven
As from the centre thrice to the utmost pole.
Oh, how unlike the place from whence they fell ! *

At the conclusion of the first Council in Pandemonium, when Satan announces his determination
to attempt the great adventure, the heralds

* *Vide* Note J.

.   .   .   bid cry
With trumpet's regal sound the great result :

and,

.   .   .   the hollow Abyss
Heard far and wide, and all the host of Hell
With deafening shout returned them loud acclaim.
Thence more at ease their minds, and somewhat raised
By false presumptuous hope, the rangèd Powers
Disband ; and, wandering, each his several way
Pursues, as inclination or sad choice
Leads him perplexed, where he may likeliest find
Truce to his restless thoughts, and entertain
The irksome hours, till his great Chief return.
Part on the plain, or in the air sublime,
Upon the wing or in swift race contend,
As at the Olympian games or Pythian fields ;
Part curb their fiery steeds, or shun the goal
With rapid wheels, or fronted brigads form :
As when, to warn proud cities, war appears
Waged in the troubled sky, and armies rush
To battle in the clouds ; before each van
Prick forth the aery knights, and couch their spears,
Till thickest legions close ; with feats of arms
From either end of heaven the welkin burns.
Others, with vast Typhœan rage, more fell,
Rend up both rocks and hills, and ride the air
In whirlwind ; Hell scarce holds the wild uproar :—

.   .   .   .   .   .

Others, more mild,
Retreated in a silent valley, sing
With notes angelical to many a harp
Their own heroic deeds, and hapless fall

By doom of battle, and complain that Fate
Free Virtue should enthrall to Force or Chance.
Their song was partial; but the harmony
What could it less when Spirits immortal sing?)
Suspended Hell, and took with ravishment
The thronging audience.   In discourse more sweet,
(For Eloquence the Soul, Song charms the Sense,)
Others apart sat on a hill retired,
In thoughts more elevate, and reasoned high
Of Providence, Foreknowledge, Will, and Fate—
Fixed fate, free will, foreknowledge absolute—
And found no end, in wandering mazes lost.
Of good and evil much they argued then,
Of happiness and final misery,
Passion and apathy, and glory and shame :
Vain wisdom all, and false philosophy !—
Yet, with a pleasing sorcery, could charm
Pain for a while or anguish, and excite
Fallacious hope, or arm the obdurèd breast
With stubborn patience as with triple steel.
Another part, in squadrons and gross bands,
On bold adventure to discover wide
That dismal world, if any clime perhaps
Might yield them easier habitation, bend
Four ways their flying march, along the banks
Of four infernal rivers, that disgorge
Into the burning lake their baleful streams—
Abhorrèd Styx, the flood of deadly hate ;
Sad Acheron of sorrow, black and deep ;
Cocytus, named of lamentation loud
Heard on the rueful stream ; fierce Phlegeton,
Whose waves of torrent fire inflame with rage.
Far off from these a slow and silent stream,

Lethe, the river of oblivion, rolls
Her watery labyrinth, whereof who drinks
Forthwith his former state and being forgets—
Forgets both joy and grief, pleasure and pain.
Beyond this flood a frozen continent
Lies dark and wild, beat with perpetual storms
Of whirlwind and dire hail, which on firm land
Thaws not, but gathers heap, and ruin seems
Of ancient pile ; all else deep snow and ice,
A gulf profound . . .
               . . . the parching air
Burns frore, and cold performs the effect of fire.
Thither, by harpy-footed Furies haled,
At certain revolutions all the damned
Are brought ; and feel by turns the bitter change
Of fierce extremes, extremes by change more fierce,
From beds of raging fire to starve in ice
Their soft ethereal warmth, and there to pine,
Immoveable, infixed, and frozen round
Periods of time,—thence hurried back to fire.
They ferry over this Lethean sound
Both to and fro, their sorrow to augment,
And wish and struggle, as they pass, to reach
The tempting stream, with one small drop to lose
In sweet forgetfulness all pain and woe,
All in one moment, and so near the brink ;
But Fate withstands, and to oppose the attempt,
Medusa with Gorgonian terror guards
The ford, and of itself the water flies
All taste of living wight, as once it fled
The lip of Tantalus.   Thus roving on
In confused march forlorn, the adventrous bands,
With shuddering horror pale, and eyes aghast,

Viewed first their lamentable lot, and found
No rest. Through many a dark and dreary vale
They passed, and many a region dolorous,
O'er many a frozen, many a fiery Alp,
Rocks, caves, lakes, fens, bogs, dens, and shades of death—
A universe of death, which God by curse
Created evil, for evil only good ;
Where all life dies, death lives, and Nature breeds,
Perverse, all monstrous, all prodigious things,
Abominable, inutterable, and worse
Than fables yet have feigned, or fear conceived.

Such is Milton's conception of Hell ; a place of promiscuous punishment, comparative gaiety, and crude theological discussion.

Now and again the poet seems to have caught a glimmering of Dante's grand and awful conception of the Hereafter ; but it is only for the moment, and not even when this is the case does the thought colour, in any perceptible manner, his conception of what *punishment* really means.

Milton agrees with both Cædmon and Dante in representing *a sense of injury* as the permanent state of mind of those in Hell. They fail to regard suffering as the logical consequence of their own wrong-doing, and attribute it, solely, to the caprice and tyranny of the Supreme, or of Society.

The "Angel of Presumption," in the Anglo-Saxon poem, exclaims on reaching God's torture-house,

" This straitened place !
Oh ! how unlike those Heavenly seats where once
In Heaven's high Kingdom we as princes reigned !
But now expelled by Him, the Almighty One,
We never more can gain that cherished realm !
How deeply hath He wronged us, who in ire,
Pours the dread flames of this infernal gulf
In full upon us and denies us Heaven ! "

At the very opening of *Paradise Lost,* Satan, referring to his defeat in the Empyrean, exclaims,

      . . .   " who knew
The force of those dire arms ?   Yet not for those,
Nor what the potent Victor in his rage
Can else inflict, do I repent, or change,
Though changed in outward lustre, that fixed mind,
And high disdain from *sense of injured merit*
That with the Mightiest, raised me to contend."

So in the interview between the Arch-Fiend and his bastard offspring, Sin and Death, after the accomplishment of the Fall of Man, the Arch-Traitor compliments them on their great feat of erecting the adamantine causey and says,

" High proof ye now have given to be the race
Of Satan (for I glory in the name,
Antagonist of Heaven's Almighty King),
Amply have merited of me, of all
The Infernal Empire, that so near Heaven's door
Triumphal with triumphal act have met

Mine with this glorious work, and made one realm
Hell and this World—one realm, one continent
Of easy thoroughfare."

This thought lies at the very root of the *Inferno*,
and pervades every portion of the poem. The free-
will, in sympathy with wrong-doing, regards opposition as an injury to be resented, and, if possible, to
be revenged.

Moreover, the three leading features in Dante's
Inferno, the subjectivity of the punishment of
wrong-doing (although represented by material
imagery); the continuity of subjective punishment;
and the discrimination between the different grades
of wrong-doing (illustrated by the various Circles
and Chasms of Inferno), are but slightly recognised in *Paradise Lost*. The grand distinction
which Dante draws between the crime of the Arch-
Traitor and that of his willing dupes,—his rebel
host,—finds no place in Milton's poem. In the
Hell of *Paradise Lost*, all of the rebel host are
punished with torments of equal intensity; or, if
there is any discrimination, it is in favour of the
dread Emperor of Hell himself.

Dante places the Arch-Traitor at the deepest
point in Inferno, wedged in a cone of ice, and held
down by the weight of a hemisphere; while his
dupes are placed among the " Pusillanimous " in

the Vestibule, or ante-chamber, of Inferno ; the neutral region where neither pain nor happiness are possible.

Milton, on the contrary, makes his Satan a proud Archangelic knight, whose palace of Pandemonium eclipses in splendour,

> . . . the wealth of Ormus and of Ind,
> Or where the gorgeous East with richest hand
> Showers on her kings barbaric pearl and gold.

He is free in limb, as in will. He can indulge freely his passion for errantry and adventure. He can even pass through the Gates of Hell; or bend his flight down through the Starry Universe. He can gaze upwards into the dazzling light of the Empyrean. He can converse with Cherubim and Seraphim. And, if his lustre as an Archangel is obscured, he is still the idol of his lone tribe, the beloved, though dreaded, leader of the forces of Hell.

His followers, however, the dupes of his inordinate ambition, suffer a common punishment of alternate fire and ice, interspersed with songs of gallant deeds, or theologic talks, or trips of exploration amid the hills and valleys of the infernal regions.

In other words, the Miltonic Satan is fully justified in his opinion that

To reign is worth ambition, though in Hell :
Better to reign in Hell than serve in Heaven.

What the opinion of Satan's followers may have been on this subject we are left to conjecture.

The subjectivity of the punishment of Hell, (as contradistinguished from the materialistic imagery of fire and ice), can be distinctly traced in germ, at least, in *Paradise Lost*.

As soon as Satan recovers from the shock of his fall through Chaos, and sees his terrible surroundings, he exclaims :

> " Hail, horrors ! hail,
> Infernal World !   And thou, profoundest Hell,
> Receive thy new possessor—one who brings
> A mind not to be changed by place or time.
>
> .   .   .   .
>
> *The mind is its own place, and in itself*
> *Can make a Heaven of Hell, a Hell of Heaven*
> What matter where, if I be still the same,
> And what I should be, all but less than he
> Whom thunder hath made greater ? "

Subsequently when he arrives in Eden,

> Horror and doubt distract
> His troubled thoughts, and from the bottom stir
> The hell within him ; for *within him Hell*
> *He brings, and round about him, nor from Hell*
> *One step, no more than from himself, can fly*

By change of place.   Now conscience wakes despair
That slumbered ; wakes the bitter memory
Of what he was, what is, and what must be
Worse ; of worse deeds worse sufferings must ensue !—

.   .   .   .

" *Which way I fly is Hell ; myself am Hell ;*
And in the lowest deep, a lower deep
Still threatening to devour me opens wide,
To which the Hell I suffer seems a Heaven,"

.   .   .   .

But the hot hell that always in him burns,
Though in mid Heaven, soon ended his delight,
And tortures him now more, the more he sees
Of pleasure not for him ordained.

These two ideas of the subjectivity of the punishment of Hell, and of the equitable gradations of
these punishments, do not seem to have appealed
to the imagination of the stern, puritan poet.   It
took the keen, philosophical eye of the Italian to
interpret the meaning of the place where " their
worm dieth not and the fire is not quenched "; and
he performed the task with marvellous skill and
power.   Indeed, on this subject of Hell, Milton's
epic does not bear any comparison with Dante's
elaborate *Inferno.*

In the following passage, Milton seems to have
caught a glimpse, at least, of the subjectivity of
happiness as delineated in the *Paradiso.*   The Arch-

angel, after the Fall, while escorting the pair from
the garden of Eden, tells Adam that if he ascend
the successive terraces of the Christian virtues and
attain to the highest step, the terrace of *love* or
charity,

> .   .   .   " then wilt thou not be loth
> To leave this Paradise, but *shalt possess*
> *A Paradise within thee*, happier far."

But this harmony of the free-will of the created
being with right-doing or Universal Order, which is
the central thought in the *Paradiso*, finds but little
expression in Milton's description of the Empyrean,
where " hymning " seems to form the chief employ-
ment of the angelic hosts.

In another passage, Milton seems to have had in
mind Dante's conception of the state of mind of those
in Purgatory, as the recoil of the free-will from wrong-
doing and its striving after right-doing.   After the
expulsion of the rebel angels from the Empyrean,
the Almighty announces his intention to make

> Another world ; out of one man a race
> Of men innumerable, there to dwell,
> Not here, *till, by degrees of merit raised,*
> *They open to themselves at length the way*
> *Up hither, under long obedience tried,*
> *And Earth be changed to Heaven*, and Heaven to Earth,
> One kingdom, joy and union without end.

But being a good Protestant, and inheriting the Protestant tradition of hatred of every dogma of Catholicism, it stands to reason that Milton could not have intended to endorse any such heretical notion.

The influence of Dante's strong imagination, however, is evident throughout *Paradise Lost*. It is not plagiarism; it is not imitation; it is the effect that must necessarily follow from the contact of one powerful imagination, strong intellect, and deeply erudite mind, on that of another, in many respects, his equal. A poem, or any other work of art, on such a subject as this, if it is the production of a man of genius, expresses and must necessarily express, the highest and deepest in his philosophy of life, and its relations to the past, the present, and the hereafter. It must be a reflection of the artist's best self, and the mode or manner of such expression must be the only way in which he could possibly convey to the world what is in his deepest heart. If this is not the case, he is not a true artist. Cædmon in his Poem, Dante in his *Divina Commedia*, and Milton in his *Paradise Lost*, have given to the world, each in his own form, his philosophy with regard to some of the most profound problems that can exercise the mind of humanity. Each poem is coloured, it is true, by the temporal environment of

the writer.   The legendary and monastic bias of
Cædmon, the Catholic and scholastic bias of Dante,
and the puritanic and classic bias of Milton, are
evident in every page of their respective writings.
Yet, below and beneath all this, we find embedded
in these poems, thoughts that for ages have agitated
the universal soul of humanity.   The pictorial
clothing of these thoughts may vary with the era or
clime of the writer ; they may be tinged by passing
speculations in philosophy or theology ; they may
reflect current views in political or national life ;
they may even be besmirched with prejudice or personal affinities ; yet, underlying all this, we see the
world-thought and heart-aspiration of the human
race, standing out in bold relief, in spite of the in-
crustations of the human weaknesses of the writer.
The soul of a poet, to be a Cædmon, a Dante, or a
Milton must sympathise, and beat in harmony with,
the universal heart of mankind, irrespective of country or of creed or of any of the accidents of life.
The clear crystal current of sympathetic world-feel-
ing must show through all surface impurities, if the
writer would touch a responsive chord in readers,
not of one nation only, but of all nations.   And this
is what Cædmon, Dante, and Milton have done.   Cædmon, by the law of poetic selection, may have drawn
many of his pictures from the pages of Rabbinical

or Biblical writers; Dante may have culled largely
from the fertile soil of mediæval fiction and scholastic
speculation; Milton may have taken many a thought
or image from the pages of his predecessors, and
have rendered more beautiful, or the reverse, the
poetic conceptions of others; but this, far from entailing any charge offensive to literary genius or
reputation, brings the poet nearer to his environment, and enables us to see him in a truer light
than we otherwise should.

But, besides this, let the poet's environment be
what it may; let him assert his individuality in any
form that best suits his fancy; let him side with any
faction political or religious; let him, in other words,
be the creature of his surroundings and caprices, yet,
if he be a true poet, the underlying world-thought
of his poetic creation can be appreciated by every
philosophical mind throughout the entire world.
Let him be monastic, scholastic, puritanic, it matters
not. The inspiration of the true poet can be discerned beneath every one, and all, of these adven-
titious conditions.

The three poems that we have been considering,
taken collectively, form one of the most interesting
niches in the whole realm of literature. They present the poetic answer to *one* phase of the great
question of Man's relation to the Infinite. The

25

Epic of the Fall of Man, or *Paradise Lost*, involving as it does, the fall of the great Archangel from the Empyrean, is the poetic expression of an infinite Past (if we may use so illogical a term) ; and of the dawn of Evil in the world. The *Divina Commedia*, on the other hand, presupposing all this, is the poetic expression of an infinite Hereafter, an immortality in which the bent which the free-will has given to the character in the Present, will have its logical issue for ever.

The philosophy of the poet may be all wrong, but it is, at least, a poetic answer to a universal cry that comes welling up from the very depths of the great heart of humanity.

The more intently and minutely these works are studied, the more overpowering becomes the sense of the grandeur of the imagination displayed. Such works to be appreciated in all their wealth of metaphor and meaning, must be *studied*, not merely *read*. Then, as time wears on, the mind of the poet will stand out in a stronger and ever strengthening light, till at length, after years of pleasurable research, the student will come to see the production of the poet's brain in all its beauty of design and perfection of finish.

Genesis in lingua Saxonica

US IS RIHT MICEL ÐÆT

we rodera weard · wereda wuldorcining ·
wordum herigen · modum lufien · he is mægna sped ·
⁊ fruma heafod ealra heahgesceafta · frea ælmihtig ·
næs him fruma æfre · or geworden · ne nu ende cymþ ·
ecean drihtnes · ac he bið a rice · ofer heofenstolas ·
heagum þrymmum · soð ⁊ fæst · sigefolcum þrea þreagl bor ·
mær heold · þa wæron gesette · wide ⁊ side · þurh geweald
godes · wuldres bearnum · gasta weardum ·
hæfdon gleam ⁊ dream · ⁊ heora ordfruman · engla þreatas ·
beorhte blisse · wæs heora blæd micel ·
þegnas þrymfæste · þeoden heredon · sægdon lustum
lof · heora liffrean · demdon drihtenes · duge
þum · wæron swiðe gesælige · synna ne cuþon ·
firena fremman · ac hie on friðe lifdon · ece mid
heora aldor · elles ne ongunnon · ræran on roder
um · nymþe riht ⁊ soþ · ær ðon engla þreatas · þurh
ofer hygd · dæl on gedwilde · noldan drihtnes word ·
heora selfra geþeaht · ac hie of wlite curfon · godes an
dsacan · hæfdon gielp micel · þæt hie wið drihtne ·
dælan meahton · wuldor fæstan wic · werodes þrym
me · sið ⁊ swegltorht · him þær sar gelamp ·
æfst ⁊ ofer hygd · ⁊ þæs engles mod · þe þone unræd ·
ongan ærest fremman · wæfan ⁊ weccan · þa he worde
cwæð · niþes of þyrsted · þæt he on norð dæle ·

[Reduced fac-simile of the first page of the Junian Manuscript.]

CHAPTER X.

The Fall of Man. Translated from the Anglo-Saxon of Cædmon.

———

M OST right it is to chant the ceaseless praise
    Of Him who guards the starry heights of bliss
And ever, with enraptured hearts, adore
The Glory-King of Heaven's Angelic host.

In Him alone, the Lord Eternal, dwells
Might uncreated.   He is Head supreme
Of all exalted creatures.   He alone
Knew no beginning and shall have no end,
Holding for evermore Almighty sway
O'er Thrones and Principalities and Powers.   10

High in His Majesty, with Justice clothed,
Omnipotent to do His Sovereign will,
He ruled the Heavenly concaves, which at first,
By power divine, were stretched out far and wide
Throughout unbounded space, celestial Home
Of those who guard the spirits of the just.

Then, had the Angelic host triumphant joy
And in the light of God's eternal Throne
Found their one guerdon of allegiance.
20 Bright messengers were they of Heavenly love
Swift to perform God's will.   In blissful mood
They praised the Lord of Life, or prostrate fell
In deepest adoration at the feet
Of Him who made them, their eternal King,
And in obedience found their highest joy.

No deadly sin or lurking, traitorous thought
Had dared assault their hearts ; in peace they lived
With their All-glorious Chief, and naught save Truth
And holy Rectitude upreared its head
30 Within the sacred battlements of Heaven
Till he, who lifted high above his peers,
The Guardian Angel of the Angelic tribes,
Fell through accursèd pride.   Full many then,
Holding in light esteem celestial Love,
Forgat their highest Good.   Presumptuous,
They thought to war against Almighty God
And erelong share, with High Omnipotence,
The unfading glory of that peaceful realm
Its sceptre, crown and bright seraphic throng.

40 Vain was their hope, delusive was their dream ;
For in the stead of rebel victory and princely power,
Hatred and pride and racking pain befell

The rebel host, and such a rancorous mind
As he possessed who first moved discontent
And horrid discord.

                Then the Archangel spake,
His soul inflamed with dark, malicious thoughts :
" In the North part of God's sublime domain
Will I a kingdom found, a palace rear,
Such is my sovereign will."   50
                    Then was God wroth
With that rebellious host, whom at the first,
With Heavenly glory and Angelic mien
He had endowed.   Forthwith, in ire, He formed
A place of banishment, an exile-house,
Filled with deep anguish and with hellish groans
And direful punishments ; a fell retreat
For those who faithless proved to their high trust.

Deep was the torture-house and void of joys ;
Home of perpetual Night, with sulphur charged,   60
With fire and cold intense, with lurid flame
And black Tartarean smoke.   The cold, He bade,
And direful flames increase a thousand-fold
That by alternate tortures Hell itself
Might be henceforth doubly unbearable.

Then, through the rebel host could nought be heard
But horrid blasphemies and bitter cries
Against their righteous King, for taking thus

Grim retribution on His fallen foes ;
70 And in fierce raging mood each rebel sware
To wrest the Kingdom from Almighty God.

But when the Archangel's Sovereign high upreared
His mighty arm against that traitor band,
Their haughty boast deceived them, for the King
Sent terror in their hearts, and prone they fell
Powerless to fight.　For in His wrath He bent
Their vengeful pride, stripped them of might and
　　state
And hoped-for triumph.　Then as abject thralls,
Joyless and shorn of Heaven's effulgent crown,
80 They stood examples of presumptuous pride.
In purpose stern and with relentless hand
The Almighty strongly grasped and might have
　　crushed
And utterly destroyed His foe.　In lieu
He seized the realms and stately palaces
Their hands had reared, and from His Kingdom
　　hurled
The faithless tribe and sent them wailing forth
Down the dark, steep, unutterable path
That leads to Hell.　No longer might be heard
The scornful vaunt ; for now their grandeur turned
90 To deepest infamy, their beauteous forms
By sin defaced, they urged their darksome way
To darker punishment.　In torments dire

Accursed they dwelt.   No longer did they raise
The loud derisive laugh ; for ceaseless woe,
Deep racking pain, grief unassuageable
And hydra-headed torture, all around,
Enthroned in blackest darkness, mocked their cries ;
Just retribution for the unholy war
They thought to wage against Almighty God.

Then, once again, there reigned celestial Peace   100
Within the walls and battlements of Heaven.
The Great Supreme, to all His servants dear,
Increased their joys, and blissful harmony,
Throughout the loyal hosts of Heaven's domain,
Held undisputed sway.
                              Strife, Fear and Hate,
Offspring of traitorous and unholy thought,
From Heaven expelled, found refuge in the dark
And joyless shades of God's great torture-house.
And now, that broad domain of Heaven's fair realm,   110
The fairest and most powerful to move
Rebellious lust, in lonely grandeur stood ;
Its palaces so richly wrought and fair,
Conceived and fashioned by rebellious skill,
Stood tenantless.   Then thought the mighty God
How, once again, those bright Angelic seats
And beauteous realms, created by His will,
He might repeople with a better race

And nobler, than the vaunting myrmidons
120 Who lightly forfeited their heaven-born right.

Then Holy God resolved, beneath the vast,
Celestial firmament (tho' still within
His boundless realms), to form a beauteous World
With overarching skies and waters wide
And earthly creatures filled, in place of those
Whom headlong He had hurled from His abode.

As yet, was naught beneath God's radiant Throne
But gloom as dark as in the cavern reigns,
And this wide-spread Abyss stood deep and dim
130 In idle uselessness, distasteful sight
To Him the source of all-creative power.
The mighty King, in mind resolved, beheld
The joyless shade and saw the lowering cloud
Lie swart and waste, like an eternal sea
Of blackest Night, beneath the effulgent glow
Of Light ineffable ; till by the Word
And fiat of the King this World appeared.
Here the eternal Lord, Head of creation,
In the beginning shaped the Universe,
140 The sky upreared, and this fair spacious Earth
By His strong might was stablished evermore.
As yet, no verdure decked the new-born World ;
The Ocean far and wide, in deepest Night,

Concealed the Universe.   Then o'er the Deep
Was swiftly borne, on bright and radiant wing,
The Spirit of the Lord.   The mighty King
Bade Light come forth far o'er the spacious Deep,
And instantly His high behest was done,
And holy Light shone brightly o'er the waste
Fulfilling His command.   150
                In triumph then
He severed Light from Darkness and to both
The Lord of Life gave name ; and holy Light,
First born of all created things, beauteous
And bright, above all creatures fair
He called the Day.   Then was the Lord well-pleased
With this beginning of creative force,
For now He saw the black and swarthy Shade
Subsiding o'er the deep and wide abyss.
Then time passed o'er the quivering face of Earth,   160
And Even first, at God's command, dispelled
The radiant Day, till onward rolled the dark
And murky cloud which God Himself called Night,
Chasing away the Even's twilight gleam.
Thus, sundered by Almighty power, they stand
Subject to Heaven's decree, and evermore
Have done their Maker's will.
                        Pale, heavenly Light,
Succeeding Earth's first Darkness, ushered in
The second Day.   Then bade the Almighty King,   170
Forth from the bosom of the ocean flood,

Rise the bright framework of the glistening stars.
On every side the waters backward rolled,
And instantly, obeying God's command,
The mighty concave o'er the Earth rose high
A solid Firmament ; and the dark waves
Beneath the lofty vault of Heaven were reft
From those above, that all might dwell secure
Beneath God's wide, far-stretching canopy.

180 Then came the third great morn swift journeying
Athwart the Earth.   As yet the fruitful Land
And mighty Oceans had no settled bounds,
But all were covered with the common flood.
Swift went the fiat forth and straightway flowed
The surging waters where the Almighty willed,
And Land and Water parted as ordained.
Soon as the great Creator saw dry land
Rise from the mere, He called the dry land Earth,
Set to the waves and swelling flood their bounds
190 And fettered .   .   .

.   .   .   .

Then to the Guardian of the skies it seemed
Unfitting that the first-born of Mankind,
The trusted Keeper of the new-formed World,
Should longer dwell alone in Paradise.
To primal Man, God's well-belovèd son,
Was given a helpmate by his Sovereign Lord

As aid and comfort in his mortal life ;
For as he softly slept, the Almighty took
A rib from Adam's side, nor caused him pain
Since from the wound there flowed no drop of blood, 200
And therewith fashioned He a woman fair,
Inspired the form with life and placed within
A soul immortal, that at last, they seemed
Like to the Angels in their sinless youth
And peerless beauty clad.
                                        No evil thought,
No evil deed or sin-bred pain they knew,
But burning love, a love divine, possessed
Their spotless souls.   Then the Creator blessed
His latest triumph of creative might   210
With blessings large, and words full fraught with
        peace.
He blessed and said : " Teem now and multiply,
Fill with your heaven-born kin the verdant Earth ;
To you I give dominion o'er the Flood,
O'er all this vast creation sole control,
And in perpetual joy your days shall pass.
Hear, then, the mandate of Omnipotence ;
Whate'er the Ocean holds, whate'er the Earth
Brings forth of fowl or cattle or wild beast,
Whatever treads the Land or is endued   220
With mystic life, e'en whatsoever moves
Throughout the whale-path of the mighty Deep
All shall pay homage and obey your will."

Then the Creator gazed with blissful joy
Upon the grandeur of His new domain.
There stood, with beauty girt and filled with gifts,
Resplendent in the golden Light, Man's home
Of Paradise.   The running stream watered
The fruitful Land ; since wind and lowering cloud
230 With rain and tempest charged were yet unborn.
The kindly Earth, adorned with fragrant fruit,
Drank of the spring-fed brook.   For at the first
One stream alone of sparkling water flowed
Through Paradise ; whence issuing it formed
Four noble rivers spreading through the world.

     .   .   .   .

" All other trees enjoy, but from that one
Strictly abstain and evermore beware
Its luring fruit, lest it become erelong
Unholy source of still unholier lust."

240 They bowed their heads in deepest reverence
Before their Heavenly King and praised His name
In sweetest melody, for all that Love
Divine had wrought or Wisdom had prescribed.
Forthwith departed Heaven's eternal King
Leaving to Man the Garden as his home.
And evermore, performing Heaven's behests
They dwelt in holy joy, nor sorrow knew ;—
Dear to the Lord their Maker while they kept
Inviolate His high decree.

Of old, 250

The King Eternal by His sovereign Might,
Ordained ten Angel tribes, of equal rank,
With beauty, power and wisdom richly dower'd
And in this host Angelic, whom in Love
He moulded in His own similitude,
He evermore reposed a holy trust
To work His Will in loving loyalty,
And added of His grace, celestial wit
And bliss unspeakable.

One of the host 260

Angelic, He endowed with peerless might
And arch intelligence.   To him alone
The Lord of Hosts gave undisputed sway
O'er all the Angel tribes, exalted high
Above all Principalities and Powers
That next to God Omnipotent he stood,
O'er all created things, lone and supreme.
So heavenly fair and beauteous was his form,
Fashioned by God Himself, that by compare
Less glorious spirits grew dim; e'en as the stars 270
In God's Fixed Belt pale in the glowing light
Of more resplendent Spheres.

Long had he reigned,

August Vicegerent of the Heavenly King,
But for presumptuous Pride which filled his heart
With dire ingratitude and hostile thoughts
Against the eternal Throne.   Then silent stood

The great Archangel 'mid the Heavenly choir.
No grateful anthem rose in meet return
280 For gifts divine.   No joyful antiphon
Burst forth responsive from his guilty lips.
Nor was it hid from God's omniscient eye
That His Archangel, though belovèd still,
Began to harbour dark, presumptuous thoughts
And in rebellion rise against his God
With words of pride and hate.

                  For thus he spake
Within his traitorous heart :

                  " No longer I,
290 With radiant form endowed and heavenly mien,
Will brook subjection to a tyrant God
Or be His willing slave.   Such power is mine,
Such goodly fellowship, I well believe
'T is greater e'en than God's own following."
With many a word of bold defiance, spake
The Angel of Presumption ; for he hoped
In Heaven to rear a more exalted throne
And stronger, than the seats he now possessed.
Then moved by traitorous guile he built in thought
300 Vast palaces within the Northern realm
And richer Western plains of Paradise,
And evermore he lived in doubtful mood
Whether 't were better in acknowledged war
To risk his high estate, or prostrate fall
Mock-loyal as his God's inferior.

At length the Archangel spake :

" Why should I toil

Who stand in need of no Superior?

Marvels as great, ay, greater in renown,

Can I perform than our Omnific Chief ; 310

A Godlier throne than His and more sublime

Can I unaided rear. Why, as a slave

Dependent on his lord for worthless gifts,

Should I His will obey and bow the head

In abject vassalage as to a King?

I, too erelong may be a God as He !

Around me, even now, are strong allies

Who will not fail me in the crucial strife ;

Unflinching heroes, warriors of renown,

Who with accordant and full-tongued assent 320

Made me their chosen Chief. Such trusty friends,

With zeal inflamed and bound by common ties

To strict fidelity, will counsel well

And lure adherents from the opposing ranks.

Then, if I win this realm, I may become

The Angels' Chieftain, Sovereign of the skies.

Why should I then cringe to Almighty God

Who does me grievous wrong? I am resolved,

No longer will I be His vassal slave."

When the All-powerful, in secret knew 330

The great presumption of his Angel-chief

And how, by folly moved, he sought to stir

Unholy war within His joyous realm,
The mighty God was wroth and straightway doomed
The apostate Fiend to expiate his crime
With sufferings greater than all mortal ills.
(For Love divine was turned to sacred Hate)
And heavenly Justice hurled him from his throne
And cast him headlong down the burning gulf
340 Which leads to deepest Hell.

      For three long days
And three successive nights the Apostate fell
Together with his lone rebellious tribe,
And all thenceforth to demons were transformed
And doomed triumphless to the swart Abyss.
There on the approach of each returning eve
The fires, rekindled, fiercely rage anew,
And Night appears immeasurably long.
Then ere the dawn leads back the joyless light,
350 Sharp biting cold and glacial blasts attack
Their fervid forms, and evermore they writhe
In lurid torture or deep, piercing cold.

Such were the apostate fiends, who at the first
Filled Hell's abyss, and such their punishment.

But erelong deep remorse and envious thought
Made willing captive each rebellious heart ;
For while the false Archangel and his band
Lay prone in liquid fire, scarce visible

Amid the surging clouds of rolling smoke
And deep infernal gloom, the Angelic host   360
Who fell not from their love still held far off
The empyreal battlements of Heaven.
This, then perceived the traitorous fiends in Hell,
And in one moment stood their folly bare
In having thus exchanged celestial bliss
For the unending torments which their pride
And groundless arrogance had thus entailed.

Then spake the haughty One, who erst in Heaven
O'er all the Angelic hosts most brightly shone,
Fairest of all God's creatures, most beloved   370
By Him who made him, till by folly moved
He warred against the Almighty.   Then the Lord
In angry mood hurled him from Heaven's heights
And gave the Fiend a name by which thenceforth
Throughout all ages he should e'er be known
Satan, the enemy of God and Man.
Then the Almighty bade this trenchant Foe
Rule o'er the swart Abyss and ne'er again
Presume with Him to wage unequal war.

Then Satan sorrowing spake :   380
               " This straitened place !
Oh ! how unlike those Heavenly seats where once
In Heaven's high Kingdom we as princes reigned !
But now expelled by Him, the Almighty One,

26

We never more can gain that cherished realm !
How deeply hath He wronged us, who in ire
Pours the dread flames of this infernal gulf
In full upon us and denies us Heaven !
That Heaven alas ! which by divine decree
390 Is destined for Mankind. 'T is this most grieves
My anxious heart, that earthborn Man should hold
My glorious seat and dwell in endless joy
While we in Hell's avenging horrors pine.
Oh ! that my hands were free ! that I might hence
But for a moment, for a winter's day ;
Then with this host would I—but now these chains
Press on me and these iron bands embrace !
Oh ! I am kingdomless ! Hell's fetters cling
Hard on each limb. Above, beneath, the flame
400 Fierce rages. Sight more horrible mine eyes
Ne'er yet have witnessed. O'er these scorching
    deeps
The fire no respite knows. The strong forged chain
With ever-biting links forbids my flight.
My feet are bound, my hands are manacled ;
Around my neck is forged this lattice-belt
Of iron strangely wrought by Angel-skill ;
And e'en the pathway to the gates of Hell
Lies thick beset with foul and horrid Shapes
That bar all exit. In this loathsome den
410 We, princes once, chained by a Tyrant's whim
Now suffer chastisement for fancied wrong.

'T is true we may not vent our dire revenge
On Him who thus denies us Heavenly light
And show our godlike strength in open war ;
Yet may we foil His will.

     " He hath devised,
'Twixt this swart Gulf and our ancestral Seats,
A beauteous World, if rumour be believed,
And hath already formed to dwell therein
A race with high intelligence endowed   420
And fashioned in His own similitude.
With this, His mignon tribe, He purposes
To fill the realms which our dread overthrow
And cruel fall left vacant. Here then lies
Our only hope of adequate rev ge , —
To ruin, if we may, this new-born Man
And on his race, eternal woe entail.
'T is futile now to cherish idle dreams
That God will e'er repent Him of His ire
Or soon restore the thrones and matchless realms   430
Which He has once usurped. Vain is the attempt
To move the Victor's mind. Whate'er we lost
Is lost beyond recall. Naught now remains
But to devise a scheme by which to thwart
The Victor's known intent and deftly strive
That Man possess not our escheated realm,
But urged by subtle craft to disobey
The stern command of his despotic God,
Forfeit celestial Grace. Then will He cast

440 These faithless creatures from His fickle heart,
And in one moment hurl them from their height
Of stainless bliss, down to this dark abode
To share our bitter torment and become
Our vassal slaves.

    " Begin we then, consult
About this war.

     " If I, of old, gave aught
Of princely treasure or rich recompense
To any warrior of my valiant host,
450 While still we held our regal eminence,
With naught more grateful could he now repay
My former favour than by speedy help,
And, passing hence through Hell's grim barriers,
Soar upward through the clouds on mighty wing
To Earth's dominion where, in bliss enthroned,
This new-born Being reigns ; while we are doomed
To bear the torture of this prison-house.
As yet in God's esteem this Adam stands
Pre-eminent, and may erelong possess,
460 (For so it is decreed,) our rightful realm.
If any one of this my sovereign host
Can counsel and devise a crafty plan
To lure his soul from loyal obedience,
Then shall he be most hateful to his Lord ;
His weal shall cease and some fell punishment
Become his lot.

    " Deeply in mind revolve

How he may be beguiled.   If he but fall,
Then shall I rest me in these chains content
And he, the daring one, who first proclaims   470
The fall of Man, seduced by crafty words,
I swear, by my eternal majesty,
Shall be exalted to the second throne
In Hell's dominion, and rewarded be
With whatsoe'er of state or wealth or power
In future ages may be proudly won
Within this fiery realm."

.   .   .   .

Without delay, the apostate Angel donned
His glistening arms ; and tightly on his head
His helmet bound, secured with many a clasp.   480
Thus armed, and with a heart deep-versed in guile
He started on his fatal enterprise.
High toward the fiery concave first he shot,
A spiral column bright with lurid flame
Showed where he took his flight.   The gates of Hell
Were quickly left behind as lion-like
In strength and desperate in fiendish mood
He dashed the fire aside.   The farthest bounds
Of that infernal kingdom passed, he urged
His venturous flight, tho' now with easier wing.   490
E'en as he upward sped, his crafty mind
Unceasingly revolved the subtlest words
Of specious flattery with which to lure,
To wicked deeds and deepest infamy,

The spotless subjects of the eternal King.
Onward he took his way and soon descried,
Far off the trembling light of this fair World.
Arrived, at length, he trod with fiendish joy
The verdant paths of Man's primeval home
500 Impatient, now to prove his mission crowned
With dark success.
           Erelong amid the shade
Of Eden's fair wide-spreading foliage,
He saw the parents of Mankind ; the Man
Whose comely form bespoke a wise design ;
And, by his side, radiant with guileless youth,
His God-created Spouse.   Above them spread
Two Trees rich-laden with immortal fruit,
The Trees of Life and Death implanted there
510 By Power divine, that Man might freely choose
Unending weal or never ceasing woe.
Far different were their fruits !   The one was fair
And glistening to the sight ; to touch most soft
And delicate.   Such was the Tree of Life.
And whosoever ate thereof should live
For evermore, neither by Age impaired,
Nor grievous sickness harmed, but live his life
And pass his days in joy ; and e'en on Earth
Should dwell beneath the smile of Heaven's high
      King,
520 And going hence in peace, should have decreed
Such honours as high Heaven alone can give.

Swarth was the other fruit and dim and dark
That on the Tree of Death hung temptingly,
Full fraught with bitterness. (For mortal man
Must know the Evil and the Good.) And he
Whoe'er should taste the baleful fruit that grew
On this accursèd Tree, his doom assured,
Must ever after live a life of pain
And sweating of the brow and sorrow dire.
Old age would from him take all youthful joys,⠀⠀⠀530
Bold deeds and lordly power, and at the last,
E'en Death would be one portion of his doom.
Awhile he might enjoy the carnal bliss
Of mortal life ; then seek that darkest land
With lurid flames illumed and be the slave
Of fiends—the direst danger of Mankind
And most enduring.
⠀⠀⠀⠀⠀⠀⠀⠀This the Foe well knew,
Satan's dark messenger who warred with God.
Then in the body of a worm he twined⠀⠀⠀540
With devil's craft around the Tree of Death,
Took of the fruit and turned his wily form
To where he knew the beauteous handiwork
Of Heaven's eternal King would surely be.
Then spake the Enemy his primal word—
A query charged with lies :
⠀⠀⠀⠀⠀⠀⠀⠀"Cravest thou aught,
O Adam, from thy God ? Hither I come
Journeying from far to bring thee His behest.

550 But little time has flown since at His side
     I sat, and then He bade me quickly hie
     To Earth with His command, that of this fruit
     Thou shouldest eat, since thus thy power and skill
     And mental grasp far greater will become,
     More radiant still thy body, and thy form
     More beauteous than before.   If aught there is
     Of treasure in the World, (so spake the King),
     E'en this shall not be wanting thy desire
     When once thy ready mind hath wrought this act
560 Of loyal obedience to the sovereign word
     Of Heaven's King, and thou in gratitude
     Hast served thy Master's will and made thee dear
     To thine own Lord.
               " I heard Him as He sat
     In dazzling brightness, praise thy deeds and words
     And speak about thy life, so must thou now
     Fulfil whate'er commands His Angel brings
     To Earth.
             " In this thy World are regions broad
570 And green and thou art lord of this domain ;
     But in the realm of Heaven, God rules supreme.
     The Lord of Men, All-powerful on High
     Deigns not at times to visit Man, but sends
     His vassals forth to speak on His behalf.
     He bids thee now by me, His messenger,
     True wisdom learn and zealously obey
     His Angel's word.   Take then this fruit in hand

Bite it and taste ; thy mind will be enlarged
Thy form far fairer, for the Sovereign God
Thy Lord, Himself this help hath sent to thee   580
From Heaven's high Kingdom."

                    Then Adam spake :
(The God-created Man majestic stood)
" When here I heard the mighty God, the Lord
Of Triumph, speak in strong and trenchant tones,
Bidding me keep inviolate His commands
And gave this bride, this Wife of beauteous mien,
To be the sharer of my blissful home,
He charged me to beware lest through deceit
My will should be seduced and I should taste   590
The Tree of Death ; since he who near his heart
Should cherish aught of sin should meet his doom
In blackest Hell.

            " I know not (since with lies
Thou mayest come and dark designing thought)
Whether or not thou art in very deed,
A messenger from Heaven ; for to say truth,
Naught do I recognise in all thy words
Or ways or subtle hints—naught do I see
In this thy journey here, or in thy speech   600
To prove thy mission true.

                " I know full well
What He Himself, the great Protector, said
When last I saw Him here, that all His words
Should be revered and cherished lovingly

And all His precepts strictly be obeyed.—
Unlike art thou to any of His host
That ever I have seen, nor dost thou show
E'en slightest token from our gracious Lord,
610 Assuring pledge of His divine command.
Thee, I will ne'er obey, so hie thee hence.
In the Almighty God, who wrought me thus
With His creative arms and placed me here
With loving hands, in Him I firmly trust.
From His high Realm, if such His sovereign Will,
He can endow His creatures with all good
Without His vassal's aid."

                Then turned the Fiend
In wrathful mood, and saw, not far away,
620 The Woman's perfect form, the beauteous Eve.
And feigning deep regret expressed a fear
Lest direst ills from henceforth should befall
Their farthest offspring through the guilty words
Her spouse had breathed :

                " Full well I know," said he,
" Our Sovereign God will justly be incensed
When, this long journey done, this tedious path
Retraced, your stubborn message I relate ;
That ye, His creatures, dare to disobey
630 Whate'er commands He now hath hither sent
From His far Eastern Throne.   Now must He come
In person to demand your quick response,
Since I, His messenger, am powerless

To carry out the task.   And this, I fear,
Will draw upon yourselves the silent ire
Of mighty God.   But if thyself wilt bow,
With willing mind submissive, to my word
'T were easy to devise the ready way.
Ponder within thy breast, that from you both
Thou may'st avert this dire, impending woe,   640
If thou wilt do as I shall now advise :
Eat of this fruit ; then will thy sight be clear
To see forthwith widely o'er all this World ;
And e'en beyond, thy sight shall pierce and see
The Throne of God Himself, and thou shalt dwell
Within the radiance of Heavenly Grace.

   If thou should'st gain the love of thy dear lord
And win his trust in all that thou dost say,
In after days thou mayest rule thy spouse.
Disclose to him the thoughts that burn e'en now   650
Within thy breast, and why thou hast performed,
By my advice, the mandate of thy God ;
Then will he quit, at once, the hateful strife
And evil answer which now rage within
The caverns of his heart.   Let us forthwith
With singleness of aim approach thy lord ;
Do thou with cautious zeal urge him to heed
And follow thy advice lest ye become
Most hateful to your Lord.
                  " If thou succeed   660
In this thine enterprise I will conceal,

O best of Womankind, from our great King
The idle words and slanders of thy lord ;
How he accused God's messenger of lies
Ay, and falsely said that I am eager
For the wrong, an ambassador of wrath
And not God's messenger.

                    "Would that he knew
My true celestial rank ; for I can tell
670 The origin of all the Angel-tribes ;
And on the vaulted dome of Heaven have gazed ;
And many an æon I, with eager will
And faithful mind, have served the mighty King
The Lord Himself. Unlike indeed am I
To Man's Arch-enemy !"

                        Thus did he lead
The Woman on with lies, and with his wiles
Allured her to that wrong ; until at length
The Serpent's counsel, deep down in her heart
680 Began to rage, (to her a weaker mind
Had the Creator given,) and now her mood
Thus straitly pressed by fiendish skill, gave way,
And from his hand she took the noxious fruit
Culled from the Tree of Death, and thus defied
The Lord's express command.

                      No greater sin
Had e'er been traced for Man than this dread
    breach
Of human loyalty.

Great wonder 't is
That Holy God should even now permit 690
His children's guileless hearts to be ensnared
With specious lies by reason of the Fall.

The fruit she ate, God's will defied and broke
His just command.

            And now with vision clear,
(Usurious gift of that malignant Foe),
Her strengthened sight pierced far and wide. All
    things
In Heaven and Earth far fairer seemed to her,
The World more beauteous and the works of God
Grander and mightier than e'er before. 700
'T was not by Man's device that she beheld
This wondrous change ; but that foul wretch beguiled
Her soul with studious care and deftly raised
The vision in her mind, so that she seemed
To see thus far o'er Heaven's extended realm.
Then spake the Fiend in secret hate : ('T was not
Her weal he sought with these fair sounding words)
" I need not tell thee, since thyself can'st see,
O Eve the Good, that since thou hast believed
My words to thee, and heeded my advice 710
No form or beauty can with thine compare.
This glorious Light, gift of a loving God,
Which I have brought, bright with the glow of
    Heaven,

Now shines before thee far along thy path
And bathes thy glistening form in golden mist
So thou may'st touch its rays.

              " Go, tell thy lord
What visions thou hast seen, what wondrous powers
My coming has revealed ; and if, e'en now
720 With modesty of mind he will obey,
The counsel that I bring, I will bestow
On him, with generous hand, that goodly Light
Which now adorns thyself.   Nor will I e'er
Reproach him for the slanders that he spake,
Unworthy though he be of pardoning grace,
For such malicious charges as he made ;—
Thus shall thy offspring ever rule their lives ;
When they do evil then shall they repent
And working works of Love avert the curse
730 Of Heaven's High King and thenceforth win His
        Grace."

Then turned she to the spot where Adam stood,
She who was fairest of all Womankind,
Most beauteous of all who e'er were born
Into this World, the handiwork of God
Himself ;—though even then unconsciously
She was undone, misled by crafty lies,
That through the Fiend's device they both might be
Hateful to God, and, through the Devil's wiles,
Lose their estate, the favour of their Lord

And forfeit Heaven's realm. 740

                   Many a time
It bodes dire woe to Man to take no heed
Of kindly warning while he has the power.

In her hands she bare the accursèd fruit,
Some on her bosom lay, that fruit which erst
The Lord of Lords strictly forbade her touch,
Fruit of the Tree of Death.

                 The glorious Chief
Had graciously revealed His will to Man,
His earthly vassal, that he might avoid 750
The greater Death. The Holy Lord prepared
For all mankind a Heavenly realm, enriched
With wide-spread bliss, if they would but forbear
To touch the fruit with bitterness fulfilled
Which hung from that fell tree, the Tree of
    Death ;
'T was this the Lord forbade.

                The foe of God,
Inspired by hate of Heaven's eternal King,
Enticed her then with lies. The woman's mind
And weaker thought fell, powerless to resist. 760
Now she began to trust his words and do
As he desired, in full believing trust,
That from her God in truth, those mandates came
Brought by the Fiend and urged so warily
With lying word and token, and his pledge

Of loyal affection and fidelity.

Then to her spouse she spake :
                              " This goodly fruit
O Adam, mine own lord, is sweet indeed
770 And pleasant to the sense ; and sure I am
That this bright messenger in very deed
Is God's good Angel, for I clearly see,
E'en in his garb, the envoy of our Lord
The King of Heaven.   Surely 't is better far
To gain his favour than his hate.   If thou
Spake aught this day to him in bitter scorn
He will forgive thy haste, if once we show
Obedience to his word.   Will hateful strife
With God's own messenger avail thee aught ?
780 We need his kindly offices to bear
Our errands to the All-powerful King of Heaven.
The promise which he gave of heavenly Light
And keener vision of the Universe
He hath fulfilled.
                    " E'en now can I discern
Where the Almighty dwells, enthroned in bliss,
Creator of the world !   And I can see
The Angelic host revolve with trembling wing
Around the Throne, of all created things
790 The greatest and most joyous company.
Who could bestow on mortal man the gift
Of such far-seeing sense but God alone,

The Ruler of the skies ?   And I can hear
From farthest point, throughout this great, wide
    world ;
And I can see o'er all the broad expanse
Of Earthly things.   And I can plainly hear
The music of the Spheres, as heard in Heaven.
Soon as I tasted this delicious fruit
All became sudden Light within the mind
And all without was Light.   800
                 " I have it here,
Mine own good lord, here in my hand, and fain
Would give it thee, my first most precious gift.
From all this messenger, with cautious words,
Lately unfolded to my wondering mind,
I doubt not that it comes brought here from God
With His command.   No likeness does it bear
To aught else on this Earth, but as I learn
(So saith this messenger) it comes direct
From God."   810
        Oft did she speak to him and urged
Him all the livelong day to that dark deed,
To break their Lord's command.
                 Meanwhile, near by,
Hell's Envoy stood, inflaming his desires
And urging him with wiles ; and followed him
With dark intent.   The Foe was near at hand,
He who had come from far, alone to wage
That danger-fraught campaign.

820   Much studious care
Had he bestowed in order to corrupt,
Mislead, and in the end to lure Mankind
Into the greater Death, that they might lose
The Almighty's promised gift, the lordly power
O'er Heaven's domain.
                    Well the Hell-miscreant knew,
When he seduced with lying words and looks
The beauteous Eve, the fairest of her race,
And bent her thought to work his evil aims
830 So that henceforth she spake his hellish will
And helped to ruin God's own handiwork,
Full well he knew that they must needs endure
God's righteous ire and endless pains of Hell
And dungeon-punishment, since God's command
They thus had disobeyed.
                    Then to her lord
Full oft she spake, fairest of Womankind,
Until at length his mind was full of doubt
From trusting to the promises she made
840 Of Light and widened vision of the World.
(But all she did was done with true intent.)
As yet she knew not that so many ills
And sinful woes must follow to Mankind
Because she deemed it wise to heed the words
Of that false messenger.   For she believed
That in the revelations which she made
To Adam's listening ear she but disclosed

A token from on High and wrought the Will
Of their exalted King.
$\qquad$ Then in his breast $\qquad$ 850
The mind of Adam changed, and all his heart
Went forth to do her will. From Eve's own hand
He took both Death and Hell ; for such it was
Though in the form of fruit. Beneath it lurked
The dream of Death, the Devil's artifice,
And loss of Eden and Eternal woe
With ruin of Mankind. Such was the food
Unholy fruit !
$\qquad$ Thus came the curse within
And stained the heart ! $\qquad$ 860
$\qquad$ Then gaily laughed the Fiend,
The bitter-purposed messenger of Hell ;
And making sport of his infernal deed
Promised to take the grateful thanks of both
To his liege Lord !
$\qquad$ His errand done, and crowned
With fell success, his fiendish joy broke forth
In deep soliloquy, addressed to him
Who reigned in Hell :
$\qquad$ " Now have I full discharged 870
The honoured trust to me decreed by fate,
Thy will performed ; for many a day to come
Are men seduced, this Adam and this Eve !
And now that through my counsel they have mocked
The orders of their King, their certain doom

3

Is the withdrawal of His love ; and hence
No longer may they claim that heavenly Realm,
But must perforce their darksome journey take
To Hell's abyss.   Surely thou need'st not bear
880 Deep sorrow in thy heart, though straitly bound
In chains ; nor mourn that here on Earth man
  dwells
In highest bliss while we, wrongly deprived
Through thy great pride, of those high palaces
And goodly courts where once we dwelt, are doomed
To naught but punishment and endless woes,
A land of darkest Night.
      " For God's fierce ire
Was stirred against us, in that we disdained,
E'en at the Court of Heaven, to bow the head
890 In mock subjection to the Holy Lord.
Nor was it congruous to our high estate
To serve in vassalage.   'T was this that made
The Almighty wrath of mood and stern of mind
So that, at length, He drove us down to Hell,
Felled in deep-scorching flames, and once again
Reared in His heavenly Realm, celestial Seats
The heritage of Man.
      " So let thy heart
Rejoice, since here on Earth both of thy dreams
900 Are now fulfilled, and all the sons of Man
Their heavenly heritage and fair domain
Will lose, and full of hate, will be thy slaves

In yonder flames.   Nor ends our victory here.
Much sorrow of the heart have we entailed
On God Himself.   Whate'er of misery
We must endure, is now on Adam's race
Fully avenged.   God's sovereign hate assured,
And the dire ruin of all humankind,
With pain of Death, my wounded pride is healed.
Around my heart great thoughts revolve. The wrongs 910
We long have borne, fruit of relentless spite,
Are all avenged.

        " At once will I retrace
My joyous steps back to the lurid flames
And seek the spot where Satan straitly bound
With tightly-woven chains, a captive lies
In darkest Hell."

        Then swiftly downward sped
That direst messenger of woe, and passed
The gates of Hell ; thence urged his toilsome way 920
Through the expanse of flame and reached at length
The point where Satan lay, his lordly Chief,
With fetters bound.

        Meanwhile, great sorrow filled
The guilty heart of Adam and his Spouse,
And oft between them words of sadness passed,
For much they feared the anger of their Lord
And Heaven's avenging wrath.   And oftentimes
They sat deep-brooding o'er their sin, and oft
In bitter anguish chided their own selves 930

For listening to the Fiend's delusive words.
Great was the Woman's grief ; for well she knew
That through seductive arts they both had lost
The love of Heaven.   And penitent in mind
She wept, for now she saw that Light depart
Which he who counselled them to do the crime
Had showed to her—false and illusive sign
Of his pretended claim.   Deep sorrow burned
Within their breasts as dark remorse displayed
940 The unnumbered ills and ghastly punishment
Their sin entailed.   At times on bended knee,
These guilty partners in a common sin,
In heartfelt prayer, invoked their heavenly King
The Lord of Victory, the source of Good,
Beseeching Him that they alone might bear
And expiate the deadly penalty
Due to their guilty act, since they alone
Had broken His command.

                 As yet no sense
950 Of human shame had marred their happiness,
(Though now they keenly felt their naked state) ;
Nor had there been by Heaven's decree assigned
A settled course of life in that fair land,
For naught they knew of toil or anxious care,
But might have lived a life of holy Rest
Had they but made the will of God their King
Their chief concern.

               Many a word of sadness

Passed between the two, for each shared deeply
In the other's woe.   960
                    " O Eve, my helpmate,"
(Thus spake the Man) " in evil hour indeed
Didst thou mark out our future path.   E'en now
Seest thou not the dark abyss of Hell
With open gates wide-yawning at our feet ?
The raging of its fires I plainly hear
E'en from this distant spot.   And how unlike
The beauteous realm of Heaven are yonder flames !
But now no fairer land than this our Earth
May we anticipate, nor can we ask   970
Such favour of our Lord, since thou didst heed
The evil counsellor who planned our woe
And urged disloyalty to Heaven's dread King,
The Ruler of the World.   Naught now remains
Save that we mourn in deepest penitence
The visit of that Fiend, since God Himself
Bade us beware that greatest of all ills,
Unending torment.   E'en at this moment
Hunger and burning thirst, warring within
Like deadly foes, already rend in twain   980
This mortal flesh !   And how shall we protect
Our fragile life or find subsistence here
When piercing winds from heaven's four quarters
     blow
And mists arise or showers of hail descend ?
When biting frost and winter's cruel cold

Bind fast the Earth in iron bands? or when
The solar Sphere sends forth its glowing beams
And radiant heat?   How can we then withstand,
In our defenceless state, each sudden change
990 Of Nature's fickle mood, devoid alike
Of shelter from the storm and present store
Of needful food?   In truth, possessing naught
Unless it be the dread hostility
Of an offended and All-puissant God?
Deeply I grieve, (since now thou hast beguiled
My loving trust and hast subjected both
To God's just ire,) that ever I invoked
The great Creator's might, bone of my bone,
To frame thy beauteous form and place thee here
1000 To share with me the joys of this fair World.
Yea, and it may repent me all my days
That e'er I gazed upon thee with mine eyes."

Then answered Eve, fairest of Womankind,
Most beautiful of wives, the handiwork
Of God e'en though undone through subtle craft :

"Well mayest thou upbraid me as thou dost,
O Adam, my belovèd spouse, and yet
Believe me, that thyself canst not bewail
More bitterly the outcome of this deed
1010 Than I do in my heart."

Then Adam spake :

" If I but knew the Almighty's sovereign Will,
What penalty awaits this fearful crime,
None couldst thou find more ready to perform
That Will than I ; e'en though by Heaven's decree
I had to plunge beneath the surging flood
And seek the Ocean's deep and sunken caves.
No depth could terrify or rapid stream
Could keep me from the abyss, if thus I might
Perform God's holy Will. 1020

   " No heart have I
For worship, now that I have forfeited,
Beyond retrieve, the favour of our King.
But let us hasten into yonder wold
And sit within the grove's protecting shade,
For naked as we are it is not meet
To tarry longer here."

    Departing thence
They sought the shelter of the grateful wold
With deepest grief oppressed, and sat apart, 1030
Awaiting now whatever righteous doom
Heaven might inflict for guilty faithlessness
To that high trust which God had erst imposed.
Then sheltered by the forest's inmost shade
They plucked the leaves and clothed themselves
  therewith.
(For they were destitute of other garb)
And every morn they knelt in solemn prayer

That God, the Mighty, Ruler of the World
Would not forget them in their great distress
1040 But graciously reveal how they thenceforth
Should live their ruined lives.

                      When many days
Had come and gone, the mighty God at length
Revealed Himself, walking at eventide
Amid the glories of that Earthly realm.
The King All-merciful, in pity stooped
To learn His children's need, and how they bare
Their ruined state, bereft of all the Grace
Which at the first adorned their mortal state.
1050 Soon as they heard the voice of Holy God
They sought, with saddened mind and shorn of joy,
The shelter of the thickest grove, and seized
With sudden dread concealed themselves within
The rocky portals of a cave.

                      Straightway,
The Heavenly Chief, the mighty Lord of Hosts,
Summoned the Warden of this Earthly sphere
And bade His son approach.

                      Then **Adam cried**
1060 In deep humility :

                " Lord of my life,
Devoid of raiment, I conceal me here
And cover me with leaves.   Great is my **guilt**
And this foul sin of mine fills me with pain
And weighs upon my soul.   I do not dare,

All naked as I am, to leave this shade
And meet Thee face to face."

                    Then spake the King :
" Tell me, my son, why seekest thou in shame
The shelter of the grove ?   Dost thou conceive   1070
That I have sense of shame ?   Whence does it
    come
That 'mid surrounding joy thou knowest aught
Of woe ? and wouldst conceal thy naked form
With clothing from the trees ?   Whence knowest
    thou
This earthly sorrow, for thou say'st, thy life
Is full of care and thou thyself full sad
With downcast mind ?   Why dost thou feel the
    need
Of clothing thus thy form, unless thou hast
Been faithless to thy trust and touched the fruit
Of yon forbidden Tree ? "   1080
                    Then in reply
The man confessed :
                    " This   beauteous   bride   of
    mine,
This virgin Wife, did place within my hand
The baleful fruit and I, O mine own Lord,
Forgetful of Thy Love, did eat, and now
Within myself plain token do I bear
Of this my sin, since day by day, I see
Fresh sorrows teeming, in upon my path."

1090 Then thus the Almighty spake, close-questioning
The guilty Wife :

"Didst thou have need of aught,
O daughter Eve, here 'midst the ample joys,
The new creations and the bounteous gifts
Of Paradise, that thou didst set thine heart
To taste the Tree of Death, and in disdain
Of my esteem, didst pluck and eat its fruit
To thy great harm? ay, and didst give thereof
To Adam, though I straitly charged you both
1100 To shun that deadly fruit ?"

The virgin Wife
In deepest shame replied :

"With artful words
Of fairest import was I sore beguiled.
Most urgently the Serpent prompted me
To this foul crime, this daring act of Sin,
Till overcome by specious argument
I basely gave the victory to the Fiend
And to my shame I seized the tempting tree
1110 And ate the fruit."

Forthwith the mighty God,
Protector of Mankind, proclaimed His will
That thenceforth should the Serpent be con-
demned
To wander far and wide :

"Thy livelong life,"
For thus He spake, "shalt thou accursèd be ;

And on thy breast shalt drag thy footless form
O'er the fair face of Earth ; and dust shalt eat
The remnant of thy days, and long as life
And breath remain—just meed of this great crime,   1120
Thy malice hath inspired.

        " And there shall burn
Within the Woman's breast, a mortal Hate
And quenchless enmity, and she shall tread
Thy hostile head beneath her feet, while thou
May'st strive, with deep and crafty plans, to snare
The offspring of this new-born race.   As long
As this fair World shall stand, a deadly feud
Shall last 'twixt her and thee.

        " Now dost thou know   1130
Thy doom, fell Scourge of Man, and canst discern
The future of thy life."

        The Holy God
To Eve in anger spake :

        " Take thyself hence
Far from these scenes of joy.   From this day forth
Obedience shalt thou yield to Adam's will,
And in the fear of him shalt expiate
The error of thy deeds, humbled and vext
By keen remorse, till Death ensue.   Meanwhile,   1140
With weeping and with moans and bitter pains
Shalt thou bring forth thy daughters and thy sons
To people Earth's domain."

        Then to the Man

The Eternal King, Lord of the Light of Life,
Announced His dire decree :

                 " Now must thou seek
Another home, a realm more joyless far,
And into exile go, in nakedness

1150 And want, shorn of the bliss which thou hast
       known
In Paradise.   And since with evil mind
Thou didst commit this crime, I do decree
That Death, at last, shall break the golden bond
Which now unites thy body and thy soul.
Henceforth thy days shall pass in arduous toil
And from the ground shalt thou thyself now seek
Thy sustenance, and eat thy daily bread
By sweat of brow so long as thou dost live,
And until fell Disease of which, alas,

1160 Thou didst partake in the forbidden fruit
Doth strike thee at the heart.   Then shalt thou
       die."

Thus did our writ of Evil take its rise
In righteous wrath, entailing World-wide woe.
The Lord of glory, Guardian of Mankind,
In goodly raiment robed the guilty pair
And bade them hide their nudeness from the gaze
Of mortal eyes.   Their sentence once pronounced
They bent their mournful steps from Paradise
To seek a narrower sphere.

Behind them closed 1170
The glistening gates of their once joyous home,
Its comforts and delights forever lost !
And at the Lord's behest, one of His host
Of holy Angels, armed with fiery sword,
Kept constant guard to hinder their return.

Thenceforth no traitorous or crime-guilty man
May enter there ; for he who guards that realm
Of blissful life, dear to the pure in heart,
Hath might and strength as Warden of the Lord.

Nor even then, would mighty God, at once 1180
Despoil the guilty pair of all their joys,
E'en though His presence He had now withdrawn ;
But for their comfort, still he let shine forth
The vault of heaven adorned with radiant stars,
And of the treasures of the Earth, He gave
With open hand ; and for their use He bade
The denizens of Earth and Sea increase
And multiply, and trees bring forth their fruit.
Sin-stained, they thenceforth sojourned in a land
More sorrowful, a region and a home 1190
More barren far of every earthly Good
Than were those blissful Seats from which alas
By Sin they were expelled.

NOTES.

NOTE A.

How much valuable literature has been lost to the world by war, by vandalism, by accident, and by ignorance, will, of course, never be known ; but we have historical data sufficient to show that treasures almost innumerable have disappeared from the face of the earth beyond reasonable hope of recovery.

It is well known, as shown by Mr. William Shepard in a recent article, that "the dramatic literature of Greece was one of its greatest glories. At the time of Aristophanes it is estimated that fully two thousand dramas had been produced : only forty-two have come down to us. From Æschylus we have only seven, out of a total of seventy ; seven also of Sophocles, out of a hundred or more ; and nineteen of Euripides, out of a possible ninety-two. The comic writers have suffered the most, and of the greatest of them, Menander, hardly a vestige remains. Goethe said that he would gladly have given one-half of Roman poetry for a single play of that master. In the few lines that have come down to us he recognized the touch of a supreme genius.

"But this is not the worst. The greatest lyric poetess of all times was Sappho. Only two odes and a few fragmentary lines are left to tantalize us with a sense of our loss. From Pindar we have some odes, indeed, but not the hymns and dirges and dithyrambs which the ancient critics considered his real masterpieces.

"Many of these treasures perished in the invasions of the Goths and Vandals, many were destroyed by the ignorant or the superstitious in the Dark Ages.

" The library of four hundred thousand manuscripts collected by the Ptolemys was burned during the siege of Alexandria by Julius Cæsar. The famous library in the same city known as the Serapeum which had been enriched by Pergamon and given to Cleopatra by Mark Antony, was partly burned, partly dispersed, at the storming of the temple of Jupiter by the Christians during the reign of Theodosius the Great.

" The shells of the German army in 1870 fired the great Strasburg library, when many manuscripts and printed books of great value were destroyed, among others the earliest-printed Bible and the records of the famous law-suits between Gutenberg, the first printer, and his partners, upon which depended the claim of Gutenberg, to the invention of the art of printing.

" Frightful losses were also sustained when the great monastic libraries were plundered in the time of the Reformation. The books and manuscripts were scattered to stuff broken windows, clean boots, and light fires, or were sold to grocers and soap-sellers as wrapping paper. One merchant for forty shillings bought two noble libraries which supplied him with paper stock enough to last for ten years. No doubt many of the most precious ancient manuscripts perished in this way as well as works more or less valuable of mediæval writers.

" A curious heap of scorched leaves, looking like a monster wasps'-nest may be seen in a glass case in the British Museum. It is a relic of a fire that occurred in 1731 at Ashburnam House, Westminster, and partly destroyed the Cotton manuscripts. By the exercise of much skill a portion was restored, though apparently charred past recognition. The remnants were carefully separated, leaf by leaf, soaked in a chemical solution, and then pressed between leaves of transparent paper.

" Ignorance has cost the world priceless treasures in books and manuscripts. Just before the French Revolution a fine copy of the first edition of the *Golden Legend* was used leaf by leaf to light the librarian's fires. A copy of Caxton's *Canterbury Tales*, with wood-cuts, worth at least two thousand dollars, was used to light the vestry fire of the French Protestant Church in St. Martin's le Grand in London some thirty years ago."

NOTE B.

FRANCISCUS JUNIUS AD LECTOREM.

Supervacuum esset, Lector benevole, pluribus verbis hoc in loco repetere, quæ non ita pridem de Paraphrasios hujus Authore attigi p. 248 Observationum nostrarum in Willeramum ; ubi quoque præclarum hunc reconditæ antiquitatis thesaurum acceptum fero summo Præsuli et nunquam non infra merita sua laudato, Jacobo Usserio, Archiepiscopo Armachano et totius Hiberniæ Primati. Per velim interim, mi Lector, abs te mihi ignosci quod editio hæc, ex uno tantum exemplari concinnata, prodit inemendatior ; futura forte correctior, si plures antiqua manu exaratos codices videre contigisset. Ne quis tamen ulla in re operam nostram desideraret, paginas ipsius Manuscripti adversis ubique virgulis inclusi, quo facilius hanc nostram editionem cum ipsis reverendi Antistitis vett. membranis conferant, quibus pretium operæ videbitur. Singulas quoque editionis hujus paginas in lineas distinxi, quo expeditius inveniri possint loca quæ posthac a nobis ex hoc Authore citabuntur, et nostras quoque in eum observationes, Deo Opt. Max. vitam viresque largiente, suis ubique paginis lineisque commodius adaptem. Vale, mi Lector, atque hac interim qualicunque opera nostra propitius fruere.

NOTE C.

Elizabeth Elstob, the author of this work, and one of the most remarkable of the literary characters of the first half of the eighteenth century, was the daughter of Ralph Elstob, a merchant living at Newcastle. Her mother, to whom she owed the first steps in her strange and extraordinary education, died when her child was scarcely nine years of age, and her guardians, on the death of the mother, strongly discouraged the young girl in her passion for literary studies, insisting that literature was not a proper vocation for one of her sex ! In spite of all opposition, however, she persistently held to her self-chosen course in life, and attained eminence as linguist, Saxonist, and *littérateur*. But after the death of her brother, she met with so little patronage and so many disappointments that she migrated to Worcestershire, where for some time she supported herself by teaching. Subsequently, she became acquainted with Mr. George Ballard and the Rev. Mr. Capon, the latter of whom kept a boarding-school in Gloucestershire, and through the kind offices of these two gentlemen, an annuity of £21.0.0 was raised among Miss Elstob's friends, in order to enable her to pursue her literary work. This annuity was assumed by Queen Caroline, who was pleased to continue it until her own death. After this, Elizabeth Elstob, mistress of eight languages besides her own, was received into the family of the Dowager Duchess of Portland [1739] as governess to her children, and remained in this position till her death, May 30, 1756.

There is a quaint note on the title-page of the *Rudiments of Grammar for the English-Saxon Tongue* that will well bear to be reproduced in this connection :

" Our earthly possessions are truly enough called a *Patrimony*, as derived to us by the industry of our Fathers ; but the language that we speak is our *Mother-tongue*, and who so proper to play the critics in this as the *Females*.

" In a letter from a Right Reverend Prelate to the author."

The full title of Elizabeth Elstob's translation of the Homily on the birthday of St. Gregory is as follows : *An English-Saxon Homily on the Birthday of St. Gregory, anciently used in the English-Saxon Church*, giving an account of the conversion of the English from paganism to Christianity. Translated into modern English with notes, etc. By Eliz. Elstob, London. Printed by W. Bowyer, MDCCIX.

We have given this title in full because it is chiefly from Nichol's *Life of Bowyer*, Elizabeth Elstob's publisher, that we have taken the brief story of her life as given above.

Note D.

There is no full description in Anglo-Saxon literature of the Mead-hall,—the building rendered famous by the death-struggle between the Grendel and Beówulf ; but from the many allusions to such a kingly and warrior resort, which occur in the poem of the *Beówulf* itself, no less than from the many hints and suggestions that we find scattered throughout Scandinavian and Teutonic literature, we can form a

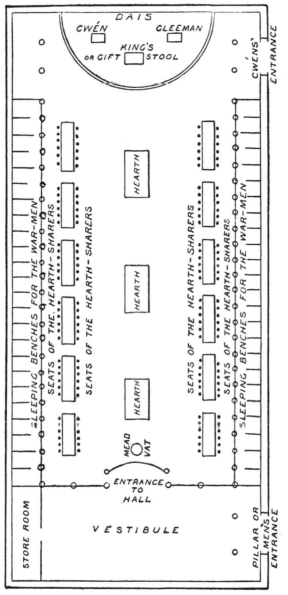

GROUND PLAN OF A MEAD-HALL.

tolerably correct idea of the general plan and internal arrangements of such a festive Hall.

Viewed from without, the Mead-hall consisted of a long building surmounted by a high, slanting roof, ornamented with curved gables, and flanked by low-roofed aisles on either side ; the whole resembling, in a very marked manner, the architecture of some of our ancient English church buildings. At each extremity of the wall of the low aisle, on the South side, was an entrance, protected by a porch ; that at the West end being the "Pillar" or men's door ; and that at the East end being the entrance for the Saxon cwéns or wives.

Internally, the Hall consisted of a spacious nave, the main roof rising high above the marble chequered floor and supported by massive pillars ; while along the whole length of the roof might be seen the heavy cross-beams which supported it, and which looked, from the floor beneath, like a frail lattice-work. Running along the sides of the Hall and extending from the eaves of the main roof, down to within some fifteen feet of the marble floor, were richly carved panels, commemorative of great battles and heroic deeds ; while the space between these panels and the floor was hung with "golden webs" or embroidered hangings that adorned the whole length of the lower sides of the Hall.

At the East or upper end of the Hall was a dais or platform,—the place of honour,—where the King, the Cwén, the chief thanes, and the King's gleeman had their stools while the King, himself, sat on a stool of state, called the "gift stool."

Down the middle of the building, at equal distances apart, were three large hearths, on which the log fires burned brightly, the smoke rising to the roof and escaping through covered outlets.

On each side of the Hall were long tables reaching from the dais on the upper end, to within a few feet of the door, on the lower end. These tables were flanked, on either side, by long rows of seats ; some of them beautifully carved and inlaid with precious metals. These were the seats of the King's "*hearth sharers*." While enjoying the festivities of the Hall, swords, and shields, and helmets were hung up against the tapestry overhead, so that the walls incessantly flashed with myriad gleams as the flames from the fires struck the polished armour.

Behind the tapestry, at night-time, when the warriors retired to rest the tapestry hangings were drawn aside, and the side aisles were exposed to view. But they contained little worth seeing. There was simply a row of benches running at right angles to the length of the Hall, and serving as couches for the warriors. Still, when the Hall was wrapped in quiet, and the fires were smouldering; when the King and Cwén, and gleeman had retired to rest, the walls of these side aisles looked, in the gloom, like a deserted armoury, for the war-men had divested themselves of their arms and each suit of mail was hung over the head of its owner.

NOTE E.

In Anglo-Saxon poetry *similes* are exceedingly rare. In the whole poem of the *Beówulf* there occur but five and these are of the simplest description. The ring-prowed bark of the hero, as it cuts through the water, is compared to a bird. The glare that shines from the eyes of the Grendel as he stalks over the moor on his murderous mission to Hróthgár's Mead-hall is compared to fire. The nails of the monster's fingers are described as hand-spurs of steel. The glow of mellow light in the subaqueous home of the She-wolf is compared to the early morning sunshine; and finally the melting away of Beówulf's sword when he strikes off the head of the lifeless eoten is likened to the melting of ice.

NOTE F.

Canon XX. of the Second Council of Nicæa [A.D. 787], commonly called by both the Eastern and Western branches of the Church the Seventh Ecumenical Council, is as follows :

" We decree that from the present time there shall be no Celibate Houses for monks and nuns together, because they lead to scandal and become a stumbling-block to the many. But if any persons with their kindred prefer to renounce the world and to follow the single life, the men must retire into a monastery for men, and the women into a monastery for women. For with that God is well pleased. But let the double monasteries which have been in existence hitherto remain in accordance with the rule of the holy Father Basil, and let them be places perfectly conformed to his arrangement. Let not monks and nuns live in the same monastery, for adultery [*i. e.*, fornication on the part of the nun who was regarded as Christ's bride] interferes with that living together. Let not a monk be permitted to talk freely and in private with a nun, or a nun with a monk. Let not a monk sleep in a monastery of women, and let not a nun eat together with a monk alone. And when the necessities of life are brought from the male part of the monastery to the nuns, let the Abbess of the monastery, together with some Sister of mature years, receive them outside the gate. But if it should happen that some monk should wish to see a kinswoman among the nuns, let him talk with her for a short time and in few words in the presence of the Abbess."

The original Greek of this Canon as given in the Πηδάλιον, published at Athens, 1841, is as follows :

Κανὼν Κ´.

Ἀπὸ τοῦ παρόντος ὁρίζομεν, μὴ γίνεσθαι διπλοῦν Μοναστήριον, ὅτι σκάνδαλον, καὶ πρόσκομμα τοῖς πολλοῖς γίνεται τοῦτο. Εἰ δέ τινες μετὰ συγγενῶν προαιροῦνται ἀποτάξασθαι, καὶ τῷ μονήρει βίῳ κατακολουθεῖν, τοὺς μὲν ἄνδρας, δέον ἀπιέναι εἰς ἀνδρῷον Μοναστήριον, καὶ τὰς γυναῖκας εἰσιέναι ἐν γυναικείῳ Μοναστηρίῳ. Ἐπὶ τούτῳ γὰρ εὐαρεστεῖται ὁ Θεός. Τὰ δὲ ὄντα ἕως τοῦ νῦν διπλᾶ, κρατείτωσαν, κατὰ τὸν Κανόνα τοῦ ἁγίου πατρὸς ἡμῶν Βασιλείου, καὶ κατὰ τὴν διαταγὴν αὐτοῦ, οὕτω διατυπούσθωσαν. Μὴ διατάσθωσαν ἐν ἑνὶ Μοναστηρίῳ Μοναχοὶ καὶ Μονάστριαι· μοιχεία γὰρ μεσολλαβεῖ τήν συνδιαίτησιν. Μὴ ἐχέτω Μοναχὸς παρρησίαν πρὸς Μονάστριαν, ἢ Μονάστρια πρὸς Μοναχὸν, ἰδίᾳ προσομιλεῖν. Μὴ κοιταζέσθω Μοναχὸς ἐν γυναικείῳ Μοναστηρίῳ. Μηδὲ συνεσθιέτω Μονάστρια καταμόνας. Καὶ ὅτε τὰ ἀναγκαῖα τοῦ βίου παρὰ τοῦ ἀνδρῷου μέρους πρὸς τὰς κανονικὰς ἀποκομίζονται, ἔξωθεν τῆς πύλης ταῦτα λαμβανέτω ἡ Ἡγουμένη τοῦ γυναικείου Μοναστηρίου, μετὰ γραὸς τινος Μοναστρίας. Εἰ δὲ συμβῇ, συγγενῆ τινα ἐθέλειν θεάσασθαι Μοναχὸν, ἐπὶ παρουσίᾳ τῆς Ἡγουμένης, ταύτῃ προσομιλείτω διὰ μικρῶν καὶ βραχέων λόγων.

Note G.

Observations on the History of Cædmon. By Francis Palgrave,
Esq. F.R.S., F.S.A., in a Letter to Henry Ellis, *Esq. F.R.S.,
Secretary.*

" It has not perhaps been hitherto remarked that the well-known
history of Cædmon has its exact parallel.   We learn from a fragment,
entitled " Præfatio in librum antiquum linguâ Saxonicâ conscriptum ;"
published amongst the Epistles of Hincmar Bishop of Rhemes (Biblio-
theca Patrum, Paris, 1644, vol. xvi., p. 609), that Ludovicus Pius,
being desirous to furnish his subjects with a version of the Holy
Scriptures, applied to a *Saxon* Bard of great talent and fame.   The
Poet, a peasant or husbandman, when entirely ignorant of his art, had
been instructed in a dream to render the precepts of the Divine Law
into the verse and measure of his native language.   His translation,
now unfortunately lost, to which the fragment was prefixed, com-
prehended the whole of the Bible.   The text of the original was
interspersed with mystic allusions ; and the beauty of the composition
was so great, that, in the opinion of the writer of the preface, no
reader, perusing the verse, could doubt the source of the poetic inspiration of the Bard.

I have endeavoured to show on another occasion (*Hist. of England*,
vol. i., p. 168), that the marvellous part of Cædmon's history, as told
by Bede, may in some degree be explained by natural causes.   But it
is scarcely possible that the same extraordinary, though not incredible,
development of poetical talent should have occurred both in Britain
and in Gaul.   And the history of the so-called Cædmon, will perhaps
rather appear as one of those tales floating upon the breath of tradition,
and localized from time to time in different countries and in different
ages.

But, whatever may have been the true history of our Anglo-Saxon
paraphrast, there are strong reasons for supposing that his real name
has not been preserved.   Most, if not all, of the Anglo-Saxon proper
names are significant ; and whenever we meet with a name which
cannot be fairly resolved into Anglo-Saxon roots, bearing a known
and intelligible meaning, we have always the strongest presumptive
reasons for supposing that it has been borrowed from some other
tongue.   Now to the name *Cædmon*, whether considered as a simple
or as a compound, no *plain and definite meaning* can be assigned, if

the interpretation be sought in the Anglo-Saxon language : whilst
that very same name *is* the initial word of the Book of Genesis in the
Chaldee paraphrase, or Targum of Onkelos : בקדמין *b' Cadmin* or
b' Cadmon, (the *b'* is merely a prefix), being a literal translation of
b' Raschith, or " In principio," the initial word of the original Hebrew
text.   It is hardly necessary to observe that the books of the Bible
are denominated by the Jews from their initial words : they quote
and call *Genesis* by the name of " *b' Raschith*," the *Chaldaic* Genesis
would be quoted and called by the name of " *b' Cadmin*," and this
custom adopted by them at least as early as the time of St. Jerome,
has continued in use until the present day.

But in addition to the value of the word *Cadmon* as denoting the
Chaldaic Book of Genesis, the name of *Adam Cadmon* (אדם קדמון)
also holds a most important station in Cabalistic theology ; the adjec-
tive or epithet (קדמון) *Cadmon* in pure Hebrew signifies *Eastern*,
Oriental, or *from the East ;* and until we can suggest a better explanation of the name given to the Anglo-Saxon poet, it will be difficult to avoid the conclusion, that using the Targum as his text, and
being also familiar with the Cabalistic doctrines, he assumed the name
of *Cadmon* either from the Book which he translated, or from the
Cabalistic nomenclature : or that, having arrived in Britain from the
East, he designated himself as the Eastern visitor or pilgrim.

The numerous episodes, especially those relating to the fallen
angels, introduced in the Anglo-Saxon paraphrase of Genesis, possess
an oriental character.   There was no Latin version of the Bible in
which they could be found, and it may be strongly suspected that they
are of Rabbinical origin.   No small portion of the allegorical literature, as well as of the philosophy, of the middle ages may be distinctly
traced to Rabbinical sources ; and the supposition that an Anglo-
Saxon might be sufficiently acquainted with the Hebrew and Chaldaic
languages to enable him to derive this information, is not attended
with any improbability.

Duns Scotus was profoundly versed in the Oriental tongues.
Venerable Bede himself could read Hebrew ; and the fervent zeal
with which the study of the Holy Scriptures was pursued during that
period of ecclesiastical history included between the age of Saint
Jerome and the eleventh century, might easily have induced an
Anglo-Saxon monk, or even a layman, during his residence in Pales-
tine, to acquire a knowledge of the language of the Old Testament,

and also of that cognate dialect in which its most valuable interpretation is preserved.

The obscurity attending the origin of the Cædmonian poems will perhaps increase the interest excited by them. Whoever may have been their author, their remote antiquity is unquestionable. In poetical imagery and feeling they excel all the other early remains of the North. And I trust I may be allowed to congratulate our Society in having determined to commence their series of Anglo-Saxon publications, by a work which belongs not only to Englishmen, but to every branch of the great Teutonic family."

Mr. Daniel H. Haigh, in his work on the *Anglo-Saxon Sagas*, has the following remarks in reference to Sir Francis Palgrave's criticism :

" The theory that sagas, originally English, were carried to the continent, and formed the basis of a very popular cycle of romances, will be found to be borne out by facts which will be adduced in the following pages, and has its exact parallel in the circumstances of the *Heliand*. We know that the poetical works of our Cædmon embraced the whole series of Scripture history, yet only a part thereof, relating the principal events of Genesis and Exodus, and a fragment treating of one of the events of the Captivity in Babylon, remain to us. The *Heliand* contains the Gospel story ; and not only is it perfectly Cædmonian in its style, but there is a tradition which evidently relates to it, that in the reign of Louis the Pious, a herdsman received poetical inspiration in his slumbers, and on awaking turned the whole Scripture narrative, of the Old and New Testaments, into excellent verse. Here is undeniably Beda's story of Cædmon, localised in Germany ; and it is very probable that the *Heliand* is one of the volumes of Cædmon's paraphrase, carried to Germany by an Anglo-Saxon missionary, and translated into the old Saxon dialect."

And Mr. Haigh adds in a note " with regard to the name, it has remained amongst us to this day (Cadmon) and in each of its elements it has its correspondents in other Anglo-Saxon names—Cædwealh, Cædbæd, Tilmon, Tytmon."

Note H.

In both poems the domain and palace of the Arch-Traitor are spoken of as being situated in the " North," or " Northwest " quarter of the Empyrean ; and so strong a hold has this idea taken on the mind of Christendom that we meet with it in the works of some of the greatest writers, as, for instance, Augustine, Tasso, and Shakespeare. In 1 *Henry VI.*, v., iii., Satan is styled "the monarch of the North." It is possible, that this tradition may have been founded on a passage in Isaiah xiv., 12, 13, "How art thou fallen from Heaven, O Lucifer, son of the morning. . . . For thou hast said in thine heart, I will ascend into Heaven, I will exalt my throne above the stars of God ; I will sit also upon the mount of the congregation, in the sides of the North."

Whether or not this is the true explanation of the widespread idea of making the North the domain of the great Lucifer before his fall, is open to question. The very name Lucifer, "son of the morning," clearly signifies a "bright star," probably what we call the morning star, and in the above passage from Isaiah it is a symbolical representation of the king of Babylon, in his splendour and in his fall. Its application, from St. Jerome downwards, to Satan in his expulsion from heaven, arises probably from the fact that the Babylonian Empire is in Scripture represented as the type of tyrannical and self-idolising power, and is especially connected with the empire of the Evil One in the Apocalypse. The fall of its material power before the unseen working of the providence of God is therefore a type of the defeat of all manifestations of the tyranny of Satan. This application of the name "Lucifer" as a proper name of the Devil is plainly ungrounded ; but the magnificence of the imagery of the prophet, far transcending in grandeur the fall of Nebuchadnezzar to which it immediately refers, has naturally given a colour to the symbolical interpretation of the passage, and fixed that application in our modern language.

NOTE I.

In his *Life of Milton*, Professor Masson says : "Since 1639, when Milton lived in the St. Bride's Churchyard lodging, he had been teaching his two nephews, and had had the younger nephew, Johnny Phillips, boarding with him entirely ; when he removed in 1640 to the house in Aldersgate Street, the elder nephew, Edward Phillips, also came under his roof ; and in 1643, after his wife had deserted him, and his father had come to live with him, he had received into his house, as boarders or day-boarders, a few additional pupils.

How many there were we do not know : probably, with the two nephews, not more than eight or a dozen at most."

Edward Phillips had four or five years' instruction under Milton and in accordance with Milton's peculiar ideas of education, and he has left an account, and a most interesting one, of Milton's method of training boys of from ten to fifteen years of age.

It is in this account that the elder Phillips tells of the text-books used by his uncle in teaching ; and in this list we find the *De Sphæra* of Joannes De Sacro Bosco. This is the famous John Holywood, an Englishman [d. 1256], whose treatise *De Sphæra*, often re-edited and republished, was the most popular manual on Astronomy during the Middle Ages.

NOTE J.

From among the many curious and interesting points of correspondence between Cædmon and Milton we may adduce the following as instances of the similarity of thought, imagery, and even of diction between the two poets.

In the Anglo-Saxon poem when Satan has recovered from the stupor caused by his fall through Chaos to Hell, and begins to realise his surroundings, he exclaims :

> Is thes ænga stede ungelíc swíthe
> Thám othrum the we áer cúthon
> Héah on heofon-rice.

> *This straitened place*
> *Oh ! how unlike those other seats where once*
> In Heaven's high Kingdom, etc.

Similarly in Milton. At the very opening of his epic, where he depicts Satan and his hosts as lying in deepest Hell, and after describing, in brief, their place of torment, the poet exclaims :

> *Oh, how unlike the place from which they fell!*

Here the similarity in *wording* is most striking.

Nor is this similarity less marked in some of the *imagery* employed by both poets.

Cædmon, in his description of the upward flight of the Fiend from the Gates of Hell on his adventurous enterprise of the ruin of Man, tells us that he,

Wand him up thanon
Hwearf him thurh tha hell-dora.

Wheeled upwards thence
Circling through the doors of Hell.

Milton tells how Satan, after his parley with the guardians of Hell-gate:

Sprang upward, like a pyramid of fire,

and his verse in several passages carries out the Cædmonic idea of spiral movement.

Again, the Junian manuscript has an illumination of the Deity pronouncing sentence on the Serpent where the reptile is depicted as

standing upright on his coils listening to his doom, and although the text itself is silent on the subject, yet the drawing shows very clearly the current tradition that before the triumph of the Devil over Man, the Serpent did not necessarily have to crawl prone on his belly.

This tradition we find fully developed in Milton's epic. He tells us that Satan :

> . . . toward Eve
> Addressed his way—not with indented wave,
> Prone on the ground, as since, but on his rear,
> Circular base of rising folds, that towered
> Fold above fold, a surging maze ; his head
> Crested aloft, and carbuncle his eyes ;
> With burnished neck of verdant gold, erect
> Amidst his circling spires, that on the grass
> Floated redundant.

These lines might be taken as the poetic description of the monastic illumination ; or, on the other hand, the drawing might equally well serve as an illustration of Milton's verse.

NOTE K.

" The three kingdoms, Inferno, Purgatorio, Paradiso, look out on one another like compartments of a great edifice ; a great supernatural world-cathedral, piled up there, stern, solemn, awful ; Dante's World of Souls ! It is, at bottom, the sincerest of all poems ; sincerity here, too, we find to be the measure of worth. It came deep out of the author's heart of hearts, and it goes deep and through long generations into ours. It has all been as if molten in the hottest furnace of his soul. It has made him lean for many years. Nor the general whole only ; every compartment of it is worked out, with intense earnestness, into truth, into clear visuality. Each answers to the other ; each finds its place, like a marble stone accurately hewn and polished. It is the soul of Dante, and in this the soul of the Middle Ages, rendered forever rhythmically visible there. Through all objects he pierces, as it were, down into the heart of Being. I know nothing so intense as Dante. Consider, for example, how he paints. He has a great power of vision ; seizes the very type of a thing; presents that, and nothing more. There is a brevity, an abrupt precision in him. Tacitus is not briefer, more condensed; and then in Dante it seems a natural condensation, spontaneous to the man. One smiting word; and then there is silence, nothing more said. His silence is more eloquent than words. It is strange with what sharp, decisive grace he snatches the true likeness of a matter; cuts into the matter as with a pen of fire. The very movements in Dante have something brief, swift, decisive, almost military. The fiery, swift, Italian nature of the man, so silent, passionate, with its quick, abrupt movements, its silent, 'pale rages,' speaks itself in his verses. His painting is not graphic only: brief, true, and of a vividness as of fire in dark night; taken on the wider scale, it is every way noble, and the outcome of a great soul. Francesca and her lover, what qualities in that! A thing woven as out of rainbows on a ground of eternal black. A small flute-voice of infinite wail speaks there into our very heart of hearts. A touch of womanhood is it, too. She speaks of '*questa forma*' so innocent; and how, even in the pit of woe, it is a solace that he will never part from her. Saddest tragedy in these *alti guai!* And the raking winds in that *aer bruno*, whirl them away again, forever! I know not in the world an affection equal to that of Dante. It is a tenderness, a trembling, longing, pitying love; like the wail of Æolian harps, soft, soft, like a child's young heart; and then that stern, sore, saddened heart! I do not agree with much modern criticism, in greatly preferring the *Inferno* to the two other parts of the *Divina Commedia*. Such preference belongs, I imagine, to our general Byronism of taste, and is like to be a transient feeling. The *Purgatorio* and the *Paradiso*, especially the former, one would almost say, is even more excellent than it. It is a noble thing that Purgatorio, Mountain of Purification, an emblem of the noblest conception of that age. If sin is so fatal, and hell is and must be so rigorous, awful, yet in repentance, too, is man purified; repentance is the grand Christian act. It is beautiful how Dante works it out. The trembling of the ocean waves, under the first pure gleam of morning, dawning afar on the wandering Two, is as the type of an altered mood. Hope has now dawned; never-dying hope, if in company still with heavy sorrow. The obscure sojourn of demons and reprobates is under foot; a soft breathing of penitence mounts higher and higher to the throne of mercy itself. 'Pray for me,' the denizens of that Mount of Pain all

say to him. ' Tell my Giovanna to pray for me, my daughter Giovanna ; I think, her mother loves me no more.' They toil painfully
up by that winding steep, bent down like corbels of a building, some
of them crushed together so for the sin of pride ; yet, nevertheless,
in years, and ages, and æons, they shall have reached the top,
Heaven's gate, and by mercy been admitted in. The joy, too, of all
when one has prevailed ; the whole mountain shakes with joy, and a
psalm of praise rises, when one soul has perfected repentance, and
got its sin and misery left behind, I call all this a noble embodiment
of a true noble thought. But indeed the three compartments mate-
rially support one another, are indispensable to one another. The
Paradiso, a kind of inarticulate music to me, is the redeeming side of
the *Inferno ;* the *Inferno* without it were untrue. All three make up
the true Unseen World, as figured in the Christianity of the Middle
Ages ; a thing forever memorable, forever true, in the essence of it,
to all men. It was, perhaps, delineated in no human soul with such
depth of veracity as in this of Dante's ; a man sent to sing it, to keep
it long memorable. Very notable with what brief simplicity he passes
out of the every-day reality into the invisible one ; and in the second
or third stanza we find ourselves in the World of Spirits, and dwell
there as among things palpable, indubitable. To Dante they were
so ; the real world, as it is called, and its facts, were but the threshold
to an infinitely higher fact of a world. At bottom, the one was as
preternatural as the other. Has not each man a soul ? He will not
only be a Spirit, but is one. To the earnest Dante it is all one visible
fact ; he believes it, sees it ; is the poet of it, in virtue of that."